Bombs, Bugs, Drugs, and Thugs

Loch K. Johnson

# BOMBS, BUGS, DRUGS, AND THUGS

## INTELLIGENCE AND AMERICA'S QUEST FOR SECURITY

New York University Press

*New York and London*

NEW YORK UNIVERSITY PRESS
New York and London

Copyright © 2000 by New York University
All rights reserved

Library of Congress Cataloging-in-Publication Data
Johnson, Loch K., 1942–
Bombs, bugs, drugs, and thugs : intelligence and America's
quest for security / Loch K. Johnson.
p. cm.
Includes bibliographical references and index.
ISBN 0-8147-4252-1 (cloth : alk. paper)
1. Intelligence service—United States. I. Title.
JK468.I6 J634 2000
327.1273—dc21 00-055027

New York University Press books are printed on acid-free paper,
and their binding materials are chosen for strength and durability.

Manufactured in the United States of America

10 9 8 7 6 5 4 3 2 1

*To Harry Howe Ransom*
*mentor and dear friend*

*and to Kristin*
*daughter and young scholar extraordinaire*

The important thing about foreign policy is this: There are a lot of important objectives: democracy is one of these, security is another, prosperity is another one, environment is another one. So you have to see how you give emphasis to these objectives at any moment in time.

—Henry A. Kissinger, interviewed by Suchichai Yoon,
*Nation,* Bangkok newspaper, March 8, 1999, A5.

# CONTENTS

# FIGURES

# ABBREVIATIONS

ADCI/A: assistant director of Central Intelligence/Administration
ADCI/A&P: assistant director of Central Intelligence/Analysis and
   Production
ADCI/C: assistant director of Central Intelligence/Collection
AFIO: Association of Former Intelligence Officers
AFMIC: Armed Forces Medical Intelligence Corps
ANSIR: Awareness of National Security Issues and Response (FBI)
ARIO: Association of Retired Intelligence Officers
BfV: German equivalent of the FBI
BND: Bundesnachrichtendienst (German intelligence service)
BNL: Bana nazionale del lavoro
BW: biological weapons
CA: covert action
CAS: Covert Action Staff
CBW: chemical-biological warfare
CDC: Centers for Disease Control
CDU: Christian Democratic Party (Germany)
CE: counterespionage
CFR: Council on Foreign Relations
CHAOS: cryptonym for a CIA domestic spying operation
CI: counterintelligence
CIA: Central Intelligence Agency
CIC: Counterintelligence Center (DCI)
CIRA: Central Intelligence Retirees Association
CMS: Community Management Staff
COINTELPRO: FBI Counterintelligence Program
COS: chief of station (CIA)
COSPO: Community Open Source Program Office
CNC: Crime and Narcotics Center (DCI)
CTC: Counterterrorist Center (DCI)

CW: chemical weapons
DCIA: director of the Central Intelligence Agency
DCI: director of Central Intelligence
DDA: deputy director for administration (CIA)
DDCI/CM: deputy director for Central Intelligence/Community Management
DDCIA: deputy director of the Central Intelligence Agency
DDI: deputy director for intelligence (CIA)
DDO: deputy director for operations (CIA)
DDS&T: deputy director for science and technology (CIA)
DEA: Drug Enforcement Administration
DEC: DCI's Environmental Center
DECA: Developing Espionage and Counterintelligence Awareness (FBI)
DIA: Defense Intelligence Agency
DA: Directorate of Administration (CIA)
DI: Directorate of Intelligence (CIA)
DNI: director of National Intelligence
DO: Directorate of Operations (CIA)
DS&T: Directorate of Science and Technology (CIA)
DGSE: French Intelligence Service
ECP: Economic Counterintelligence Program (FBI)
EOP: Executive Office of the President
EOS: Earth Observing System (NASA)
EPA: Environmental Protection Agency
ETF: Environmental Task Force (MEDEA)
EWG: Environmental Working Group
FAS: Federation of American Scientists
FBIS: Foreign Broadcast Information Service
FIAS: Foreign Intelligence Surveillance Act
FOIA: Freedom of Information Act
FPD: Free Democratic Party (Germany)
GAO: General Accounting Office (Congress)
GATT: General Agreement on Trade and Tariffs
GDIN: Global Disaster Information Network
GDP: Gross Domestic Product
GRU: Soviet military intelligence
GSG: German counterterrorism service

HPSCI: House Permanent Select Committee on Intelligence
HUMINT: human intelligence (espionage)
IC: Intelligence Community
ICBM: intercontinental ballistic missile
ICS: Intelligence Community Staff
IDP: imagery-derived products
IG: inspector general
IMINT: imagery (photographic) intelligence
INF: intermediate-range nuclear forces
INR: Bureau of Intelligence and Research (Department of State)
IOB: Intelligence Oversight Board
ISCAP: Interagency Security Classification Appeals Panel
ISI: Inter-Services Intelligence (Pakistani intelligence agency)
I&W: indicators and warning
JCS: Joint Chiefs of Staff
Jstars: Joint Surveillance Target Attack Radar Systems
KGB: Soviet foreign intelligence and secret police
KLA: Kosovo Liberation Army
MASINT: measurement and signatures intelligence
MEDEA: Greek mythological nickname for the Environmental Task
    Force (CIA)
Mossad: Israeli intelligence service
MRBM: medium-range ballistic missiles
MRC: major regional conflict
NAC: National Assessment Center (proposed)
NASA: National Aeronautic and Space Administration
NAFTA: North American Free Trade Agreement
NBC: nuclear, biological, and chemical (weaponry)
NEOB: New Executive Office Building
NFIP: National Foreign Intelligence Program
NGO: Non-Governmental Organization
NIC: National Intelligence Council
NIE: National Intelligence Estimate
NIMA: National Imagery and Mapping Agency
NIO: National Intelligence Officer
NISD: National Intelligence Security Directive
NOAA: National Oceanic and Atmospheric Agency

NOC: nonofficial cover
NPC: Nonproliferation Center (DCI)
NPIC: National Photographic Interpretation Center
NRO: National Reconnaissance Office
NSA: National Security Agency
NSC: National Security Council
NSCID: National Security Council Intelligence Directive
NSDM: National Security Decision Memorandum
NSTC: National Science and Technology Council
NTM: National Technical Means (mechanical spy platforms)
OMB: Office of Management and Budget
ONI: Office of Naval Intelligence
OPA: Office of Public Affairs (CIA)
OPEC: Organization of Petroleum Exporting Countries
OSINT: open-source intelligence
OSIS: Open-Source Information System
OTI: Office of Transnational Issues (CIA)
PDB: President's Daily Brief
PFIAB: President's Foreign Intelligence Advisory Board
PLO: Palestine Liberation Organization
PM: paramilitary
PRC: People's Republic of China
ROSE: Rich Open Source Environment (CIA computer system)
SAS: British intelligence service
SDO: support to diplomatic operations
SHAMROCK: cryptonym for NSA domestic spying operation
SIGINT: signals intelligence
SISDE: Italian intelligence service
SMO: support to military operations
SPD: Social Democratic Party (Germany)
SSCI: Senate Select Committee on Intelligence
Stasi: East German intelligence service
TECHINT: technical intelligence
UNSCOM: United Nations Special Commission
USAMRIID: U.S. Army Medical Research Institute for Infectious
  Diseases
USAMRMC: U.S. Army Medical Research and Material Command

USC: United States Code
USTR: United States trade representative
VA: Veterans Administration
VX: a deadly nerve agent used in chemical weapons
WHO: World Health Organization (UN)
WMD: weapons of mass destruction

# PREFACE

As with my earlier research on intelligence over the past twenty-five years, this book has benefited enormously from the help of others. The footnotes and bibliography in this volume attest to the valuable literature produced by those writing on intelligence: works by former government officials, media correspondents covering this elusive beat, and a growing number of academic scholars. I thank them one and all.

I am pleased to pay special tribute to a number of individuals who assisted me more directly with this volume. Mark S. R. Heathcote offered thoughtful insights into the question of economic security (the subject of chapter 2, based on a lecture I presented at St. Antony's College, Oxford University, in 1999). Scott A. Hershovitz, my former undergraduate honors student and currently a Rhodes scholar at Balliol College, Oxford University, tackled some of the research problems in chapter 3 (environmental intelligence). Diane C. Sawyer, a former CIA officer and now a private-sector manager, brought a valuable perspective to chapter 4 (health intelligence) and conducted some of the research. Kevin J. Scheid, a budget expert, led me through the maze of national security procedures followed by the Office of Management and Budget and worked closely with me in drafting an earlier version of chapter 6 (intelligence funding). Thomas P. Lauth, a friend and colleague at the University of Georgia and a public finance expert, also read an early version of chapter 6 and made useful suggestions, for which I am grateful. Annette Freyburg, my former graduate student and freshly minted Ph.D., researched shoulder-to-shoulder with me on an earlier version of chapter 7 (foreign intelligence liaison) and was especially helpful with the German literature review. Mark M. Lowenthal and H. Bradford Westerfield, whose writing in this field has been exemplary, generously read the entire manuscript and offered enormously valuable guidance.

My understanding of contemporary intelligence issues has benefited, too, from an opportunity to serve as special assistant to Les Aspin, chair of the Commission on the Roles and Missions of the U.S. Intelligence Community (the Aspin-Brown commission, Washington, D.C., 1995– 96). During and since the commission's proceedings, I have been able to discuss a range of intelligence topics with its members and staff, as well as with several of the witnesses who testified before the panel; their insights are greatly appreciated. In addition, I served as an assistant to Senator Frank Church (D, Idaho) on the U.S. Senate Select Committee on Intelligence (1975–76); as the issues director in Church's presidential campaign (1976); as the staff director of the Subcommittee on Oversight, U.S. House Permanent Select Committee on Intelligence (1977– 79); and as a foreign policy consultant to the White House during the Carter administration.

My knowledge of intelligence issues has benefited as well from informal discussions with scholars and a variety of government officials, both here and abroad. I thank the following good people (who, along with the others I have mentioned in this acknowledgment, are in no way responsible for any errors of fact or interpretation that may appear in these pages): Christopher Andrew, John B. Bellinger III, Richard A. Best, Cliff Blaskowsky, Ann Z. Caracristi, David Charters, James R. Clapper Jr., Charles G. Cogan, Richard N. Cooper, Jack Davis, Linda England, Linda C. Flohr, Ambassador Wyche Fowler Jr., Richard H. Giza, Allan E. Goodman, Representative Porter Goss (R, Florida), David D. Gries, Sir David Hannay, Glenn P. Hastedt, Michael Herman, Sarah B. Holmes, Douglas M. Horner, Arthur S. Hulnick, William Hyland, Rhodri Jeffreys-Jones, James H. Johnston, Frederick M. Kaiser, Wolfgang Krieger, William T. Kvetkas Jr., Edward Levine, John Macartney, Ernest R. May, Brendan G. Malley, Phyllis Provost McNeil, John Millis, John H. Moseman, Joseph S. Nye Jr., Hayden B. Peake, Charles Peters, Walter Pforzheimer, John Prados, Harry Howe Ransom, Jeffrey T. Richelson, L. Britt Snider, Robert D. Steele, William P. Sullivan, Stafford T. Thomas, Gregory F. Treverton, Michael Turner, Richard R. Valcourt, Wesley K. Wark, David Wise, and Paul D. Wolfowitz.

Several intelligence officers also spent time explaining their work to me, and I thank them profusely while maintaining my assurance of their anonymity. At least I can publicly acknowledge the insightful guidance (through conversations, interviews, and correspondence) of all the directors of Central Intelligence (DCIs) since and including Richard

Helms, as well as the admirable patience of the CIA public affairs officer David French. I am grateful to two of my student research assistants, Amy Elizabeth Early and William Gillespie, for their careful library and Internet searching, and to the University of Georgia for its ongoing support, especially the travel assistance from the Office of the Vice President for Research and a pleasant working environment provided by the political science department. Bertis and Catherine Downes offered me an opportunity to write in the tranquillity of their sylvan retreat, Wood House, nestled in the mountains of North Carolina. I thank them for these quiet times and for their friendship.

I would also like to thank the following journals and institutions for allowing me to draw on earlier research for this book: Espace Europe, *Freedom Review, Intelligence and National Security, International Journal of Intelligence and Counterintelligence*, the German Historical Institute, *Journal of Conflict, Public Budget & Finance*, Research Institute for European Studies, St. Antony's College at Oxford University, and St. Ermin's Press.

Finally, I wish to express my appreciation to Niko Pfund, the inspiring editor in chief of New York University Press for his encouragement, which sustained me during the inevitable frustrations of research and writing; to Despina Papazoglou Gimbel of the press for her guidance; and to my wife, Leena, for bringing sunshine and flowers into each day.

# INTRODUCTION

> Certainly nothing is more rational and logical than the idea
> that national security policies be based upon the fullest and
> most accurate information available; but the cold war
> spawned an intelligence Frankenstein monster that now needs
> to be dissected, remodeled, rationalized and made fully ac-
> countable to responsible representatives of the people.
>
> —Harry Howe Ransom, "Reflections on
> Forty Years of Spy-Watching," 1994

## The Importance of Intelligence

"Every morning I start my day with an intelligence report," President
Bill Clinton once observed. "The intelligence I receive informs just
about every foreign policy decision we make."[1] Intelligence has influ-
enced the decision making of most presidents, and during the cold war
it played a key role (sometimes helpful, sometimes not) in many fateful
choices. Among them were the provocative deployment of American
troops near the Yalu River during the Korean War (1950–53), the Bay of
Pigs fiasco in 1961, the Cuban missile crisis in 1962, and the attempted
rescue of the *Mayaguez* in the South China Sea in 1975. Yet despite an
increasing number of studies written on intelligence, the topic is often
confused in the public mind with the fantasy world of Ian Fleming. To
remedy this confusion, my book underscores the significant role played
by real-world intelligence in the conduct of contemporary American foreign policy.

Guiding the secret agencies has been a daunting leadership challenge
for American officials. In 1947, President Harry S Truman vowed to coordinate America's espionage apparatus more tightly. No more surprise
attacks like the one that nearly destroyed the Pacific fleet at Pearl Harbor. Yet his hope for more integrated information on global affairs remains substantially unfulfilled, stymied by fractious bureaucratic rivalries
inside the intelligence "community."

## The Secret Agencies

This nation's intelligence community—a misnomer if there ever was one— is composed of the Central Intelligence Agency (the CIA or simply "the Agency") and a dozen other entities that conduct mostly hidden activities on behalf of the federal government (see figure 1). These organizations are responsible for three primary missions: the collection and interpretation ("analysis") of information gathered from every corner of the globe; the protection of U.S. government secrets against hostile intelligence services and other spies ("counterintelligence"); and the clandestine manipulation of events in foreign lands on behalf of America's interests through the use of propaganda, political activities, economic disruption, and paramilitary operations (collectively known as "covert action" or "special activities").

The collection of intelligence relies on technical means (satellites and reconnaissance airplanes, for example, or, in the professional acronym, technical intelligence or TECHINT); on human means (classic espionage or human intelligence, HUMINT); and on the sifting of information available in the open literature (newspapers, public speeches, and the like, sometimes referred to as open-source intelligence or OSINT).

Of the United States' thirteen intelligence organizations, eight fall within the framework of the Defense Department. These agencies include those in the four military services (army, navy, air force, and marines), which are concerned chiefly with gathering tactical information for battlefield purposes, as well as the Defense Intelligence Agency (DIA), which runs the Department's Defense HUMINT Service (a network of military espionage agents overseas) and assesses intelligence for the military and civilian personnel up the Pentagon's chain of command. Other military intelligence agencies are the National Security Agency (NSA), the nation's code breaker and collector of worldwide electronic transmissions (notably signals intelligence or SIGINT)—potential tips about what is about to happen somewhere in the world; the National Reconnaissance Office (NRO), responsible for building and launching spy satellites and their in-space supervision; and the National Imagery and Mapping Agency (NIMA), in charge of interpreting satellite photography ("imagery" intelligence or IMINT, a look at what is happening in the world).

*Figure 1.* The U.S. Intelligence Community

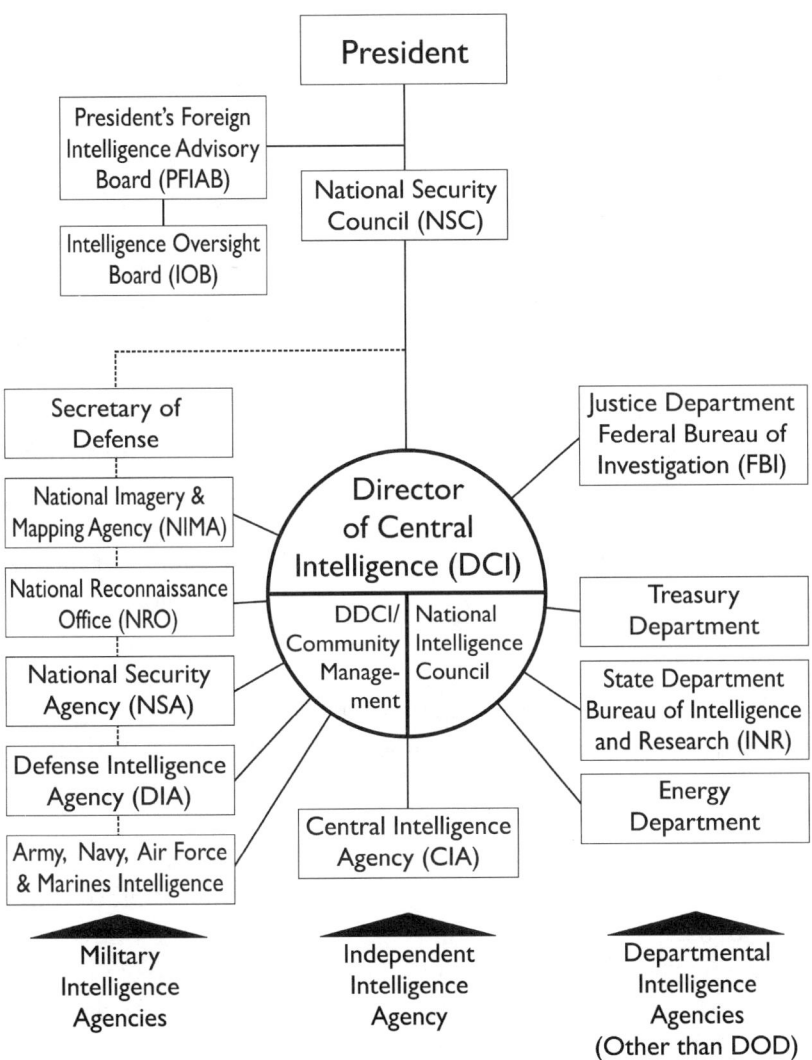

In addition, NIMA, the newest intelligence agency, prepares world maps used by everyone from crisis managers in the White House Situation Room to fighter pilots and foot soldiers in combat (and also for targeting coordinates built into the electronic brains of cruise missiles and other "smart" weapons). Just how important accurate mapping can be was underscored in 1999 during the war precipitated in the Balkans by a Serbian takeover of Kosovo. Out-of-date mapping data on Belgrade went from the hands of intelligence analysts into the cockpit of a NATO B-2 bomber pilot headed for the Yugoslav city. Under the impression that an improperly identified building was an arms depot, the pilot dropped part of his payload on what proved to be the Chinese embassy.

Four cabinet departments have nondefense intelligence agencies: the Energy Department, with one intelligence unit that tracks the worldwide flow of nuclear materials and another brand-new agency created to improve security at the nation's weapons laboratories; the State Department, whose Bureau of Intelligence and Research (INR) serves the secretary of state and the diplomatic corps and draws heavily on the highly touted political reporting of foreign service officers; the Treasury Department, which supervises intelligence units within the Secret Service and the Internal Revenue Service (IRS); and the Justice Department, home of the counterintelligence corps of the Federal Bureau of Investigation (FBI) and the intelligence division of the Drug Enforcement Administration (DEA).

Finally, the CIA is an institutionally independent entity, situated in neither the organizational framework of the Pentagon nor that of any of the other cabinet departments (although it does collect and analyze strategic military information from abroad, in addition to its responsibility for a wide range of nonmilitary subjects). The CIA enjoys a special stature in the intelligence community by virtue of its early creation in 1947, predating most of the other agencies. More important, the main office of the leader of the entire intelligence community—the director of Central Intelligence (DCI)—is located on the seventh floor of the CIA's headquarters building in Langley, a neighborhood in the Virginia suburb of McLean, near Washington, D.C.

Surrounded by an electric barbwire fence and patrolled by stern-faced guards in dark blue fatigues with black pistols at their hips and German shepherds at their heels, the CIA is a 219-acre leafy, campuslike compound on the west bank of the Potomac River. The DCI also has an office in the Old Executive Office Building adjacent to the White House but spends little time there outside of attending the occasional meetings of the president's Foreign Intelligence Advisory Board.

## The Ups and Downs of Intelligence

Despite the enormous expense of maintaining this information system—the largest ever devised to assist in the governance of a nation—these thirteen agencies are often blindsided by important world events. The following are some recent events that took American intelligence by surprise:

- North Korea's 1999 testing of a three-stage missile.
- North Korea's 1998 attempt to place a surveillance satellite in space.
- The 1998 bombing of the American embassies in Kenya and Tanzania.
- India's and Pakistan's nuclear tests in 1998—"a good kick in the ass for us," ruefully conceded a senior intelligence official.[2]
- Gerhard Schroeder's 1998 ascension to the German chancellorship (the CIA predicted that Helmut Kohl would win).
- The 1996 bombing of a U.S. military apartment complex in Dhahran, Saudi Arabia.
- The threat of Japan's Aum Shinrikyo organization, which attacked the subway system in Tokyo with nerve gas in March 1995 and had plans to attack U.S. cities as well.
- Iraqi President Saddam Hussein's extensive nuclear, chemical, and biological weapons programs, discovered in the aftermath of the Persian Gulf War.

One of the unfortunate facts of life is that no intelligence community, no matter how large or expensive, can know everything that is going on in the world. The planet is simply too vast. Moreover, nations and groups such as terrorist cells are clever at hiding their activities. Still, much can be done to reduce the number of intelligence failures and thereby better protect Americans against threats from abroad. This is the main interest of this book.

The intelligence agencies have had successes. As a senior intelligence official correctly claimed, "We're in a different class, compared to any other nation in the world—thanks to our satellites and SIGINT."[3] Satellites provide photographs snapped from space, such as high-resolution images of enemy troops and weapons, and experts in signals intelligence can intercept revealing conversations held by those who intend harm to the United States. But even when they save lives (the main purpose of intelligence), these achievements usually go unheralded, since the secret agencies try to conceal successful methods that they might use again against future threats. Nonetheless, some victories have made their way into the public record, including the rounding up of more than fifty international terrorists in the past five years; effective support for U.S. military operations in the Persian Gulf, Bosnia, and Kosovo; the destruction of Colombia's Cali drug cartel; the disruption of terrorist Osama bin Laden's activities; and an important role in the effort to prevent the outbreak of war between Turkey and Greece.[4] Certainly America's intelligence agencies have also made their share of mistakes. Their close watching of Soviet military activities, however, may well have helped (along with the nuclear deterrent) to prevent the cold war from mushrooming into a thermonuclear war--the most important contribution of these agencies since their establishment.

So, as with all human ventures, the intelligence ledger has its pluses and minuses. To reduce the debts in the twenty-first century will not be easy, as America's current advantage in imagery is rapidly diminishing. In 1999 the civilian sector launched a surveillance satellite that is almost as good as the NRO's best space "platforms" and whose photographs are for sale to anyone with cash or a credit card. During the Persian Gulf War, the United States enjoyed a nearly perfect view ("transparency") of the Iraqi battlefield, allowing American commanders to pinpoint targets and call in "smart" weapons that demolished enemy positions with much greater success than in previous wars. In contrast, the Iraqi military remained in a fog about the American side of the battlefield. Within a few years, however, Iraq and other rogue nations will have access to their own satellites—or commercially available substitutes (the Rent-a-Satellite option)—to acquire battlefield transparency for themselves.

America's SIGINT capacities are declining as well, approaching what one authority has referred to as a "crisis" situation.[5] The NSA's listening satellites capture microwave telephone transmissions from the air. But the world is rapidly switching to underground (and undersea) fiber-optic modes of communications, which are much harder for this agency's technicians to tap and so are leaving the NSA with an increasingly irrelevant constellation of SIGINT satellites. Furthermore, the NSA has traditionally depended on its considerable skills at decoding foreign diplomatic communications to gain access to secret information. But nations and terrorist groups are growing more and more clever at encrypting their messages using complicated mathematical, computer-based technologies that can stymie even the most experienced NSA cryptologists. Moreover, under pressure from the profit-oriented U.S. software industry and the Department of Commerce, the Clinton administration decided in 1999 to allow the export of advanced American software that encrypts electronic communications, making it even harder for the NSA and the FBI to break into the communications of foreign entities that might intend harm to the United States.

There is an additional shortfall on the human side of the intelligence community. Currently, the agencies do not have enough spy handlers ("case officers") abroad to recruit foreign agents ("assets"), especially in places where the United States has never had much of a presence (such as in China and various Arab nations). As a result, the human intelligence flowing back to the CIA is insufficient as well. Even if this HUMINT problem could be solved, the community would still have another, equally serious human deficiency: brain power. The secret agencies lack enough talented information interpreters ("analysts") to make sense of all the data that stream into their offices each day. On the eve of the Persian Gulf War, for instance, the DIA had only two analysts assigned to study the intelligence on Iraq.[6] Imagery analysis has also suffered from inadequate attention. An intelligence supervisor on Capitol Hill reported that "less than half of the pictures taken by our satellites ever get looked at by human eyes" or, for that matter, "by any sort of mechanized device or computerized device detecting change."[7] The United States does not have enough imagery analysts, many of whom chose to retire rather than be uprooted from the CIA and sent to the new NIMA.

Across the board of the various "ints" (intelligences), America's analytic depth is uncomfortably shallow. The first generation of U.S. intelligence officers hired in the 1950s began retiring in the past few years and has yet to be replaced with an adequate number of fresh recruits. The intelligence community is thus undertaking its largest recruitment effort since the early days of the cold war. But even after the newcomers are trained and sent overseas, it takes years—decades usually—for them to mature into effective officers with a productive network of assets in foreign capitals. "We need to recruit talent, grow it, and nurture it," emphasized a ranking CIA official, "and this means paying and promoting area experts in a way that is competitive with the private sector."[8]

Lacking, too, are adequate connections between the various collectors and analysts inside the intelligence community at home, on the one hand, and U.S. military and civilian personnel overseas, on the other hand. Also missing is an effective pooling of the findings and insights produced by all the agencies in the intelligence community (a desirable "all-source" intelligence capability). "We need a smoother electronic communication of intelligence *everywhere*," stressed a recent director of State Department intelligence.[9]

In a nutshell, the secret agencies must recapitalize or become obsolete. They need better technology, more officers in the streets of foreign capitals, additional analysts at home (though with more frequent travel abroad than is presently the case for these desk-bound thinkers),[10] and a greater integration of all phases of intelligence, from the gathering and analysis of information to its timely dissemination. These goals can be achieved while at the same time (with a thoughtful shifting of priorities) reducing the overall size and expense of the intelligence community. The preferred model is a smaller, more efficient intelligence service—not as limited as Britain's secret service, since the United States has broader global responsibilities than Great Britain does, but similar in its leanness and agility.

Any ornery mule can kick down a barn; building one is harder. Similarly, the various shortcomings that plague the intelligence agencies are relatively easy to outline, whereas coming up with workable solutions is a more difficult assignment. Nonetheless, this book hopes to contribute toward that end. The starting point is a look at the array of threats that confront the United States in this new and uncertain world, for which intelligence is expected to provide the first line of defense.

# PART I

# An Intelligence Agenda
# for a New World

# ONE

# A Planet Bristling with
# Bombs and Missiles

I believe the proliferation of weapons of mass destruction presents the greatest threat that the world has ever known . . . perhaps the greatest threat that any of us will face in the coming years.

—Secretary of Defense William S. Cohen,
*Confirmation Hearings*, U.S. Senate
Armed Services Committee, 1997

## The More Things Change . . .

When the Soviet Union disappeared in 1991, so did the central concern of U.S. intelligence. Throughout the cold war, most of America's intelligence resources were focused on the USSR and its activities at home or abroad. The primary goal of U.S. foreign policy was to curb the spread of Communism.[1] Now, in the new order of things, the CIA and its companion agencies have had to reshuffle their missions and targets and, skeptics warned, perhaps even invent some new ones to justify the continuing existence of a large bureaucracy with an annual budget in excess of $27 billion.

According to a former DCI, Robert M. Gates, the demise of world Communism ushered in "a set of tasks assigned to the Agency [that] are both more complex and more numerous than during the cold war."[2] Debate over the proper objectives of a refashioned intelligence agenda heated up during the Clinton administration as it attempted to navigate the uncertainties of a new age without the reliable compass of the containment doctrine.

Observers of American foreign policy wondered whether life after the omnipresent Communist threat would produce a dramatically different approach to international affairs in Washington, D.C., as befitting the radical change in global politics. Within the secret confines of the National Security Council (NSC), the Pentagon, and the intelligence community, planners drew up fresh lists of enemies—real and potential—now arrayed against the United States. The White House and Congress created a special panel of inquiry, "The Roles and Capabilities of the United States Intelligence Community" (the Aspin-Brown commission), viewed widely as an opportunity to revamp the nation's secret agencies for a different kind of threat environment. Public officials and media pundits claimed that economics would now replace the nation's more traditional concerns about military security.

The intelligence community adapted fairly quickly to the changed environment, contrary to the expectation that the secret agencies (in the caricature of bureaucracies) would prove sluggish and resistant to change. By 1994, the CIA had extensively reoriented its global operations, dedicating only about 15 percent of its assets to Russian intelligence collection and analysis. Gates, the first post–cold war DCI (1991–93), referred to this new orientation as a "massive reallocation of resources."[3] The former Soviet empire, once hidden behind an "iron curtain," was now on view to outsiders. Russia alone had hundreds of neophyte independent newspapers, magazines, and other media outlets, as well as a handful of competitive political parties. Secrets were fewer, so the need for espionage by the CIA was less.

This impressive reshuffling of duties notwithstanding, America's foreign policy goals remained relatively static in the post-Communist world. To be sure, the list of adversaries had changed, with "rogue nations" like North Korea and Iraq moving to the forefront to take the place of the Soviet Union. Attention to economic globalism fell short, however, of what the hoopla over the creation of a new National Economic Council seemed to foreshadow early in the Clinton administration. Moreover, the Aspin-Brown commission was able to make only modest adjustments to, rather than a sweeping reform of, the fifty-year-old CIA and the rest of the intelligence community. In the highest councils of government, military security continued to hold sway over other agenda items, and the military intelligence agencies still received the lion's share (85 percent) of the annual budget for espionage.

## Old Wine in New Bottles

### Military Security

The needs of human beings follow a certain priority, from basic survival to enlightened self-actualization.[4] Nations, likewise, set priorities according to their needs. "Our first and most important foreign policy priority is peace—for ourselves and for others," stated the director of the Policy Planning Staff in the Carter administration.[5] In a bipartisan echo, the Reagan administration's State Department emphasized the importance of "seeking to protect the security of our nation and its institutions, as well as those of our allies and friends."[6] Above all during the cold war, America would keep up its military guard, carry a big stick, and—if necessary—use it.

But with the demise of the Soviet Union, it seemed for a moment that military matters might be less pressing. A series of arms accords adopted near the end of and soon after the cold war on intermediate-range nuclear forces (INF), strategic arms reduction talks (START I and START II), and chemical weapons appeared to foreshadow a decline in military confrontations in the world. And in fact, around the globe, democracy took root in once inhospitable soil. Juntas fell in Latin America, and liberated citizens cast aside Communist regimes in Central Europe. For the first time in history, a majority of nations were experimenting with some form of representative government.

But even though the U.S.-Soviet standoff had ended, many nations (and ethnic and tribal factions) continued to regard the use of force as an attractive option in pursuit of their objectives. Indeed, much of the world looked just as it had during the cold war: India and Pakistan exploded nuclear devices underground in 1998, and North Korea fired a test missile over Japan's home islands in 1999, and in 1999, too, the American people learned that China had evidently engaged in widespread espionage activities inside the United States.

Some nations ventured further. Iraq invaded Kuwait in 1990, and as the century's last decade ended, savage internecine warfare broke out in Somalia, Burundi, Rwanda, the Balkans, and East Timor. Reports of mass rape and genocide in Central Africa, Bosnia, and Kosovo became part of the evening news throughout 1998 and 1999. Despite the end of the cold war, the world remained a hostile place.

Nations become not what they may wish to be but what they must be. Accordingly, in light of the enduring military threats in the world after the cold war, the United States was forced to set aside thoughts of a peace dividend, particularly since the country had been thrust into a new leadership position. Less by aspiration than by fait accompli, the United States had become the world's foremost power. Reinforced by the dynamics of the military-industrial complex (alive and well even without the Soviet threat), Washington officials maintained U.S. defense and intelligence budgets at near cold war levels—indeed, using the excuse of the Kosovo crisis in 1999, GOP legislators sought and obtained large spending increases for national security.

If America now was the world's leading power, it also had to have a credible military capability to intervene when necessary—or so the nation's leaders seemed to think. The intelligence community would have to monitor potential military threats around the globe, from tracking the proliferation of major weapons systems and anticipating chemical and biological terrorist attacks against the United States to gathering information vital to American military operations whenever they might take place.

## Political Security

As Clausewitz pointed out, war is the pursuit of politics by other means. The United States must understand the political machinations of other nations as well as the location and capabilities of their war machines. The twenty-first century has not changed the concentration by America's intelligence agencies on both military and political concerns, what is often referred to as "strategic" interests in contrast to economic and humanitarian considerations.[7] Does North Korea intend to start a war against South Korea or Japan? Do the leaders of China have imperialist intentions in Asia, perhaps beginning with an invasion of Taiwan? Has Iraq resumed its quest for nuclear weapons? How friendly will the new president of Russia be toward the United States?

## Economic Security

Because of the United States' abiding interest in the military and political dimensions of international affairs, its goal of economic prosperity has usually been relegated to second position in the list of America's leading foreign policy (and, therefore, intelligence) objectives.[8] At the beginning of the Clinton years, however, it seemed as though issues of international economics were about to displace America's long-standing central interest in military and political security. With the cold war now in the hands of the historians, the new administration decided that it could afford to concentrate more on domestic policy considerations. "The Clinton administration has given priority to 'commercial diplomacy,' making the promotion of American exports a primary foreign policy objective," observed a foreign policy expert in 1997.[9] Or as President Clinton's U.S. trade representative put it in the early months of the administration, "The days when we could afford to subordinate our economic interests to foreign policy or defense concerns are long past."[10]

The president's first DCI, R. James Woolsey, reinforced these sentiments. "The days are gone," he said, "when international economics could be labeled low politics to separate it from the higher, loftier plane of political-military issues."[11] President Clinton's undersecretary of state for political affairs further stressed that "our economic interests are paramount,"[12] and the director of the FBI, Louis Freeh, added, "We've entered a phase and a century where our economic independence and security and strength [are] really identical to our national security."[13] Throughout his presidential honeymoon, Bill Clinton appeared determined to focus on rebuilding the American economy. His administration believed, according to a trade expert, that "international issues (other than commercial ones) could be for the most part marginalized."[14]

Then the pressure of security problems began to crowd in on the president's economic aspirations: Iraq, Somalia, Burundi, Rwanda, North Korea, Bosnia, the terrorist Osama bin Laden (hiding in Afghanistan under the protection of the Taliban regime), mainland China's threats against Taiwan, Israeli-Palestinian flare-ups, tensions between India and Pakistan, and the war in Kosovo that threatened to embarrass—some said unravel—NATO, America's second oldest defense alliance (signed in 1949, two years after the Rio Treaty provided for regional security in the Western Hemisphere). International economics no longer enjoyed the front seat in the bus.

"Most of the threats to global stability—and ultimately to the security and integrity of American civilization—have had less to do with the intricacies of "geoeconomics," wrote a foreign policy specialist, "than with a primal fact of international politics, namely, states and peoples intimidating one another by force of arms."[15] While some authorities continued to argue that American foreign policy had become largely a battle over international economic supremacy,[16] by 1996 the Clinton administration knew better. It was up to its ears in problems that chiefly involved the Pentagon and the Department of State, not the Departments of Commerce and Treasury or the U.S. trade representative.

This is not to say, of course, that trade no longer matters. It has always mattered, from the days of Thomas Jefferson's naval duels with the Barbary pirates in the Mediterranean (an early use of military force to protect economic interests) to contemporary diplomatic struggles with Japan and China over worrisome trade imbalances. Today, as a *New York Times* foreign affairs columnist writes, "Economic crises can spread rapidly from one continent to another."[17] Although America cannot afford to ignore the ramifications of an increasingly global economy, the Clinton administration's initial euphoria for things commercial gave way to a greater concern for military and political affairs.[18] Intelligence has mirrored these policy interests, focusing more on economic intelligence from 1993 to 1997, after which intelligence support for military operations gained ascendancy when the Iraqis again got out of control and President Slobodan Milosevic started his policy of ethnic cleansing in Bosnia and Kosovo.

### The Security of a Quality Life with Human Dignity

The United States' foreign policy goals extend beyond the military, political, and economic. Though generally less well supported by the American people,[19] a cluster of lifestyle issues that threaten humanity attract the sympathies of many citizens, issues such as adequate health care, quality housing and education, clean air and water, protected woods and streams, defense against drug dealers and other international criminals, and freedom from the biggest killer of all, infectious diseases.[20]

Many Americans care, too, about global injustice, particularly the violation of human rights in other lands. A major impetus for U.S. military involvement in Africa and the Balkans since the end of the cold war was a heartfelt concern for the suffering of the people in those regions, whether they were victims of hunger or armed conflict. Americans also hope to see the benefits of democracy spread worldwide, a dominant theme in the Clinton administration, with its goal of democratic "enlargement" taking the place of Communist containment as the centerpiece of American foreign policy.

Expressions of cold war nostalgia are commonplace among intelligence officers and other members of the national security establishment in the United States. "During the cold war, life was simpler for intelligence agencies," reminisced a senior intelligence officer. "There was a reasonably clear consensus about who the bad guys were, about what countries were legitimate targets for intelligence collection. Today, the situation is much more complicated."[21] This complication arises from the host of claimants for the intelligence dollar that was once dedicated almost exclusively to anti-Communist activities. With Communism now largely in ruins, policy officials have turned to other threats facing the nation. While most of these perils are military, political, or economic (like the wars in the Persian Gulf and Kosovo, the byzantine political maneuvering in Moscow, and the recent Asian financial crisis), some are more novel and have stimulated debate over the so-called New Intelligence Agenda, characterized by a greater awareness of how intelligence might be used to improve the quality of life for Americans and to make the world more humane.

In 1994, the director of the DCI's National Intelligence Council (NIC) created a new position: a national intelligence officer, or NIO, for global affairs. This analyst's portfolio gave special attention to "soft power," the director's label for issues of human rights, international ethics, and other cultural and ideological influences related to the quality of life and human dignity around the world, as distinguished from the "hard power" of traditional military, political, and economic might.[22] This large basket of responsibilities contains everything from global ecology issues and the danger of infectious diseases to world hunger and violations of basic human rights. While the NIC global affairs position is new, the concern for such matters is not. In preparing his speech to announce the Marshall Plan in 1947, General George C. Marshall crossed out a reference in an early draft to "the Communist threat." Instead, the enemies of humanity that he chose to emphasize were "hunger, poverty, desperation and chaos."[23] The NIO for global affairs is expected to monitor such conditions and to report on their likely consequences for American and allied interests abroad. The growing importance of soft power is unmistakable. As a leading newspaper reported with respect to the war in Kosovo, the United States has raised human rights "to a military priority and a pre-eminent Western value."[24]

To what extent the intelligence community should reorient its resources toward issues of soft power is a matter of considerable debate in Washington, with interest in soft power on the ascendance. During the recent Balkan wars, for instance, government officials here and abroad displayed a strong interest in the capacity of U.S. spy satellites to look for evidence of genocide. From hundreds of miles deep in space, these satellites' high-powered cameras were able to discern evidence that mass graves may have been freshly dug in the villages of Pusto Selo and Izbica in Kosovo during 1999.[25] This imagery then allowed UN investigators on the ground to search for further evidence of atrocities that might be used in trials against the murderers.

During the war in Kosovo, U.S. satellite cameras filmed the countryside several times a day, recording the pathways of enemy troops and tanks, locating burning villages, and searching for signs of civilian carnage. Low-flying pilotless aircraft augmented the satellite data by crisscrossing the province each day with cameras fastened to their bellies. The surveillance operations of two piloted radar planes, called "Jstars" (Joint Surveillance Target Attack Radar Systems), further contributed to the goal of battlefield transparency.[26] When the war ended, Apache helicopters (never used in actual combat in Kosovo) flew intelligence reconnaissance missions over the region, aiming the cameras in their cockpits at any individuals on the ground suspected of foul play—Serbs and their opponents and the Kosovo Liberation Army (K.L.A.), alike. After the cameras recorded the criminal activity, the Apaches swooped in to make an arrest.[27]

Valuable, too, both during and after the war, were HUMINT reports on the activities of Serbian military and police forces. More broadly, HUMINT has grown into an important component of the U.S. efforts to judge the state of human liberty around the world, as summarized in the State Department's annual appraisal of human rights in every foreign nation. Intelligence, often sneered at as an unsavory business, has become a knight errant in the cause of human rights, uncovering foul deeds and helping apprehend the bad guys.

The objectives of America's external relations are, above all, the physical protection of the United States and its allies (a shield relying on knowledge about foreign powers' military strength and political schemes), followed by a concern for economic prosperity. Also on the agenda—though often an interest more rhetorical than real—is the well-being of people in other nations and their freedom from coercion. This is the moral impulse in America's external relations that has long buttressed foreign aid programs, cultural exchanges, support for struggling democracies, the Peace Corps, and, more recently, selected military interventions abroad (notably Kosovo in 1999).

Using this rich intelligence agenda in the post-Communist era, this and the next chapter offer illustrations of the role played by intelligence in support of America's traditional military, political, and economic objectives, beginning with a look at intelligence efforts to prevent the spread of weapons of mass destruction. The following chapters examine two key dimensions of the New Intelligence Agenda, environmental and health security. The purpose is not to offer a definitive survey of the current intelligence agenda; after all, one could write a separate book on military intelligence activities alone, or political intelligence, or economic intelligence. Rather, the purpose is to provide a glimpse into some of the threats to this nation that warrant monitoring by the secret agencies.

## Military and Political Security

The USSR has vanished, but Russia and its bombs remain—including six thousand nuclear warheads capable of striking the United States. With great fanfare, Moscow supposedly removed the United States from its long-range missile targeting, just as this nation no longer aims its ICBMs at Russia; yet these hospitable gestures provide little comfort, since the missiles can be retargeted in minutes. The fact remains that when a foreign nation has the capacity to annihilate one's society in the span of an unthinkable half hour, it concentrates one's attention and remains, in the words of the incumbent DCI, "a major preoccupation for U.S. intelligence."[28] So while the amount of the CIA's overall resources devoted to

Russia has sharply declined, high-quality espionage against this part of the world continues, including the use of the NRO's most expensive satellite platforms. The purpose is to alert the United States if Moscow makes any untoward changes in its relations with the West, particularly with respect to military posture.

Even though Russia is now more open, it still hides information about its military capabilities and intentions, just as it did during the cold war. So does the United States. Moreover, Russia's pro-American sentiments in the aftermath of the cold war have been fickle at best. In 1999, NATO's bombing of Serbia produced mass protests against the United States, leading a *New York Times* correspondent in Moscow to report that "Russia . . . seems at times almost gleefully anti-American and, yearning for empire, is considering new unions with Belarus and Yugoslavia itself."[29]

All nations and other entities (such as terrorist organizations) that have the ability to inflict grievous harm on the United States stand high on its list of intelligence targets. The Clinton administration (as did each of its predecessors during the cold war) carried out a global "threat assessment" exercise soon after entering office. The purpose was to sort out from the nations of the world those that were both well armed and hostile (or ambivalent) toward America. The White House expected the intelligence agencies to watch these top-level threats with special scrutiny, especially to find out as much as possible about their military and political capabilities and intentions.

This objective can be difficult. Nations are becoming ever more sophisticated at hiding their weaponry. North Korea has cavernous underground bunkers at Kumshang-ni and elsewhere, large enough to house a plutonium production facility and possibly a reprocessing plant as well.[30] Inside these hideouts, technicians can construct nuclear bombs, free from the probing cameras of U.S. surveillance satellites. Likewise, officials in India knew when the NRO's satellites would be passing over their territory and, in synchrony, camouflaged their nuclear-testing preparations.[31] At least, though, TECHINT (supplemented by HUMINT) has been able to monitor most significant nuclear weapons developments. The U.S. intelligence community had a good track record of knowing where Soviet missiles and tanks were during the cold war, especially after the Cuban missile crisis when U.S. surveillance satellites became more sophisticated and plentiful. Much harder to fathom have been the political intentions of leaders in Moscow, Baghdad, Belgrade, and Pyongyang, for in these places one needs a HUMINT asset with access to the inner sanctums where decisions are made.

## The Importance of Nonproliferation

High on the list of military-political intelligence objectives is a problem that cuts across national boundaries: the proliferation of nuclear, biological, and chemical (NBC) weapons, as well as the development of radiological agents for military purposes. Nations acquire advanced weapons for a number of reasons, sometimes as a means for discouraging an adversary from trying to topple nation-state "dominoes" that might eventually fall toward their own shores (a fear of the United States with respect to Soviet military operations in the developing world). Or because they seek status (Great Britain) or are curious about the ability to master the technical problems (a potential fascination for Sweden and Switzerland). Some countries consider themselves in a state of siege and view weapons of mass destruction as the ultimate deterrent (North Korea, Israel). Others appear driven by a lust for power and hegemony (Iraq, Iran) or a sense of fatalism (the Japanese terrorist group Aum Shinrikyo).

Disturbing reports at the end of the cold war suggested that a surge in the spread of NBC weapons was rampant, including nuclear programs in Iraq and North Korea; aggressive efforts by Iran to purchase fissionable materials; the sale of advanced conventional weaponry by North Korea and other nations to Iran, Algeria, Pakistan, Syria, and Libya; the suspected sale of missiles by China to Pakistan; the near outbreak of a nuclear war between Pakistan and India; and the fear of international crime rings attempting to steal and sell weapons.[32] According to public opinion polls, the American people view the spread of dangerous weapons as the single most important threat facing the United States in the aftermath of the cold war.[33]

Of special concern to weapons experts is the threat of biological warfare (BW). Biological weapons—employing such agents and toxins as anthrax bacteria, botulinum toxin, smallpox virus, tularemia, cholera, and plague bacillus—are cheaper to produce than nuclear weapons are (costing millions rather than billions of dollars). Moreover, they are easier to conceal and can cause a larger number of casualties (although the dissemination is vulnerable to winds and other weather conditions). For delivery, one could even use a crude system of aerosol sprayers attached to an aircraft, a boat, a truck, or simply a portable device strapped to a terrorist's back. By weight, BW materials are hundreds of thousands of times more potent than the most toxic chemical warfare (CW) agents (such as the sarin gas used, fairly ineffectively, in the Tokyo subway system in 1995 by the Aum Shinrikyo terrorist organization). However, if the terrorist does know how to disseminate the agent or toxin efficiently, BW provides ground coverage that is far more expansive than any other—including nuclear—weapons.

Existing BW agents can also be modified by genetic engineering, making the materials even more pathogenic or infectious. Even benign microorganisms can be converted into pathogenic or toxin-producing BW agents by inserting into these organisms genetic material from harmful species. "With recombinant DNA technology, for example," notes an unclassified government report, "it is possible to produce new organisms, exploit variations on organisms, or induce organisms to respond in new ways, such as producing synthetic bioregulators or chemical toxins."[34]

## The Arms Control Legacy

America's intelligence agencies became deeply engaged in monitoring foreign weaponry during the cold war. As a result of advances in satellite technology, the United States (and, on its side, the Soviet Union) was able to count precisely the number of missile silos constructed by its adversary, and it could estimate with a high level of confidence each missile's accuracy and throw weight. By way of surveillance from space and other TECHINT methods, both nations were able to verify each other's compliance with arms control accords within tolerable parameters of error.

Even though they made mistakes from time to time, U.S. intelligence officers in the CIA's National Photographic Interpretation Center (NPIC) and the DCI's Arms Control Intelligence Staff contributed significantly to world peace through their painstaking analysis of technical and human intelligence on the adherence of nations (especially the

USSR) to arms accords. Modern espionage made the world much more transparent, which permitted a greater sense of security within the ideological camps of both the East and the West during the cold war, thereby helping minimize the risk of a global conflagration.

## A More Complicated World

The job of monitoring weapons production and deployment in the Soviet Union was a daunting challenge, but U.S. intelligence responsibilities are now in some ways more daunting still. As DCI Woolsey once observed, although the Soviet dragon has been slain, "we live now in a jungle filled with a bewildering variety of poisonous snakes."[35]

Even as the intelligence agencies have become more skillful at collecting and analyzing data on weapons proliferation, they are not infallible. In the waning months of the twentieth century, their failures included North Korea's unexpected test of a long-range missile; the lack of verification of a suspected weapons plant in Sudan bombed by American cruise missiles; the failure to know the precise whereabouts of the Osama bin Laden, leader of the Al-Qaida terrorist faction, during a military strike against his base camp in Afghanistan (he was more than a hundred miles away when the missiles struck the Zhawar Kili region of Afghanistan's Paktia Province);[36] and surprise Indian and Pakistani nuclear tests.[37] These intelligence shortcomings—though offset by a much longer list of successes, many of which remain classified—serve as a reminder of the uncertainties that human beings (whether intelligence officers, policymakers, stockbrokers, or academics) face when trying to predict what is about to happen in the world.

The case of India is a good example. The intelligence community expected the Indians to accelerate their nuclear program; after all, that is what the top-level Indian politicians were saying publicly that they were going to do. The surprise was how quickly the program escalated. The Indians had also become more clever at deception. The cables normally moved into place for a nuclear test were nowhere to be seen in U.S. satellite photographs of the test sites, because the Indians had devised less visible ignition techniques. Moreover, during the cold war South Asia received limited attention from U.S. intelligence agencies, compared with their concentration on the Soviet Union and its surrogates; therefore, building up a HUMINT espionage infrastructure in this region after the cold war took considerable effort and still was far from finished at the time of the Indian-Pakistani tests.

The Sudanese case is instructive, too. In 1998, the CIA's biosensor devices sniffed out the chemical weapons precursor Empta (required for the production of the deadly nerve agent VX) in a pharmaceutical factory near Khartoum. The intelligence community had also collected SIGINT and HUMINT information linking the factory in the past with the terrorist bin Laden. Putting two and two together, analysts estimated with a high degree of confidence that the factory was indeed producing chemical weapons, even if the Sudanese strenuously claimed that the only chemicals produced by the plant were aspirin and other common medicines.[38] Such detective work is difficult and imprecise, and "the turning of a few values can mean the difference between a pharmaceutical company and a chemical or biological plant," lamented the CIA's leading proliferation specialist.[39]

As an indication of the growing complexity faced by the intelligence community with respect to proliferation, its experts note the existence of at least sixteen countries with active chemical weapons programs and a dozen or so pursuing offensive biological weapons programs.[40] Furthermore, fifteen developing nations are likely to produce their own ballistic missiles during the first year of the new century.[41] The intelligence community has responded to these events with some new ideas, including intensified intelligence targeting, the creation of a new organization focused on proliferation, improved methods of tradecraft, and a redirection of counterintelligence and covert action capabilities toward proliferation targets. India's nuclear test has also led to a number of postmortems—"watching the football game films," in the words of the director of the DCI Nonproliferation Center—in search of ways to avoid comparable mistakes in the future.

## Countering the Spread of Weapons

### Targeting

According to former DCI Robert Gates, after the cold war the CIA "took scores of scientists and engineers out of the old office of Scientific and Weapons Research, took them off of Soviet weapons programs and put them onto proliferation."[42] Under Gates and his successor, James Woolsey, renegade states like Iraq, Iran, Libya, and especially North Korea became the proliferation targets of highest priority.

Additional targets have included companies engaged in commercial transactions that aid and abet the spread of weapons of mass destruction, such as the German corporations that assisted the Iraqi weapons buildup and the construction of the large chemical-weapons plant at Rabta in Libya.[43] Other intelligence concerns are the whereabouts of former Soviet nuclear scientists (the Russian "brain drain" danger),[44] the buyers of uranium ore, the dealings of international mobsters involved in weapons theft, the activities of shipping companies that might be transporting weapons parts or fissionable materials, and the governments of major powers known to sell missiles and related matériel.

In this last category, the most immediate concern is the movement of matériel and expertise from the former Soviet Union, especially Russia's cooperation in the development of Iran's weapons and missile programs. Worrisome, too, is China's sale of missiles to Pakistan and Iran. A senior intelligence officer reported that "Russian entities have helped the Iranian missile effort in areas ranging from training, to testing, to components," and "North Korea's sales of [missiles and related technology] over the years have dramatically heightened the missile capabilities of countries such as Iran and Pakistan."[45]

Also high on the nonproliferation agenda is the future of India's and Pakistan's nuclear programs (and their implications for other potential proliferators like Iran); the status of weapons development in Iraq now that the United Nations Special Commission (UNSCOM) inspection team has been thrown out of the country; and North Korea's weapons program, especially its ongoing development of powerful, multistaged missiles (the Taepo Dong series) that could strike the United States with nuclear warheads. The intelligence community has dedicated substantial resources to penetrating foreign biological and chemical weapons programs, especially with an eye toward blocking the use of weapons of mass destruction by terrorists. Scores of analysts have been assigned to the routine but important jobs of strengthening existing arms control and export control regimes. More resources have been directed to aggressive operations against proliferators, such as the "substantial" use of covert action for disruptive purposes.[46] Finally, a new buzzword among intelligence officers is "consequence management," preparing to help Americans cope with an NBC weapons attack, should one take place.

### The Nonproliferation Center

When he was the DCI, Robert M. Gates tried to coordinate the government's intelligence-related activities with respect to proliferation. In September 1991, he established the Nonproliferation Center (NPC) and gave it added authority in April 1992. The NPC grew out of a realization among policymakers in the wake of the Persian Gulf War that they needed better information about potential proliferation culprits like Iraq's Saddam Hussein, whose weapons programs had proved far more advanced than the CIA had estimated.

The NPC, like other newly created centers designed to concentrate communitywide intelligence resources on selected problems (counterterrorism among them), is made up of an interdisciplinary corps of officers from the various secret agencies. Housed at the CIA headquarters in Langley, the NPC has been dominated from the beginning by CIA personnel. Nearly all the Agency's analysts covering biological and chemical weapons, missile and nuclear technology, and proliferation supplier networks have been reassigned to the Center. Its professed early goal was to recruit at least 40 percent of its more than two hundred members from non-CIA agencies within the community by the year 2000, but the CIA staff has thus far remained at 80 percent. "Participation [of the full community] is broad but not deep," concedes the NPC director, though he is quick to emphasize that the FBI, the NSA, the DIA, the military intelligence units, the Customs Service, and the Department of Commerce all have representatives in the Center.[47]

To offset the possible dominance of CIA analysts, the director has insisted that the Center's staffers rotate for part of their careers (for one to two years) into some other entity, such as the Office of Naval Intelligence or the CIA's Operations Directorate. The director also serves on several interagency nonproliferation committees (such as the intelligence community's Nonproliferation Committee and the Intelligence Subgroup of the Weapons of Mass Destruction Preparedness Working Group), which he believes provide him with extensive communitywide views on the subject. The director also establishes from time to time "tiger teams" made up of personnel from several different centers and agencies to focus on specific short-term problems, such as how to stop bin Laden's terrorist activities. "Virtual teams" are becoming increasingly popular, too, in which analysts throughout the community work with one another on proliferation issues, linked together by their computer workstations as they follow key developments as a group (say, the money flow of suspected weapons proliferators). Both of these efforts are innovative attempts to overcome the community's centrifugal forces, although a recent commission concluded nonetheless that America's research on the status of foreign chemical-biological weapons programs remained "fragmented among the CIA, the Army and [Energy Department] laboratories."[48] The NPC director also has sought outside expertise, recently hiring a leading private-sector virologist to serve as the DCI's science adviser on weapons proliferation. The scientist schedules conferences with academic and think-tank experts and brings in private-sector consultants and contractors to discuss the technical ramifications of ballistic-missile technology.

The NPC, the White House, and the NSC communicate daily through short classified reports and answers to specific queries on proliferation activities. The Center also incorporates its principal findings into the President's Daily Brief (PDB), the highest-level intelligence document sent each morning to the president and a dozen other top policy officials.

### Tradecraft

The prerequisite for curbing weapons proliferation is information about when the proliferation is likely to occur, where it will take place, and its probable forms. This requires close surveillance of several important sites where proliferation decisions are made. Besides the inner councils of those foreign governments suspected of violations, other intelligence targets are the offices of matériel suppliers and their intermediaries, front companies, the international scientific community, worldwide banking networks and other financial institutions, customs houses, and weapons laboratories overseas.

If the president of the United States decides to destroy another country's facilities used for weapons production (as George Bush did in Iraq during the Persian Gulf War), intelligence agencies must be prepared to provide the U.S. military with detailed maps of the suspected locations. As demonstrated by the mistaken bombing of the Chinese embassy in Belgrade, even obtaining reliable maps may be difficult, especially when a nation (like North Korea) is less open to on-the-ground HUMINT verification opportunities than Yugoslavia was.

## Counterintelligence

The arcane discipline of counterintelligence (CI) contributes to the nonproliferation effort, too, and the NPC closely coordinates its activities with the Counterintelligence Center (also located at the CIA). The purpose of counterintelligence is to thwart the operations of hostile intelligence services, including their efforts to undermine U.S. nonproliferation objectives. During the cold war, inflating rubber submarines was a crude method that the Soviets used to try to fool U.S. satellites into overcounting them as warships. The Kremlin then offered to destroy these "subs" in exchange for the destruction of real American counterparts, a zany deception operation detected by U.S. satellite cameras and the experienced eyes of counterdeception imagery experts at NPIC and on the CIA's Counterintelligence Staff.

Similarly, figuring out how Saddam Hussein and other outlaws may try to conceal weapons lies within the domain of counterintelligence, and this information was secretly shared with UNSCOM weapons inspectors during the Clinton years to help them locate Iraqi weapons caches. Other responsibilities of counterintelligence specialists are interrogating defectors about weapons programs in their native countries and helping America's weapons industries protect their technologies against theft by foreign intelligence services and rival businesses. In 1999, the spy scandal at the Los Alamos labs, investigated by the Cox committee on Capitol Hill, revealed that counterintelligence had been negligent at the nation's weapons laboratories, which U.S. officials have vowed to correct,[49] just as similar vows were made to strengthen it at the Central Intelligence Agency following the Aldrich H. Ames spy scandal in 1994.

## Covert Action

The most extreme method used to stop the spread of weapons is direct military strikes against foreign weapons laboratories, nuclear reactors, or weapons caches, as in the case of Israel's bombing an Iraqi nuclear facility at Osirak in 1981. Escalation to full-blown war, though, is a last resort. Instead, policymakers usually prefer the "quiet option," a euphemism for covert action, or the secret interference in the affairs of other nations. Here the purpose is to undermine a nation's proliferation activities through clandestine operations, without using overt force. Covert actions of this kind might be propaganda placed in foreign media that disclose a nation's involvement in improper weapons activities or articles designed to persuade a nation not to make a proliferation decision (for example, a newspaper article encouraging Taiwan to concentrate on satellite technology rather than rocketry).

The CIA might also try to plant a virus in the computers of hostile weapons laboratories or see that faulty equipment is provided to foreign manufacturers involved in proliferation. More risky would be a paramilitary operation designed to set back or eliminate a renegade nation's weapons production programs, perhaps by blowing up an underground weapons lab. Under the Iraq Liberation Act of 1998, Congress granted $97 million for lethal and nonlethal aid to seven dissident groups dedicated to overthrowing Saddam and destroying his weapons programs through covert actions.[50]

## The Value of Nonproliferation Intelligence Operations

In this way, the uses of America's secret agencies to help slow, if not end, weapons proliferation are numerous. Eventually, though, the problem of proliferation must be resolved through diplomatic initiatives, backed up by trade inducements, foreign aid, and related economic incentives (as exemplified by the recent U.S.-North Korean negotiations, which seem to have at least retarded the development of Pyongyang's nuclear program). On-site inspections and related confidence-building measures for arms monitoring are important, too, though the experience of the UN inspectors in Iraq (until they were expelled by Saddam in 1998) was not encouraging. The inspections in Iraq were the most extensive ever carried out against a sovereign nation. Even so, in a territory as large as California, the inspectors felt sure they had missed many tons of Iraqi chemical-weapons matériel and other suspected caches.[51]

The intelligence community's essential proliferation task, according to the NPC director, is not so much curbing the flow of all armaments around the world but, rather, helping "delay the spread of weapons of mass destruction until nations come to their senses."[52] The hope is to reform the attitudes of foreign leaders who might be thinking about adopting an NBC weapons program. "Long-term obstruction works," declared a seasoned British diplomat.[53] Would-be proliferators must be convinced that weapons of mass destruction are unnecessary for either security or status, as Brazil and South Africa finally concluded.

In the meantime, America's diplomats, military leaders, and politicians continue to seek guidance from the intelligence agencies on how to counter the spread of NBC weapons into irresponsible hands. From time to time, when outlaw nations threaten the international community, the secret agencies may be called on to take more aggressive covert action. In some circumstances, a clandestine approach is preferable to direct hostility and the inevitable casualties of noncombatants.

Another avenue holds promise for fighting the spread of weapons without resorting to extreme measures: intelligence liaison, that is, a greater emphasis on sharing information about proliferation activities among national intelligence services and international organizations (discussed in chapter 7). Presidents Bush and Clinton have already taken some steps in this direction. Both authorized the DCI's Iraqi Task Force (part of the Nonproliferation Center) to share intelligence—particularly satellite photography—with UN arms inspectors to an "unprecedented" degree.[54]

In 1993, President Clinton extended America's intelligence sharing (on a limited basis and over the objections of CIA counterintelligence personnel worried about security breaches) to a number of nations working together to monitor and control global arms trafficking.[55] This could lead to the eventual development of an effective UN intelligence arm for tracking proliferation activities, relying on member states for satellites and other surveillance equipment and also analytic expertise. A greater emphasis on liaison—the intelligence services of peaceful nations working together against the world's renegades—may prove to be the most valuable of all the nonproliferation programs conducted by the United States.

# TWO

# Stocks and (James) Bonds

## Spies in the Global Marketplace

War and commerce are but two different means of arriving at the same aim, which is to possess what is desired.
—Benjamin Constant, quoted in Hirschman, *National Power and the Structure of Foreign Trade*, 1945

### In Defense of Prosperity

An understanding of foreign military threats and the politics that fuel them has been and will continue to be the first responsibility of the U.S. intelligence community. These, after all, including the still-present specter of nuclear annihilation, are matters of life and death. Nevertheless, matters of economic security, too, have always been high on the national security agenda. An intelligence expert explained why economic intelligence is important to a nation: "In its most basic form, intelligence of this nature is designed simply to assist government leaders to better manage the economy."[1]

As the interest in economic intelligence surged to the forefront for a brief time during the first term of the Clinton administration, the government devoted at times (as on the eve of important international economic conferences) roughly 40 percent of the intelligence community's resources to matters of international economics.[2] Even during the cold war when Moscow's political and military maneuvers attracted most of the community's attention, the secret agencies still allocated an enormous amount of funding and human talent to monitoring the Soviet economic system, the "largest single project in social science research ever undertaken."[3] The CIA managed to track closely the demise of the Soviet economy during its final stages between 1984 and 1991, despite failing (like everyone else) to anticipate its complete collapse.[4]

Economic security, then, is by no means a new entry on the New Intelligence Agenda, but specific economic issues of interest to policymakers (and, as a result, to the managers of the intelligence community) have fluctuated over time. Wheat production in the USSR and oil pricing by the Organization of Petroleum Exporting Countries (OPEC) were significant intelligence priorities in the 1970s, for example, while the effectiveness of trade sanctions against Iraq and the flow of petroleum into Serbia were preeminent in the 1990s. The generic economic categories considered important by intelligence planners have, however, remained fairly constant. They include information about and insight into global economic trends, international financial and trade issues, the availability of critical resources, negotiating strategies at international economic conferences, and worldwide technological developments. They do not include industrial espionage.

### Industrial Espionage

The purpose of economic intelligence is to give policymakers in the U.S. government information about the economic decisions and activities of foreign *governments*, not foreign businesses. This support is based on insights derived from sources both open (legal) and closed (illegal espionage), in a ratio of about 95 to 5 percent, respectively.[5] For a variety of reasons, the intelligence community has rejected industrial espionage, that is, providing clandestinely derived intelligence to private American companies.

In the first place, these companies have rarely asked for assistance. The largest corporations already have their own capacity for spying on foreign competitors, often hiring former CIA and FBI officials. In addition, the network of agents recruited by U.S. intelligence and in place around the world are burrowed into governments, not companies. (In some nations, though, certain industries such as aerospace and telecommunications are run by the government, and so this becomes a distinction without a difference.) Moreover, if a CIA agent were caught with his hands in the Toyota headquarters' safe at midnight, the repercussions on

U.S.-Japanese relations might be so severe as to make the attempt counterproductive in the extreme, especially since Japanese autos are often assembled in America through joint ventures that create jobs at home for U.S. workers.

Given the intermingling of American and foreign components in automobiles and other manufactured goods, along with the multinational boards and stockholders of the major corporations, the CIA would run into baffling dissemination problems even if it gathered intelligence against a "foreign" company. Would the company that the CIA decided to help be sufficiently American to receive the top-secret information? The Boeing aircraft company in the state of Washington is a good illustration of the complications inherent in today's global economy. If the CIA provided secret intelligence to Boeing about Airbus (its European competitor), might this not harm another American company, General Electric, which produces jet engines for Airbus? Some U.S. firms make a greater profit in overseas markets than they do in the United States (General Motors, for one) and do not want these markets jeopardized by a spy scandal. Furthermore, given a choice of three or four competing American industries, which would receive the information? Should both labor and management be informed? And if the answer were yes to all of these questions, could the sensitive sources and methods on which the intelligence is based be kept secret?

Commerce among nations has become so interwoven and complex that industrial espionage by the U.S. intelligence community would raise many red flags. Employing a different metaphor, a former defense secretary warned that the hazards of industrial espionage by America's secret agencies would be not just a slippery slope but a "ravine."[6] As a result of these considerations, the CIA has decided that it will "not conduct economic espionage against foreign firms for the benefit of U.S. companies," a position firmly endorsed by DCIs Gates and Woolsey while they were in office (and since).[7] This policy stance also is popular among intelligence officers, one of whom has proclaimed (with a modern geo-economic twist to Nathan Hale's famous declaration), "You know, I'm prepared to give my life for my country, but not for a company."[8]

This is not to say that everyone endorses a hands-off attitude toward industrial espionage. Former DCI Stansfield Turner (1977–80) was convinced that the U.S. intelligence community's rejection of this option was tantamount to a form of disarmament, and unilateral as well, given the support for this approach by nearly all the other industrial nations.[9] In Turner's opinion, in light of the growing world trade competition, economic secrets might help the United States as much as military secrets, and so they ought to be pursued in the same fashion with the same amount of determination.[10]

So far, Turner's argument has not been heeded. Sometimes, though, in the course of their normal espionage activities, the intelligence agencies do come across seemingly important economic intelligence about specific foreign companies, and they are allowed some discretion over whether to pass this information along to the Commerce or State Department. Once inside these departments, the intelligence is stripped of telltale signs that might reveal sources and methods and then from time to time is forwarded to U.S. companies in what can only be described as an evolving ad hoc relationship between the government and various U.S. businesses.[11] These murky arrangements are poorly conceived, follow no uniform guidelines, and, if they contain classified information, are vulnerable to disclosure, however inadvertent.

## On the Defensive

The intelligence community does help the American business community more systematically and legitimately through counterintelligence. According to DCI Gates in 1992, some twenty nations have engaged in economic espionage against the United States since the end of the cold war.[12] Four years later, a Senate document reported that the number of nations that had tried to obtain advanced technologies from American industries through clandestine means had climbed to more than fifty.[13] Another survey in 1996 claimed that China, Canada, France, India, and Japan have been (in descending order) the most aggressive nations in their conduct of non-defense-related economic espionage against the United States, with Germany, South Korea, Russia, Taiwan, England, Israel, and Mexico close behind.[14] In 1999, the Cox committee discovered a remarkable Chinese espionage effort directed against U.S. defense targets as well,[15] and another recent study pointed to aggressive economic espionage operations against the United States carried out by France, Israel, and South Korea.[16]

"There are no friends or allies in this international [economic] spy game," cautioned an FBI agent,[17] a point of view reinforced by none other than a former director of the French intelligence service, Pierre Marion. "It would not be normal that we do spy on the [United] States in political matters," he confided on the NBC TV show *Exposé* in 1991. "We are really allied, but in the economic competition, in the technological competition, we are competitors; we are not allied."[18]

Through such training programs as Developing Espionage and Counterespionage Awareness (DECA) and the Economic Counterintelligence Program (ECP), the FBI advises U.S. companies on protecting themselves against espionage, whether by a foreign company or a foreign intelligence service.[19] A more recent bureau program, Awareness of National Security Issues and Response (ANSIR), educates and warns American firms about foreign intelligence activities that might be directed against them. During fiscal years 1993 and 1994 alone, the FBI reported briefing almost twenty thousand companies about safeguarding proprietary information. The bureau has conducted comparable seminars for universities, laboratories, and local governments,[20] although as the Chinese spy scandal of 1999 indicates, the lessons apparently failed to protect the nation's nuclear secrets at the Los Alamos labs. As an additional deterrent to industrial spying, the Economic Espionage Act of 1996 made it a federal crime to steal trade secrets.[21]

The State and Defense Departments occasionally block some of the Commerce Department's commercial sales programs, to prevent sensitive scientific information from falling into the hands of potentially hostile nations. Such action illustrates how America's export-control laws may be used to curb or at least slow the spread of military technologies around the world. A recent instance is the prohibition against selling a Hughes Space and Communications satellite to China to establish a mobile telephone network that would cover much of Asia. Officials at the State and Defense Departments feared that the technology to place the satellite in orbit might also improve the accuracy of China's long-range missiles.[22] This is but one of many battles that have taken place between the Department of Commerce, with its domestic orientation and interest in advancing U.S. business deals, and the more traditional departments like State, Defense, and Treasury, with their greater focus on security issues.

## The Purposes of Global Economic Espionage

Industrial espionage aside, the intelligence community is busy enough simply responding to policymakers' requests for information about more globally oriented issues, according to a former vice chairman of the National Intelligence Council (NIC), the panel of communitywide senior analysts located at the CIA.[23] "We are being asked today to do much more on a whole set of world economic issues," testified DCI Woolsey in 1995.[24]

### State Economies

Foremost among the intelligence community's global economic responsibilities is helping America's leaders better understand the "objectives, motivations, and constraints" that shape the economic decisions of other nations.[25] America's secret agencies attempt to track the progress of economic reforms in Eastern Europe, for instance, as well as in the former Soviet republics.

The economic future of Russia is in itself a subject of obvious significance. The intelligence community can ill afford to ignore the question of economic stability in a nation armed with thousands of nuclear-tipped intercontinental ballistic missiles and marked by a lingering hostility toward the United States.[26] According to Russia's top prosecutor, Yuri Skuratov, half of Russia's commercial banks are run by criminals, who also control about half of the country's gross domestic product.[27] A poll taken in 1998 indicated that Russians believe that power in their nation is far more likely to be in the hands of "criminal structures and mafia" than in the presidency or the national assembly (Duma) combined.[28] This is a situation that warrants American scrutiny,[29] and the CIA and the FBI may be the best able to provide reliable information on these unfortunate internal conditions in Russia.

To combat international criminal activities, DCI Woolsey in 1994 created the Crime and Narcotics Center (CNC) at the CIA, by renaming and expanding the duties performed by the Counternarcotics Center (established in 1989). The new CNC consists of about two hundred people, 90 percent of whom are CIA personnel, the standard pattern for DCI centers. Any group that is suspected of transnational criminal activities and that has more than two hundred members as well as a hierarchical structure becomes a target for the CNC—that is, if the director thinks the center has a chance of successfully opposing the group. Prominent targets include organizations inside Russia (some of which operate in the Western Hemisphere), Nigeria (active in eighty nations), and various Asian countries.

The three main areas of concern for the Crime and Narcotics Center are business fraud (corrupt business practices, counterfeiting, and financial fraud, for example), threats to Americans (from drug dealers, terrorists, international child pornographers, and other criminals), and issues of global stability (such as arms trafficking).[30] The overlap between the missions of the CNC and other DCI centers—especially Counterterrorism and Nonproliferation—is obvious, and they readily share information and personnel. Cooperation with the FBI on crime matters is also "better than I've seen it in thirty years," claimed the CNC director, adding: "It has to be, since the intelligence community now has more problems in the world to deal with."[31]

Valuable, too, is intelligence on economic conditions in closed and unfriendly societies like North Korea and Iraq, for again such information is often difficult to acquire through means other than espionage. Knowledge of a nation's economic health can reveal much about its prospects for stability as well as its military capabilities, making it doubly important for foreign policy officials to acquire.

Many U.S. government agencies often have information that is as good, if not better, than the intelligence community's. First-rate economists at the Departments of Treasury, Commerce, and State may know more about particular questions of international finance than any CIA analysts do. Yet often the intelligence community can provide a perspective that other agencies and departments may have overlooked, especially "nuggets" of secret information derived from, say, a telephone tap or an asset deep within the trade ministry of a foreign economic rival.

Moreover, sometimes the more open U.S. government departments (especially the State Department) are simply too busy and understaffed to prepare detailed economic reports for U.S. officials. Even the basic task of collecting open information on economic topics overseas has been eroded by substantial cutbacks in State Department personnel posted in U.S. embassies around the world. In response to these staff cuts, officials have turned increasingly to the intelligence community to take up the slack on a wide range of foreign policy issues. According to one experienced government official, "Intelligence analysts—essentially DI [the CIA's Directorate of Intelligence] analysts—do 90 percent of the analysis of the USG [U.S. government] on foreign affairs."[32]

George Tenet, the current DCI, argued further that the policy departments already have a heavy load without taking on the added task of gathering and disseminating information. "If the CIA did not pull [information] together, sort it out, and present it, who would?" he asked. "Some argue that individual agencies, such as State and Defense, should do it; but, in my view, this would place an unfair burden on them. Our democratic system obliges these agencies to formulate policies on behalf of the president and to defend them in public and before the Congress. That is a heavy responsibility."[33]

Nor do the various policy departments have a good track record for cooperating and sharing information among themselves or with the intelligence agencies. "Many policymaking entities jealously guard their analytical functions," accurately noted an observer of international economic policy as practiced in Washington, "and [they] see intelligence service analysis as an unwanted and not very useful intrusion into their territory."[34]

Such obstacles to the contrary notwithstanding, the CIA has taken a leadership role—just as it did with arms control issues during the cold war—in providing useful economic information to policymakers. The Agency has stepped forward because it has the headquarters staff and the worldwide espionage network needed to carry out these tasks. Moreover, the CIA boasts elaborate around-the-clock publishing facilities that help analysts prepare eye-catching, four-color graphics of economic statistics printed on glossy paper and attractively bound. The CIA has become skillful, too, in writing reports that are easily understood by busy policymakers with limited training in econometrics.

Besides these advantages of institutional resources is the secret information the CIA can incorporate into its open-source reporting. An additional flourish is the "SECRET" or "TOP SECRET" classification the Agency stamps on its reports, which fairly shouts "Read Me First!" to harried officials. Finally, the Agency has developed over the years a quick distribution system for inserting its reports into the in-boxes of the government's highest echelons in Washington.

Even though the secret agencies are not necessarily smarter on international economic questions than the rest of the government, they are outstanding at processing and disseminating information. "The capacity to handle both open and clandestine sources of information for now remains uniquely within the intelligence community," observed an expert, "rendering it the sole choice for all-source intelligence."[35] The policy departments wisely understand another advantage of letting the CIA and its sister agencies fill their information gaps: analytic support from the intelligence community is available to them at zero marginal cost.

As a result of these capabilities, the intelligence community frequently takes the initiative in preparing the economic portfolios sought by policy officials. As the DCI's chief economic analyst stated in 1995:

> The intelligence community is not a source of mainline economic analysis. Our strength—and our principal mission—lies in winkling out the key bits of nonpublic information and then blending this nonpublic information with, typically, a much larger volume of openly available material to build a picture of foreign government plans and intentions that is comprehensive (the phrase we often use is "all-source") and, equally important, tailored to the specific immediate needs of U.S. policymakers.[36]

The resourceful policy official also pays attention to the economists in the Departments of State, Commerce, and Treasury, along with those in the Federal Reserve Board, the Office of the U.S. Trade Representative (USTR), and various international organizations. In addition, the prudent decision maker draws on information gleaned from leading newspapers and periodicals, trusted business lobbyists, and opinion on Capitol Hill.

### Level Playing Fields

Also high on the list of economic intelligence priorities, and a newer role, is monitoring unfair trade practices by foreign governments, a responsibility that DCI Woolsey reportedly approached "with particular gusto."[37] The goal here is to ensure fair access for American businesses in the global marketplace or, in the popular Washington cliché, to seek "a level playing field," such as when American companies are bidding for contracts against foreign competitors (insofar as "American" and "foreign" can be ascertained in this age of multinational corporations). The CIA's worldwide network of agents watches for signs that a foreign government might be rigging bids on a contract, giving preferential access to information, taking bribes from foreign firms, receiving kickbacks, or otherwise engaging in inappropriate business practices that would place the United States at a disadvantage.

"We collect intelligence on those efforts to bribe foreign companies and foreign governments into, for example, awarding an airport contract to a European firm rather than an American firm," Woolsey explained. The State Department then warns the offending government that it is about to jeopardize its relations with the United States. "Frequently, but not always, the contract is rebid and the American firm gets a share of it."[38] The Aspin-Brown commission reported that diplomatic interventions of this kind netted billions of dollars in foreign contracts for U.S. firms between 1993 and 1996 alone that otherwise would have been lost.[39]

### Dossiers for Diplomats

The intelligence community also gathers information that might be helpful to U.S. negotiators at international trade conferences, what a former intelligence official has referred to as "tactical tidbits."[40] While en route to a conference on (say) the North American Free Trade Agreement (NAFTA), American diplomats may benefit from studying intelligence insights into which coalitions are likely to form around what issues and how various nations are apt to vote. As one intelligence officer put it, "We can't go into this kind of thing [trade negotiations] disarmed."[41]

In 1993, American intelligence assets in the European Union are said to have provided information that aided U.S. diplomats in preparing for the Uruguay round on international trade negotiations.[42] In 1995, the intelligence community reportedly gained access to revealing data on Japanese negotiating positions regarding automobile trade with the United States.[43] During the final negotiations with the Japanese in

Geneva, a team of intelligence officers continually briefed the U.S. trade representative and his aides on the latest HUMINT and SIGINT findings on the Japanese negotiating positions, along with assessments on just how far the Japanese side could be pressed.[44]

Popular among U.S. negotiators are personality profiles prepared by the CIA on the people they will be facing across the bargaining table. This information is organized into a "baseball card" format for easy reading and carrying, and sometimes is interspersed with juicy tidbits about the foreign diplomats' private lives. Telephone intercepts of conversations held by foreign negotiators on the eve of an economic conference (courtesy of the NSA) are often helpful. Wise recipients of this information understand, however, that signals intelligence can be a risky source of knowledge, as it is subject to deliberate deception, or the individuals being recorded may be poorly informed. According to a reliable newspaper report, the U.S. negotiators have occasionally found valuable the daily "int" tidbits (such as SIGINT telephone taps) but have been less impressed by the intelligence analysts' broader assessments.[45]

The economic agenda for diplomats and spies expands from time to time. In 1999, for instance, President Clinton encouraged the International Labor Organization to adopt a treaty that would prohibit the most abusive forms of child labor practices, including the exploitation of children in prostitution and pornography. In support of the proposed treaty, the president issued an executive order that mandated the preparation of a list of countries and companies that might be engaged in forced child labor.[46] The collection of these data will no doubt require clandestine, not just open, inquiry, and the intelligence community will be handed yet another assignment related to international economic policy.

### Monitoring Sanctions

Just as the United States has increasingly turned to the use of economic sanctions in recent years as punishment against nations opposing its global interests, the intelligence community has been asked to gauge their effectiveness. This involves tracking the activities of individual foreign trading companies, including their ties to international banks and their use of various communications channels (telephone, fax, e-mail). In addition, the CIA is expected to watch the flow of oil, international transportation, and arms into and out of offending nations.

For these purposes, the CIA houses interagency teams that keep an eye on sanctions, following shipping and other modes of trade involving Iraq, Pakistan, Iran, China, and Serbia. The information analyzed by these teams is then forwarded to the Treasury Department, whose Office of Foreign Assets Control is in charge of enforcing trade sanctions. Should the president order the U.S. Navy to check on suspicious ships at sea bound for (say) Iraq, the CIA is able to conduct a quick computer run on each ship to see whether its owners have previously attempted to violate an international blockade.

## America for Sale

The international community keeps track of foreign attempts to invest in the United States or to purchase American real estate and other assets. This responsibility, known in the government as "foreign acquisitions review," requires the community to provide information about such activities to the Committee on Foreign Investment in the United States, an interagency panel in which the Commerce Department is a major player.

## Protection against Predators

In the CIA's rich database on international economic activities are detailed profiles of companies that have been engaged in unsavory business activities, such as violating sanctions, laundering money, spreading weapons and fissionable materials, or selling to known terrorist organizations. These are the "bad actors" of the global marketplace. The Federal Reserve Board, the Treasury Department, and the Commerce Department also have extensive corporate memories in this regard, but the intelligence agencies are often able to contribute useful information to the government's storehouse of knowledge on disreputable foreign companies. The intelligence community funnels these data to the Department of Commerce and the Department of Treasury's Office of Foreign Assets Control, and they alert American banks and firms to stay away from those companies.

## Drug Busting

In the shadowy domain of "underground economics," the intelligence community has been drawn into the war against international organized crime, especially drug trafficking (highlighted by a recent DCI as the "main money-making venture" of international criminals).[47] America's secret agencies have taken on this counternarcotics mission only reluctantly, sensing that law enforcement officials in the FBI and the Drug Enforcement Administration (DEA) are more experienced and better armed to deal with the low-life—and dangerous—thugs who peddle cocaine and heroin in the back streets of urban and even rural America.

The DCI Crime and Narcotics Center is the repository for information collected by the intelligence community on drug dealers' profits—so-called narcodollars—and money-laundering operations. Suspected ties between drug cartels and international banks are monitored for tip-offs on illegal drug deals, and the CNC alerts FBI and DEA officers if the opportunity for an arrest seems ripe.

While this concept of intelligence support to law enforcement agencies may sound good in theory, in reality the narcotics cartels are winning the drug war hands down, even though a few of the major cartels (including the notorious Cali drug lords) have been "brought down" by the U.S. government. Indeed, of the total amount of illegal substances bound for the United States, only about 30 percent is apprehended. Although this is an improvement over the 10 percent interdiction rate of a decade ago, this statistic is still discouraging, since the remaining 70 percent more than meets the U.S. demand for illegal drugs.[48]

Some five hundred to six hundred tons of cocaine are produced each year in Peru, Bolivia, and Colombia, of which three hundred tons are shipped to the United States and the rest chiefly to Europe.[49] In the last year of the twentieth century, production in Peru and Bolivia dropped markedly, but that of Colombia more than made up for the slack. Almost two-thirds of the cocaine bound for the United States comes through Mexico and about one-third through the Caribbean, with Haiti the fastest-growing transit point (currently at some four tons a month).[50] Some three hundred tons of heroin are refined from opium each year, mainly in Burma and Afghanistan (where production is spiraling upward); ten tons are shipped to the United States, with much of the rest going to Russia and eastern Europe.[51] This losing effort has led critics to conclude that success lies not in intercepting drugs, which is akin to finding a needle in a haystack, given the thousands of ships, airplanes, and motorized vehicles that enter the United States each year. Rather, success lies in discouraging the desire of American consumers to purchase harmful drugs in the first place.[52]

Clearly, the United States must more aggressively educate Americans about the physiological dangers of illegal narcotics, especially America's main drug users: white, affluent males in their late twenties and early thirties.[53] The current funding of about $18 billion per year has proved inadequate to defeat what President George Bush often referred to during his first year in office as America's "public enemy number 1." Important to a more extensive education campaign would be publicity debunking various drug misconceptions, including the widespread belief that inhaling heroin (as opposed to injecting it with a needle) avoids addiction.[54] Necessary, too, are more effective treatment programs for current addicts.[55] The constructive role that intelligence agencies (or, for that matter, the FBI and the DEA) can play in counternarcotics is relatively limited compared with the results that could be derived from allocating additional resources to improve anti-drug education and health care, that is, shifting attention away from the supply side to the demand side.

## A Period of Transition

As these examples illustrate, America's secret agencies expend considerable resources on international economic matters. Yet, according to a senior intelligence official, just how important this assignment really is was still not "resolved" as the twentieth century came to an end: "We are still in a transition period."[56] The Asian financial crisis in the last years of the century revived interest in collecting international economic intelligence. Questions linger, however, about whether the secret agencies really can add much beyond the information and assessments already provided by the Departments of Treasury and Commerce as well as other government agencies, not to mention the well-regarded reporting on economic issues by the *New York Times,* the *Wall Street Journal,* and *The Economist.*

In support of the CIA's economic role, its officers are quick to emphasize that the needs of Washington officials are often quite different from those of Wall Street investment analysts. Besides, they maintain, the CIA has become adept at "making things easier to understand" for distracted Washington officials.[57] The Agency focuses on economic problems at the top of the policymaker's tray for "Action This Day," delivering information and insight that are timely, lucid, and attractively presented, a composite of open and secret sources of information directly relevant to the official's immediate concerns. That, at any rate, is the goal but, as discussed in chapter 8, is not necessarily what really happens in the hurly-burly daily life of Washington, D.C.

The CIA has recently tried to concentrate on carrying out three activities especially well with respect to economic intelligence.[58] First, it attempts to serve the needs of the National Economic Council (NEC), created during the first year (1993) of the Clinton administration as an economic companion to the National Security Council. Bo Cutter, the NEC's deputy director, developed the council into an important focal point for economic intelligence, treating the CIA as an extension of his own staff and giving strong credibility to the Agency's "value added" in this domain. The NEC has been particularly interested in trying to understand the politics of shifting coalitions at international trade conferences, and according to Cutter, the CIA has been helpful.[59] Most important, though, has been the daily "tactical" information the Agency has provided about economic events around the world, everything from world crop production to maps tracing international oil shipments.[60]

Second, the CIA has tried to rise above its past focus on the economies of individual countries. Shaken by the Asian financial crisis of 1997–98, Bo Cutter and other consumers of economic intelligence in the executive branch have sought a broader assessment of the world economy, an "integrated transnational analysis" in the current Washington jargon. Knowing what is going on inside a particular country is no longer enough; more important is an understanding of the economic global interactions among nations and the unexpected dynamics they may create. Recently, the National Intelligence Council conducted a one-day "game simulation" involving intelligence officers and policymakers (chiefly deputy assistant secretaries). Participants considered the experience useful for the sense it gave them of the dynamics of contemporary geoeconomics.[61]

Third, intelligence analysts in the community, from the most senior NIO down to the newest employee, are attempting to write more detailed economic assessments. These days, economic intelligence reports are filled with possible scenarios, laying out a panoply of likely directions the international economy might take and assigning probabilities to each pathway. The intention is to remind policymakers that intelligence analysts—mere mortals like the rest of us—never know for sure what is going to happen; rather, they are able only to draw on their experience and expertise to suggest the odds of certain events unfolding. Unlike during the cold war era, policymakers are now presented with fewer black-and-white intelligence assessments. Shades of gray are the order of the day. Although this approach is often frustrating for the nation's leaders, who seek sure guidance and definitive answers, it is also less misleading, conveying to those who must make decisions just the best-guess hunches for various options.

## The Importance of Economic Security

"Our national security is inseparable from our economic security," declared President Clinton's first secretary of state, Warren Christopher.[62] Similarly, President Clinton vowed that despite Chinese spying on the United States, he would pursue better security at the nation's weapons labs *and* improved economic engagement with the Chinese, "because both of [these objectives] are in the national interest."[63]

Most of the economic information sought by U.S. policymakers can be acquired through open sources. Accordingly, officials read newspapers and journals, as well as interpretations of economic trends by economists in the Departments of Treasury, Commerce, State, the Federal Reserve, the Office of the U.S. Trade Representative, the International Trade Commission, the National Economic Council, and Capitol Hill. Still, the CIA has demonstrated a skill for sifting through open foreign materials (especially hard-to-find "gray" sources, such as speeches by Saddam Hussein or esoteric papers delivered by Japanese economists at scholarly meetings) and then combining them with valuable bits of information and insight derived from clandestine operations. This service has been a generally appreciated time-saver for busy policymakers.[64]

The trick is to ensure that the assessments of analysts in both the open and the secret agencies are brought to the attention of key decision makers in a timely, synergistic manner. Here, unfortunately, one runs into the problem of institutional fragmentation that has long plagued the U.S. intelligence community. During America's clumsy response to the Mexico financial crisis of 1995–96, a noted historian and intelligence scholar observed that "neither the Treasury nor the Federal Reserve had a comfortable relationship with the intelligence community."[65] Unfortunately, this institutional estrangement still prevails (the subject of chapter 5).

Even though military and political security concerns most of the time crowd out other interests at the top of America's foreign policy agenda and even though a vast amount of valuable data on international commercial matters can be found in the public domain, the intelligence community will remain a player of consequence in the U.S. government's deliberations over global economic policy. The secret agencies are well staffed for, and experienced in, providing timely information to policymakers on events and conditions related to military, political, *and* economic affairs (which is not to say the agencies are always correct in their assessments). The intelligence community will continue to shoulder the counterintelligence assignment of helping U.S. firms protect themselves against economic espionage by other nations and foreign companies. Finally, the White House will occasionally order the CIA to employ disruptive economic covert actions ("special activities") to counter America's adversaries. During the 1980s, this disruption took the form of mining harbors and blowing up power lines in Nicaragua (considered a Marxist adversary by the Reagan administration) to cause commercial havoc. For as long as nations seek trade advantages in the global marketplace and an understanding of the economic underpinning of hostile military forces, economic intelligence will remain an important assignment for America's secret agencies.

## Balancing the Old and the New

Far less fixated on Moscow since the end of the cold war, Washington's policy officials and intelligence managers have been able to give their attention to other threats that jeopardize U.S. security interests. Strategic security concerns such as weapons proliferation and the danger of ethnic confrontations (which could to a wider war and draw in the major powers) have always been paramount, closely followed by geoeconomic considerations, particularly in the new era of tightly interwoven patterns of international trade.

Less pressing are foreign policy issues related to human dignity and the quality of life for people around the world. Yet these considerations are gaining greater attention as the twenty-first century begins. The intelligence community has been expected to provide insights into a much wider range of threats than it did during the cold war, including environmental and health security, the subjects of the next two chapters.

# THREE

# The Greening of Intelligence

"Of late I have been tempted to look into the problems furnished by Nature rather than those more superficial ones for
which our artificial state of society is responsible."
—Sherlock Holmes, in Arthur Conan Doyle,
"The Final Problem"

## Environmental Security

The expression "environmental security" refers to the potential effects of global environmental scarcity and degradation on the well-
being of a nation or group.[1] Even though America's intelligence
community devoted only limited resources to this question during
the cold war, environmental topics were not completely ignored. The
CIA studied (and carried out, though without much success) ways
to disrupt weather conditions in North Vietnam during the Vietnam
War, for example, and even researched the potential environmental
consequences of a large asteroid's striking the earth. (The conclusion: it could happen, but the chances are so remote that we humans
ought to spend our time and resources on more immediate perils.)[2]
Since the end of the cold war, however, policymakers have asked the
intelligence agencies to address a much wider range of environmental issues.

Some intelligence officers remain skeptical about the new emphasis on
nature watching, dismissing the notion as a "rather squishy" mission and
evoking the risible image of Agency assets creeping around the mountains of Patagonia counting the number of blind rabbits, victims of retina
damage from the ozone hole over Argentina.[3] For some observers,
though, the government's growing environmental agenda is heartening,

however belated. "The cold war is now over," declare a pair of researchers, "and the 'green war' is about to begin."[4]

## A World of Environmental Dangers

Threats to the world environment may be grouped into three categories: those having global consequences, those affecting individual states and their immediate neighbors, and, narrower still, natural disasters occurring at the local level.

### Threats of Global Consequence

Some environmental problems affect the entire world and can be alleviated only through a multilateral response. The United States cannot significantly reduce global warming, for example, simply by changing its own consumption habits; progress requires a worldwide reduction of greenhouse gas emissions. Furthermore, environmental conditions that necessitate extensive international cooperation have become a matter of national security concern for the United States because they may affect the health and lifestyles of American citizens.

The intelligence community has the potential to contribute to the resolution of such problems in three ways. First, they can use their specialized technical capabilities to gather information about the threat by, say, using powerful satellite cameras to track the growth of the earth's flora resulting from global warming. Second, and the most traditional environmental mission for the intelligence agencies, they can provide information to improve the United States' negotiating position during international conferences on environmental issues. And, third, they can verify the signatories' compliance after they ratify an international environmental agreement.

### Environmental Conflict within and between States

While environmental issues are rarely the sole cause of conflict between states or among factions within a state, they can clearly contribute to political, social, and economic tensions. As two leading environmentalists pointed out,

One state's behavior can radically change the amount of resources available to other states—drift net fisheries of one country may devastate a fishing ground used by all—and in the realm of management of the atmosphere there is no problem that does not cross national frontiers: acid rain, greenhouse gases, and ozone depletion are salient at this writing.[5]

An important example of the transboundary character of environmental threats can be found in the Middle East, where the 12 million people of Israel, Jordan, and Palestine receive as little rainfall as does Phoenix, Arizona, thereby creating a situation that, according to an international group of scientists, will cause "significant water stress in the near future."[6] Another illustration comes from Scandinavia where even though Norwegians themselves produce virtually no dangerous amounts of sulfur dioxide and nitrogen oxide, they have one of the worst acid-rain conditions in the world, thanks to industrial pollution drifting northward from Great Britain, Germany, and a few other neighbors.[7]

Another example is the island nation of Haiti in the Caribbean, whose local ecology has been ravaged by government corruption and poor resource management.[8] The soil in Haiti has become so badly eroded that almost no crops can grow, and in 1994 this condition resulted in the mass exodus of a hungry population, headed for the United States in a flotilla of small boats. The ensuing crisis caused by the outburst of refugees toward Florida led the Clinton administration to prepare for a military invasion of Haiti to stem the tide and restore order. This intervention was barely averted through the skillful diplomacy of three private American citizens—former President Jimmy Carter, former Senator Sam Nunn, and retired General Colin Powell—brought in by the administration for a last-ditch try at resolving the crisis peacefully.

Another site of disputes related to environmental conditions is the Tigris-Euphrates Valley, whose rivers nourish the "Fertile Crescent" in the Middle East. Dams in the eastern (Kurdish) parts of Turkey punctuate these rivers, thereby making Syria and Iraq vulnerable to Turkish influence. In this region of the world, "water is power."[9] Other areas of environmentally related conflict are Indochina, Nigeria, and the Great Lakes region in Central Africa. To facilitate negotiations designed to keep the peace in these strained regions, America's intelligence agencies give the White House and the Department of State assessments of local demographic conditions that affect U.S. security interests—American diplomats have learned that what may appear to be a traditional military, political, or economic source of unrest can often have deeper environmental roots.

## Local Environmental Emergencies

Environmental calamities may strike more confined localities, such as an earthquake or severe flooding. In such a situation, the intelligence community is sometimes able to help the Federal Emergency Management Agency (FEMA) and other domestic agencies respond to such crises with information gathered by its airborne collection platforms.

With the encouragement of Vice President Al Gore, the government established its Global Disaster Information Network (GDIN), operated by the U.S. Geological Survey and furnished with data from open agencies like the Environmental Protection Agency (EPA), as well as the secret agencies. For example, in 1989, intelligence managers redirected the spy satellites' cameras to help determine the extent of earthquake damage in California. The secret agencies also answer requests for assistance in rescue operations, as in 1997 when U-2 spy planes aided the search for an air force fighter plane that had crashed in Colorado.

## The Producers of Environmental Intelligence

Only a few organizations in the intelligence community gather and distribute environmental information. One is the National Intelligence Council, staffed by the nation's most senior analysts, the national intelligence officers (NIOs). The NIO for global affairs takes the lead in producing analytic reports on environmental topics (along with many other responsibilities, including interpreting world events related to such diverse topics as narcotics, crime, humanitarian problems, UN affairs, and international ethical issues). Important, too, are the CIA's Directorate of Science and Technology (DS&T) and the Office of Transnational Issues, or OTI, which is housed in the Agency's Directorate of Intelligence.

The CIA's success with a number of internal centers led to the creation of the DCI Environmental Center (DEC). Established in 1996 during the tenure of DCI John Deutch, this latest center has become the focal point for the greening of U.S. intelligence. Lawrence Gerswin, at the time the NIO for global affairs and currently the NIO for science and technology, was the crusading spirit behind the establishment of this, the smallest and most tightly focused of the DCI centers. The DEC lacks the generous resources lavished on some of the other centers (especially the one dealing with counterterrorism). In fact, it has just one analyst concentrating on Chinese environmental issues and only one with expertise on the Russian environment. All together, the DEC has just two dozen analysts, half from the CIA and the others on loan from such places as the EPA, the National Imagery and Mapping Agency (NIMA), and the National Oceanic and Atmospheric Agency (NOAA). Despite its limited resources, the center has prepared several high-quality reports in its short lifetime and is beginning to attract favorable, if sometimes begrudging, attention from the intelligence community.

As with every significant topic of national security concern, the government also has a high-level interagency environmental working group, which meets once a month and is chaired by an NSC senior staff member. Other participants engaged in environmental intelligence work are the intelligence units of the four armed services: the army, navy, air force, and marines, which monitor global environmental developments that could affect American military operations. The National Security Agency's SIGINT collectors have certain words in their computer "watch lists" (such as "pollution") that are used to sort through the deluge of electronic data captured by NSA's worldwide listening posts, filtering out information that the Environmental Center might find useful.[10]

If the environmental information gathered by these military agencies is deemed important by intelligence managers (say, information related to the dumping of radioactive materials in the Arctic Circle region by Russian military personnel), they pass it along to civilian and military analysts in the CIA and the Defense Intelligence Agency (DIA) for closer study and evaluation. As with economic intelligence, the greatest value added by SIGINT in the environmental domain has been to inform U.S. diplomats regularly about the likely negotiating positions of other countries at international conferences.

Traditional HUMINT reporting may be relevant to environmental concerns. By having agents visit (or even work inside) aging nuclear reactors in the former Soviet republics, the CIA or military intelligence units might be better able to judge the risk of additional nuclear-plant meltdowns, like the 1986 Chernobyl reactor accident in then-Soviet Ukraine. Other local assets can complement satellite surveillance with close-up reports about the extent of flooding in Bangladesh or drought conditions in Africa. The National Photographic Interpretation Center (NPIC), now part of the newly established NIMA, is responsible for interpreting satellite photographs of such environmental matters as earthquakes, fires, floods, hurricanes, volcanoes, and oil spills; but it is the "ground truth" of local agents that fills out the picture, especially with respect to how well the indigenous government is coping with the crisis.

## The Consumers of Environmental Intelligence

Like every other form of intelligence, the environmental dimension also has a consumer side, the policymakers who use the information gathered by the secret agencies. Currently, the principal customers are the Office of International Affairs in the EPA; the staff and principals of the National Security Council, which has a new office with environmental responsibilities (promoted by Vice President Al Gore) and is particularly interested in questions of global climate change; and the Department of Defense, which also has a new environmental office run by a deputy undersecretary of defense for environmental security.

The Pentagon's leading field commanders are especially interested in environment intelligence, since struggles within or between nations that are caused by ecological disputes—say, over water shortages—can erupt into to armed conflict that may require U.S. intervention (either unilaterally or through the auspices of the UN or NATO). Moreover, when the United States sends troops into unfamiliar places, field commanders need to know about local environmental conditions that may affect the deployments.

Legislators on Capitol Hill, each with a more or less important environmental constituency, also find intelligence reports a useful guide to global environmental issues. Traveling home to their states and districts, they are able to cite unclassified versions of these reports that have been specifically prepared for them by the CIA. Then, in public meetings with voters, they are able to project an aura of expertise on the latest ecological issues. Private-sector and university scientists also find intelligence data on global ecological conditions useful for their scholarly research.

## Environmental Security Initiatives

Policymakers inundate the intelligence community with information requests (called "requirements" by intelligence professionals). A complex "tasking" process follows, in which requests are evaluated according to priority and assigned to collectors (from spies to satellites). Data are requested on such topics as global warming, stratospheric ozone depletion, the rise in the frequency of catastrophic weather conditions, and the loss of biodiversity. Information is also sought on state conflicts with an environmental dimension, such as disputes over water rights in the Middle East or the likelihood of conflict breaking out between north and south China over access to water. Finally, from time to time, policymakers have asked for the intelligence agencies' help during specific local emergencies inside the United States itself.

### The Analysis of Global Environmental Issues

Two NIOs on the National Intelligence Council, one responsible for global affairs and the other for science and technology, have joined with the CIA's Office of Transnational Issues and the DCI Environmental Center to provide intelligence leadership for the nation's core environmental-security objectives: analyzing global ecological data, supporting America's diplomats at international environmental conferences, and monitoring international environmental accords.

### In Search of Accurate Ecological Data

The intelligence community tries to give policymakers timely and reliable reports on environmental threats to America and its allies. During the cold war, these threats included the cumulative ecological effects of Soviet submarine accidents and the concomitant spilling of radioactive materials. Since the cold war, leaks from nuclear storage sites in contemporary northwestern Russia have been a concern, along with the ongoing dumping of various contaminants into the world's oceans that has been condoned by Russian authorities (the focus of a recent national intelligence estimate, or NIE, prepared by the NIO for science and technology).

Russia is not the world's only environmental culprit. Environmental researchers report on the unloading of waste products by a variety of rogue ship captains "sailing the seas in search of unsuspecting ports in the South, abandoning leaking drums of toxic waste at dockside in developing countries, or dumping it under cover of night."[11] These and other environmental crimes are of concern to the United States, and policymakers rely on the secret agencies to uncover such behavior. Environmental data are valuable, too, for efforts by the United States to help clean up the now abandoned foreign military bases and oil depots in the former Warsaw Pact countries.

The nuclear reactor accident at Chernobyl reminded Americans how small today's world has become. Indeed, an environmental disaster or crime in a country that seems far away can quickly reach the United States. As an example, within two weeks of the Chernobyl accident, research scientists at the University of California in Irvine discovered floating in the air above their seaside campus fission products released from the nuclear facility.[12] The CIA's efforts to track the dumping of radioactive materials by the Soviet Union in the Arctic Ocean is an illustration of the Agency's involvement in collection operations related to environmental security. Relying on the technical collection capabilities of its Directorate of Science and Technology, the CIA has kept Washington officials up-to-date on the frequency of this dumping and its likely effects.

Several topics have been taken up by the DCI Environmental Center, the Office of Transnational Issues, and the NIC, displaying the wide breadth of the intelligence community's involvement in environmental studies since the end of the cold war. Almost all the research has focused on ecological degradation at the global level.[13] Global battlefield conditions have attracted research funding inside the community, especially the ecological effects of Iraq's sabotage of Kuwaiti oil fields and the ensuing oil slick during the Persian Gulf war. More generally, the community has explored a wide range of questions about pollution, including the feasibility of monitoring complex chlorofluorocarbons, or CFC emissions (which many scientists believe are depleting the earth's protective ozone layer that blocks out harmful solar ultraviolet radiation). As suggested earlier, the dumping of hazardous materials into oceans, lakes, and rivers around the globe, along with the effects of nuclear weapons testing on atmospheric pollution (even modern underground tests, mandated by the 1963 Nuclear Test Ban Treaty, leak radioactive substances into the air) and the status of nuclear power reactors in various countries, are ongoing concerns.

The extent to which global resources have been depleted has drawn the attention of scientists in the secret agencies: such matters as tropical deforestation research in support of U.S. efforts to secure an international treaty on forest protection, climate change in support of international agreements on reducing greenhouse gas emissions, global water supplies, the environmental effects of narcotics cultivation, global food shortages, the environmental implications of mass refugee movements in Kosovo and elsewhere, and the environmental implications of world population growth. In addition, the government has turned to the intelligence community for research on natural calamities, including studies of the effects of earthquakes and flooding around the globe.

Scientists in the intelligence community also study future environmental challenges, such as the likely cost of coping with environmental stresses and what technological advances the United States can anticipate to combat global environmental problems. Some analysts examine the environmental issues faced by individual countries, and others explore the prospects for the electoral success of "green parties" in foreign countries.

The DCI Environmental Center is especially enthusiastic about the statistical modeling of environmental futures. "It tells us where to focus," explained a DS&T scientist affiliated with the center.[14] Besides detailed case studies of environmental disputes that have led to inter- or intrastate conflict, the DEC is improving its measures for "I&W" (indications and warning) with respect to the environment, alarm systems to alert U.S. policymakers that an impending ecological event could affect America's security interests.

## Support for America's Diplomatic Initiatives

The second and third major environmental objectives are closely related to each other and entail supporting diplomats involved in international agreements (treaties, statutory agreements, or executive agreements) on matters affecting the global commons. This support ranges from marshaling data to buttress the American position during the early stage of bargaining over the content of pacts through monitoring compliance by the signatory nations on specific agreement provisions.

Support for agreement making has become a steadily expanding responsibility for the secret agencies as the United States enters into more and more environmental accords with other nations.[15] Analysts in the DCI Environmental Center (DEC) and the Office of Transnational Issues (OTI) examine the likely negotiating tactics of other nations at multinational conferences on the environment. Then they provide probability forecasts of where the participants are apt to lean during the working sessions and on final votes. The DEC uses both qualitative modeling and more quantitative gaming methods to simulate international conferences. A recent game focused on the issue of climate change. The players were able to test negotiating positions and float "trial balloons" that might be used in real conferences. Analysts in the OTI also supply empirical data on existing environmental conditions in whatever part of the planet may be of concern to the international conferees, so that U.S. negotiators are not forced to rely on the environmental-impact statistics pushed by those countries that seem more interested in protecting their own economic interests than in seeking a fair international accord that will help all nations.

The following, in chronological order, is a selection of conferences for which intelligence analysts provided support to U.S. negotiators. They represent, however, only a small sample of the nine hundred international agreements on ecological problems that have been a part of the recent U.S. agenda for environmental diplomacy.[16]

- International Tropical Timber Organization (1983)
- Montreal Protocol on Substances That Deplete the Ozone Layer (a landmark negotiation) (1987)
- Basel Convention on the Control of Transboundary Movements of Hazardous Wastes (1989)
- London Conference on CFCs (1990)
- Framework Convention on Climate Changes (1992)
- UN Conference on Environment and Development, UNCED (the "Earth Summit" in Rio de Janeiro, 1992)

- UN Convention on Biological Diversity (1992)
- UN Commission on Sustainable Development (1993)
- Summit of the Americas (1994)
- Intergovernmental Panel on Global Forests (1995)
- UN Convention on Combating Desertification (1996)
- Kyoto Conference on Greenhouse Emissions (1997)

The intelligence support was notably useful, according to a senior EPA official who participated in many of these conferences, in calculating "how far to push" U.S. environmental objectives.[17] Added a manager of the National Intelligence Council, "It was very helpful for U.S. negotiators to know, based on information provided by intelligence analysts, that illegal shipments of hazardous wastes were being made from certain countries who were—at the very same time—engaged with [the United States] in negotiating the Basel Convention on the Export of Hazardous Wastes."[18] The intelligence community was able, too, to uncover instances in which CFCs, the focus of the Montreal Protocol, had been improperly shipped abroad by nations participating in the conference—additional information helpful for U.S. diplomats to have at hand.

The demands on the intelligence agencies to support environmental diplomacy is unlikely to diminish. Other negotiating challenges that loom on the horizon are establishing agreements to control international commerce in toxic chemicals; grappling with land-based sources of marine pollution; improving international forestry agreements; and dealing with a broad range of environmental, health, and ethical issues related to genetically engineered organisms. Preparing solidly researched and clearly written international agreements is only part of the challenge for the United States; equally important are assurances that they will be implemented according to the letter and spirit of the negotiations that produced them. This means keeping a close eye on the diligence with which signatories honor the principles of their agreements and each of the specific provisions.

### The MEDEA Program

Among the Directorate of Science and Technology's most valuable assets is its extensive ecological database, gathered over the years by spy satellites and other collection platforms. Coincidental to their traditional (mainly military) intelligence duties, these platforms' images have mapped the development of the earth's surface. As one CIA officer put it, "We have photographed the evolution of the planet,"[19] or at least some parts of the earth since the late 1950s.

While still a member of the U.S. Senate, Al Gore (D, Tennessee) became a leading advocate for releasing portions of these archives to the American scientific community. He further proposed that a cross section of this nation's scientists be given the opportunity to recommend the kinds of environmental data that the intelligence agencies should gather from various regions of the world, beyond the well-photographed topography of the Soviet republics.

In response to Gore's urging, in 1992 DCI Robert M. Gates and the DS&T management team invited seventy prominent American scientists to visit the CIA. The scientists represented ten different disciplines—including geologists, ecologists, and hydrologists[20]—and the program was initially called the Environmental Task Force (ETF), but within a year it acquired a more informal moniker that stuck: MEDEA (pronounced "ma-day-a"). The word is not an acronym but, rather, a reference to the sorceress of Colchis in Greek mythology, who helped Jason of the Argonauts steal the Golden Fleece.

With their permission, the CIA ordered background investigations of the scientists (if they did not already have the necessary clearances, as many did), along with the Agency's standard polygraph tests. The concept behind the project was to have these experts, some of the best scientific minds in the country, evaluate the CIA's potential for collecting environmental intelligence that would be useful to America's scientific community. The MEDEA scientists were, in essence, a kind of search party assembled to pore over some thirty years of data collected by satellites (mostly imagery, plus some SIGINT) to assess their value for private-sector ecological inquiry. In return, the scientists made available their expertise to help the DS&T interpret environmental conditions that might threaten U.S. security interests, and they helped design new environmental sensors.

According to interviews with DS&T personnel and public comments from outside participants, the imagery shared with the MEDEA scientists has proved valuable for civilian environmental research.[21]

Among the topics in which the CIA and the scientists have had a mutual interest are predictions of natural disasters, with experiments under way on improving the accuracy of forecasts of volcanic eruptions and early warnings of forest fires.[22] They also are measuring global warming and tropospheric water content and looking for buried oil trenches, water run-off contamination, other waste site examinations, oil spills and seeps in the oceans, and biomass burning (a significant source of greenhouse gases).

Included in the secret agencies' environmental research are studies of cloud-size variability, which affects infrared radiation flows in the atmosphere; observations of snowfall, glaciers, and permafrost, important to understanding the growth of vegetation and related animal habitats, as well as global climate warming; and measurements of sea-ice thickness, useful for calculating the exchange of heat between the ocean and the atmosphere and a significant factor in modeling global climate change (not to mention the obvious interest in this subject by military planners responsible for strategic submarine operations). Other studies have examined geological erosion, mapped wetlands, and tracked industrial air pollution, population growth, urbanization, and industrialization. Intelligence sensors have been used for oceanographic research and fine measurements of trends in vegetation, desertification, and deforestation.

The deforestation studies illustrate how the intelligence community can enhance the research of nongovernmental scientists. Satellites and other national technical means of intelligence collection allow a more detailed mapping of small deforested areas than is currently feasible with civilian sensors. Moreover, the MEDEA program permits the examination of a larger number of land-cover categories than currently available through civilian remote-sensing data sets. Finally, intelligence sensors more accurately estimate changes in existing carbon stocks in tropical forest regions.[23]

In general, the intelligence community's surveillance equipment offers greater topographical detail in its earth photography ("reduced mixed pixel ambiguities for improved interpretation" in DS&T lingo).[24] Intelligence satellites can spot a small forest fire more quickly than civilian satellites can, for instance, although the civilian sector is rapidly improving its camera resolution and is likely soon to match the government's surveillance capabilities. Currently, the NRO satellite resolutions are measured in inches, whereas the best commercial satellite (the *Ikonos*, launched in September 1999 by the U.S. firm Space Imaging) has greater than a one-meter resolution.[25] Just a few years ago, only the government could capture even one-meter-resolution imagery with its satellite cameras. This photographic clarity allows analysts to count the number of people swimming in a backyard pool, but so far, only the NRO's satellites can identify each of the swimmers—or, more to the point for intelligence purposes, distinguish a tank from a jeep.

One of the MEDEA projects on the drawing board is to set up two hundred "global fiducials," or earth zones, which the intelligence community's satellites will watch for signs of ecological change. Another possible topic of interest to the civilian scientists is the status of corral reefs throughout the world, a topic also amenable to analysis based on satellite photography.

Cooperation between the CIA and the outside scientific world has not always gone smoothly. They disagreed over what the scientists—unaccustomed to having their work censored by a government review board—would be allowed to publish based on these classified archival data. In addition, several of the scientists refused to take a polygraph and insisted that this requirement be waived. And the CIA has frequently complained that the relationship is, to quote a top DS&T manager, "mostly a one-way street—toward the scientists."[26]

The CIA concedes, nonetheless, that the scientists have provided valuable insights into such questions as how much arable land exists in China and how well the Chinese will be able to feed their large population over the next few decades. As another example, in 1998, the MEDEA scientists studied the condition of the Russian boreal forest, the coniferous woodlands just south of the Arctic tundra zone, as these woods are important reservoirs for more than one-fifth of the world's carbon found in terrestrial biomes. The scientists sharply disagreed with the Russian scientists' projections of this forest's capacity to absorb atmospheric carbon and chided them for underestimating the fire, insect, and logging disturbances likely to affect the trees' carbon-removal potential. The American scientists then called for more data on the forest to be collected by both government and private-sector satellites, coupled with on-the-ground field investigations by civilian researchers.[27]

The scientists in the MEDEA program have also been interested in reviewing intelligence imagery archives on the world's rain forests. As the Harvard University ecologist Edward O. Wilson pointed out, the rain forests are home for some two-thirds of the earth's life species.[28] At the beginning of the twentieth century, the tropical forests that had been in existence for the last twenty centuries remained intact; but in just the last one hundred years, half of them have vanished, and they continue to disappear at the rate of one hundred acres per minute. If this trend continues, all the rain forests will be lost within the next century. Scientists have made clear one of the potential effects of this catastrophe: "The home of nearly half our plant's known species will be destroyed, including those that may hold the secrets to curing cancer, AIDS, heart disease, and other diseases."[29]

As a consequence of MEDEA's enthusiastic evaluation of the potential for important scientific research resulting from access to the intelligence community's imagery, President Clinton signed executive order no. 12591 in 1995, releasing to the public photographs from the Corona, Lanyard, and Argon generation of intelligence satellites. This amounts to a staggering 860,000 images from 1960 to 1972. Under the auspices of DS&T, the MEDEA scientists have met periodically with Russian scientists to exchange views and unclassified data on the subject of remote sensing for the purpose of better environmental monitoring. Under urging from Gore and the DS&T, the National Reconnaissance Office has been willing to "tweak" its satellites from time to time (as DS&T officials put it) to meet specific environmental tasking requests from other parts of the government, including the National Aeronautics and Space Administration (NASA) and NOAA. The nongovernmental MEDEA scientists also are sometimes permitted to use these platforms.

At the present time, only 1 percent of the intelligence community's total satellite collection capacity has been released for environmental research, precisely the level at which the NRO and other elements of the intelligence community (including the DS&T and the CIA) intend to keep the support for environmental science. According to intelligence officials, spy satellites are not well equipped technically for environmental research. The band length of the imagery used by the NRO's satellites is designed to spot the location of weapons and troop movements on the surface of the earth, not to penetrate the planet's crust for precise ecological measurements. Although the intelligence community can be of some help to ecologists (the spy satellites are good at taking photographs of flora above ground), roughly 85 percent of the information of interest to outside scientists regarding environmental matters cannot be addressed by the community's collection platforms as they are presently configured. So the nation's collection capabilities for environmental intelligence can only modestly supplement the research being conducted in other, more open government agencies (like EPA and NASA) and in the private scientific laboratories of industry, academia, and the think tanks.

Despite these limitations, the intelligence community anticipates contributing to environmental research in a number of ways. The MEDEA program will continue to be developed, including the nurturing of U.S.-Russian scientific cooperation on environmental problems. In addition, America's intelligence community will continue to assist civil government agencies with their environmental studies, toward which the higher-resolution imagery of its spy satellites can provide important "ground-truth" referents (at any rate, until commercially available satellites equal the intelligence community's machines in their degree of imagery resolution). "We're trying to make these [satellite surveillance] systems more available to a wider set of U.S. government entities," the NRO director stated, "especially imagery for use by FEMA in disaster relief."[30] Moreover, the intelligence community intends to make its classified ecological databanks more user friendly to a wider array of government agencies interested in environmental issues. Finally, intelligence managers are studying ways to make additional archival data on the environment available to the general public.

One outgrowth of the MEDEA experience was the formation in 1995 of the U.S.-Russian Environmental Working Group (EWG), the brainchild of Vice President Gore and former Russian Prime Minister Victor S. Chernomyrdin. Drawing on the MEDEA experience, the EWG envisions a bilateral relationship between the two nations that is devoted to encouraging cooperation among scientists and intelligence agencies on a host of environmental questions, an unanticipated form of intelligence liaison between the former adversaries. Russian and American environmental specialists and intelligence officers have already exchanged unclassified information on such matters as environmental cleanup efforts, accurately calculating the extent of forest defoliation, evaluating oil and gas exploration risks, and accurately assessing earthquake damage. This cooperative research also draws on selected classified data collected by both nations' intelligence agencies.

### Emergency Aid to FEMA

Sometimes the intelligence community receives requests from the Federal Emergency Management Agency (FEMA) to direct its spy satellites toward U.S. territory in times of domestic environmental upheavals, say, an earthquake in California, a hurricane in South Carolina, or volcanic activity in Washington State. This form of tasking requires high-level authority, given the sensitivity of directing intelligence satellites against U.S. domestic targets.[31] Thus far, such authority has been quickly granted in times of emergency. But such requests for emergency assistance are complicated by the need to protect from disclosure the sensitive sources and methods used by the NRO and other agencies to gather intelligence, such as specific camera-lens capabilities that could prove useful to America's foreign adversaries seeking to develop countermethods to escape the eyes of America's cameras in space. To solve this problem, intelligence photo-interpreters work with artists to redraw the precise images acquired by the satellites ("imagery derived products" or IDP, in the inescapable Washington acronym) into cruder, but still valuable, maplike depictions. This conversion process protects the secret details of satellite camera capabilities but still manages to convey the essential information necessary to aid FEMA in its rescue operations.

An example of cooperation between FEMA and the intelligence community occurred during the 1994 earthquake in Northridge, California. Intelligence on postquake conditions began within five hours of the event, and analysts in the National Photographic Interpretation Center (NPIC, at the time still a part of the CIA) gave FEMA officials preliminary damage assessments on the same day. This form of assistance has also been supplied to other nations that have suffered a major natural disaster. In 1994, for instance, NPIC's analysis of the Vozey oil field spill near Komi, Russia, disclosed numerous, long-term leaks throughout the pipeline system, though it found no evidence of a single catastrophic spill—important information for Russia's emergency workers and a source of their enduring goodwill toward the United States.

## An Assessment of Environmental Intelligence

Reports on environmental issues prepared by the National Intelligence Council and the Office of Transnational Issues remain a low-level concern for the intelligence community and the drafters of intelligence authorization bills on Capitol Hill. "This is not biological warfare and it's hard for [DCI George] Tenet to sell," commented a senior manager of the DCI Environmental Center. Nevertheless, as DCI Robert M. Gates often liked to repeat, the environment and other nontraditional intelligence responsibilities are important to the president, Congress, and others in our government. As a result, he concluded, the managers of the secret agencies should "enhance our capabilities in some of these newer areas, while continuing to monitor more traditional concerns."[32]

An indication of the intelligence community's rising interest in environmental topics is the recent preparation of the NIC's first national intelligence estimate on the global environment, accompanied by a raft of other reports.[33] An example of a key finding in this research relates to Russia. Intelligence analysts concluded that water pollution is the most serious environmental concern facing that nation, with less than half of its people having access to safe drinking water.[34] But some of the studies produced by the Office of Transnational Issues and the DCI Environmental Center have merely duplicated comparable research conducted by NASA, EPA, and other open agencies. An example is the OTI's examination of CFC emissions, which the EPA had already researched extensively. In sum, the secret agencies' most important contribution to environmental security is their use of all sources of intelligence to assess the compliance of other nations that have signed international environmental accords with the United States. Scientists at the CIA acknowledge that this will remain their comparative advantage in the coming years, rather than the replication of studies that can be carried out by well-qualified experts in more public agencies like the EPA. Still, according to some consumers, the intelligence community's raw (unevaluated) intelligence on such matters as CFCs is a useful supplement to the environmental studies by EPA scientists and others, and they have expressed a desire to continue to have access to information of this kind gathered by the secret agencies.[35]

The NIC, the DCI Environmental Center, and the OTI have had little luck making known to policymakers the benefits of their environmental research. Interviews with staff personnel at the EPA and the NSC revealed that policymakers still do not know what environmental services are available through the intelligence community. For instance, a senior EPA official found useful the community's raw intelligence on and analysis of suspected Russian radioactive dumping in the Arctic, of industrial plants illegally producing CFCs in different parts of the world, and of evidence of pollution in sundry global watersheds. Yet he was surprised to learn that the secret agencies also give senior policymakers throughout the government (on request) daily briefings on international topics of interest to them, including information on fast-breaking environmental news around the world. This official also did not know that some policymakers have intelligence "forward observers" in their own buildings, that is, liaison officials from the secret agencies who convey classified information and requests for further analysis back and forth between the policymakers and intelligence analysts. Furthermore, he was surprised to learn that policymakers may regularly request from the intelligence community written materials on specific topics of interest to them, so-called niche intelligence. This official expressed an interest in having all these services to support his global environmental responsibilities.[36] Similarly, a senior NSC official in charge of environmental affairs had had little contact with either the NIC or the individual intelligence agencies and was unaware of the environmental services available from the community.[37]

Blame for this failure of communication between the producers and the consumers of intelligence lies on both sides. Policymakers could be more assertive in seeking assistance from the intelligence community; but clearly the community could advertise its products better. As one high-level EPA official complained, "The intelligence community must become more user friendly."[38]

As for the MEDEA program, the CIA's Directorate of Science and Technology is making some modest and useful contributions to ecology by providing archived imagery to outside scientists for analysis. The DS&T contributes by occasionally collecting material requested by other government agencies and private researchers, if it can be done without significantly diminishing the traditional missions of the NRO's platforms. Although processing the environmental data does cost money, it is a small amount so far and will be further reduced through cost-sharing arrangements with consumers. Officials in the DS&T are skeptical about expanding the intelligence community's environmental responsibilities, however, because their spy satellites are not generally well suited for most forms of ecological research. Thus, these officials anticipate at best a complementary, not a central, role in the collection and analysis of ecological data. The secret agencies can, however, continue to assist FEMA and other governments in times of earthquakes and other national disasters.

The National Aeronautic and Space Administration is in the process of developing the Earth Observing System (EOS), a planned flotilla of twenty-six satellites to measure the earth's climatic system in greater detail than ever before. The intelligence community is also contributing its expertise to this project. Unlike the incidental involvement of America's secret agencies in ecological research, the EOS was specifically designed to address the most important environmental questions facing the world today.[39] The managers and scientists in the secret agencies view their role as complementary at the margins to NASA's more extensive focus on the earth as an ecological system. The intelligence community's main contribution thus will be the occasional redirection of spy satellites and aircraft to scrutinize environmental phenomenon of interest. But at least into the foreseeable future, intelligence managers intend to keep the resource commitment for such assignments at no more than 1 percent of the community's total collection capacity.

## The Prospects for Environmental Intelligence

The CIA's Directorate of Science and Technology has cooperated with outside environmental scientists, including a number of leading American ecologists and even (chiefly on an unclassified basis) some Russian scientists. This work should be encouraged, as it shows how the secret agencies and outside society can join together to address selected security problems facing the United States. Still, it is worth emphasizing again that the DS&T's contribution to environmental security will be small, in large part because spy satellites have only limited value for ecological research. NASA's Earth Observation System shows more potential in this regard, as the DS&T management readily acknowledges. Hence, dramatically greater funding to collect environmental intelligence is not warranted, although the MEDEA program and related activities do deserve continued and even somewhat greater funding.

The CIA's Directorate of Intelligence should be encouraged to create a larger group of analysts to support international negotiations on ecological issues and to monitor the compliance of signatories to environmental treaties and other international agreements. Moreover, the DI should maintain its presently small group of analysts who study global environmental issues. Yet because the government already has a large number of environmental researchers working on these issues, analysts at the NIC, the DEC, and the OTI should concentrate on the comparative advantage they can bring to the table as a result of their access to clandestine information, which can fill in the gaps in open-source information on environmental topics.

This is where the Directorate of Operations (DO) could be more involved. Its case officers usually regard environmental issues as beneath their station. "I'm concerned about questions of military and political instability," declared one. "If the DEC wants to know if the Dnieper River is polluted, they can go find out for themselves."[40] This case officer has a point. After all, a U.S. embassy scientific officer would be better trained for this mission. Nevertheless, occasionally the DO may be in a position to sniff out useful environmental information that no one else has detected. In sum, the DCI's Environmental Center has failed to clarify adequately the importance of its interests to DO operatives in the field. It is not enough to express concern about tree cutting in Gambia. Quite rightly, DO officers (and intelligence budget-planners on Capitol Hill) need to understand exactly what military, political, or economic threat the tree cutting might pose. What is the strategic intelligence concern for the United States? Until this is adequately explained, the DEC is likely to see further resistance to the environmental mission.

The intelligence community should continue to cooperate with FEMA, providing rapid imagery of key locations in times of natural disasters in the United States and, when feasible, abroad. The secret agencies should also consider sharing its archival materials on the world's environment with international organizations. This sharing would have to be carried out within the constraints of protecting sources and methods, but as the cooperation among the NRO, CIA, and FEMA has demonstrated, it is possible to offer useful information gleaned from advanced satellite imagery without revealing technical secrets.

The intelligence community should also consider accepting specific environmental assignments from international organizations, either at cost or perhaps in partial compensation for dues that the United States has been reluctant to pay to the United Nations. This cooperation would be particularly admirable in times of global natural disasters, when reconnaissance satellites might be able to provide valuable information to save lives or when outlaw nations are suspected of violating environmental international agreements (say, by dumping hazardous materials in the oceans) and richly deserve to have their misbehavior publicly documented and widely disseminated.

Last, the intelligence community should continue to improve its program of outreach to consumers, both inside and outside the government, who are interested in environmental security and ecological research. So far, the secret agencies have not been able to explain adequately the value of their environmental products. How does deforestation in Brazil relate to climate change and quality of life in the United States? What risks to Americans are presented by Russian radioactive dumping in the Arctic? Or to our allies the Norwegians, who are much closer to the dumping sites? Because these questions have never been answered satisfactorily to policymakers (and to the public), they know little about the value of the intelligence community's environmental data collection.

The secret agencies have resources that can contribute to the understanding and management of environmental-security concerns without sacrificing their preeminent role of protecting the United States against hostile military and terrorist threats. America's intelligence agencies should not, however, waste their time trying to serve as additional EPAs or NASAs but, rather, should concentrate on gathering and interpreting environmental data that other agencies or the public cannot acquire, information derived from clandestine sources and cutting-edge satellite technology.

# FOUR

# Spies versus Germs

## *A Worldwide Resurgence of Bugs*

> The traditional idea of intelligence is the spy who provides
> the enemy's war plans. Actually, intelligence is concerned
> not only with war plans, but with all the external concerns
> of our government.
>
> —declassified CIA mimeograph statement
> to the Church committee, 1974

### Debate over a New Intelligence Agenda

The legislation that established the Commission on the Roles and Capabilities of U.S. Intelligence (the Aspin-Brown commission) in 1994 required its investigators to examine

> whether the roles and missions of the intelligence community should extend beyond the traditional areas of providing support to the defense and foreign policy establishments, and, if so, what areas should be considered legitimate for intelligence collection and analysis, and whether such areas should include, for example, economic issues, environmental issues, and health issues.[1]

Although often referred to as the New Intelligence Agenda, the topics examined by the commission were in fact not new at all to the intelligence agencies. As noted in chapter 2, economic intelligence has been a subject of interest to policymakers and intelligence officers throughout the nation's history, and during the cold war, America's secret agencies closely monitored a number of environmental concerns, including the dramatic drying up of the Aral Sea between Kazakhstan and Kyrgyzstan.

Still, nontraditional intelligence topics have largely been allowed to simmer on the intelligence community's back burner. Its managers continually dipped into this small budget for funds to cover the more immediate responsibility of containing the global communist threat. But when the Soviet empire fell apart, resources once intended for the USSR became increasingly available for the New Intelligence Agenda. The back burner, though, is precisely where many critics inside and outside the secret agencies would like to keep these nontraditional consumers of the limited resources available for intelligence. From their point of view, military threats—the whereabouts of Russian missiles and warheads, the likelihood of renewed Indian and Pakistani nuclear testing, the extent of Iraqi and North Korean nuclear weapons production, the ongoing sale of Chinese missiles to Pakistan and other nations, a renewal of paramilitary operations by the Serbs or the Kosovo Liberation Army in the Balkans, and potential terrorist attacks against U.S. personnel at home or abroad—must remain the primary concern of officials responsible for protecting the American people and their global interests.

In reaction to the runaway defense spending of both superpowers during the cold war, U.S. government officials tried to rebalance the federal budget and draw down the national debt. This popular political movement toward reducing government expenditures has worked against expanding intelligence requirements without strong support and whose direct relationship to national security and foreign policy may not be as readily apparent as warheads and missiles in the hands of rogue nations. Intelligence managers are dismayed, too, at the rising number of unfunded mandates emanating from Congress and the White House.

In contrast are those who maintain that Americans can no longer afford to define this nation's security in narrow, traditional terms. If the ozone layer disintegrates, if the rain forests vanish, if the Ebola virus spreads across continents, or, for that matter, if a large asteroid strikes the planet, the American people may be just as endangered, or dead, as they would have been under a massive Soviet nuclear attack during the cold war. Thus, to define the nation's security strictly in terms of foreign military dangers is delusive. An obsession with the USSR once distracted America from these other dangers, but now the old-fashioned views of threat assessment must be redefined in the climate of uncertainty characterizing the post-Communist world.[2] As one specialist remarked with respect to global public health, "Infectious diseases are potentially the largest threat to human security lurking in the post-cold war world."[3]

As for balancing the budget (continues the argument in favor of shifting resources toward the New Agenda threats like environmental and health security), the fresh set of targets can be covered in part by reorienting those technical systems—satellites, for instance—once directed toward the Soviet Union. Experts maintain that the United States invested too much money in gold-plated collection platforms in the first place, equipped as they are with every conceivable bell and whistle. An official at the National Security Agency, for instance, accused the National Reconnaissance Office of "building Cadillacs" instead of smaller satellites that could just as well meet America's security needs.[4]

Improved intelligence gathering with respect to the New Agenda items could actually save the United States money, according to some reports. The president's Office of Science and Technology Policy calculated that the lack of early warning about a resurgence of drug-resistant tuberculosis (TB) "undoubtedly contributed to the more than $700 million in direct costs for TB treatment incurred [by the United States] in 1991 alone." The office added that surveillance of this form of tuberculosis "was not reinstated until 1993, by which time multi-drug-resistant TB had become a public health crisis and millions of Federal dollars had been allocated."[5]

Support for attention to nontraditional intelligence topics comes from the highest levels of government. In *The National Security Science and Technology Strategy*, a report issued in 1996 under the guidance of the National Science and Technology Council (NSTC, a cabinet-level panel), President Clinton stated that "no country is isolated from the consequences of newly emerging diseases, environmental degradation, or other global threats—even if the roots of these problems lie in distant parts of the world."[6] As an example, he offered the tragedy of AIDS.

## Global Disease Surveillance

This was not the first expression of presidential concern about the AIDS pandemic. In the mid-1980s, President Ronald Reagan issued a directive ordering federal agencies to develop a model that could predict the global spread of AIDS and its demographic effects. Working under the

auspices of the State Department, the CIA led this research in cooperation with a number of other government entities (including the Departments of Energy and Defense).[7] The initial focus was on Africa, where
the AIDS epidemic originated, and researchers sorted the infected
groups according to such standard demographic variables as age, gender,
and rural-urban residence. The model was subsequently expanded to include Latin America and Asia and also took into account infection by the
AIDS virus (HIV) through intravenous drug use, homosexual transmission, and blood transfusion.

The worldwide rise of disease continues, despite hopes to the contrary
in this age of advanced medical knowledge.[8] Yellow fever haunts Benin,
viral meningitis has surfaced in Romania, polio in Albania, bubonic and
pneumonic plague in India, and cholera in the Philippines. Tuberculosis
has undergone a global renascence, too, and in a recent epidemic in
Madagascar, a strain of plague proved resistant to standard treatments
with ampicillin and tetracycline, raising fears that this strain "could ren-
der plague untreatable."[9] As reported by the World Health Organization
(WHO, an arm of the United Nations), malaria, plague, diphtheria,
cholera, yellow fever, and dengue have reemerged around the globe.[10]
Each year, there are 300 million to 500 million new cases of malaria, with
a child dying of the disease every twelve seconds.[11] In 1999 a new and
highly infectious tropical virus, never seen before by scientists, killed
dozens of people in Malaysia.[12] At least thirty-three new disease-causing
organisms have been identified since 1976, including HIV, hepatitis C,
the Ebola virus, sabia, and rotavirus, along with previously unseen strains
of bacteria resistant to antibiotics.[13]

These diseases have no country borders. In this era of modern transportation, more than 200 million people arrive in the United States each
year from foreign locations, by land, sea, and air.[14] This high volume of
human traffic links the world's cities "in a close-knit matrix of vulnerability. . . . Diseases that once took months to cross the Atlantic with
Columbus or the Pilgrim Fathers could now circumnavigate the globe in
a single day."[15] With this vulnerability in mind, the White House issued
a stern warning:

> Diseases affecting humans, plants, and animals are spreading rapidly as a
> result of trade and travel and, especially when combined with malnutrition,

threaten public health and productivity on a broad scale. The rapidly growing human population, widespread pollution, and the deterioration of other environmental factors that contribute to the maintenance of good health, as well as the lack of dependable supplies of clean drinking water for fully a fifth of the world's people, contribute to the acceleration and spread of such diseases.[16]

Concern over world health risks must not diminish America's vigilance against potential military threats from abroad, always the first priority on the intelligence agenda, whether traditional or new. As outlined in chapter 1, the world remains an angry place where weapons of mass destruction are abundant and the specter of swift and devastating carnage still stalks the planet—as does the prospect of terrorist attacks using chemical or biological agents. Yet the less prominent topics mandated for investigation by the Aspin-Brown commission, including economic and environmental security, are not inconsequential and warrant close scrutiny by policymakers and the public they serve if U.S. officials are to make thoughtful judgments about competing intelligence resource priorities. Among these topics is perhaps the least understood of all: global public health intelligence, the subject of this chapter.

## The Significance of Global Disease Surveillance

At first glance, it is easy to dismiss public health intelligence as having limited relevance to the secret agencies. After all, the United States already has more medical journals and more Nobel laureates for medicine than any other country. The open literature, both scientific and popular, on health matters is vast. Furthermore, the federal Centers for Disease Control and Prevention (CDC for short) and the Carter Center, both based in Atlanta, monitor and report on health conditions and threats throughout the world, as do the United Nations and a number of private organizations like the Federation of American Scientists (FAS).

With all the open sources of information on possible threats to the health of American citizens, why, then, spend limited intelligence resources on this subject? Even the Aspin-Brown commission, which agreed that a "legitimate role for intelligence" existed with respect to global health conditions, devoted just a quarter-page to the topic in a 151-page report and offered virtually no evidence to support its endorsement.[17]

## Health Intelligence Scenarios

Yet as one begins to probe beneath the surface of the limited information available on this subject, it becomes apparent that public health intelligence warrants more serious attention than it has received. Imagine the following scenarios:

- AIDS is spreading rapidly throughout the population of a developing nation with mineral resources important to America's industrial base. Indeed, in the previous year, about one-third of the children in the nation's capital city were born HIV positive. The National Security Council is concerned about the stability of the currently pro-U.S. regime, since some members of its government appear to have symptoms of AIDS. The president's national security adviser wants to know to what extent the government's higher echelons have been infected by AIDS and the likely effect this will have on the regime's stability. The CDC does not collect information about foreign leaders, and even if it did, many countries hide the truth about the prevalence of AIDS within their own borders—and certainly within their own ruling councils. In addition, the CDC and its staff would not be qualified to write an accompanying analysis of the military, political, and economic implications of the AIDS-induced instability.

- The secretary of state is worried about the widespread unrest in another developing country that seems to be a result of extensive poverty and disease. Particularly disquieting is the near endemic nature of debilitating intestinal afflictions in its northern territories. The secretary wants an analysis of what might be causing the illnesses. Although this information may be available somewhere in the files of the United Nations, she wants it right away and with an analysis that will explain the implications for American foreign policy toward the country. The secretary is especially anxious about the potential of infected refugee populations moving across national borders into neighboring states, further spreading the disease throughout the region.

- American troops are ordered by the president to join a UN peacemaking mission in the heart of Central Africa. Among the field commander's responsibilities is ensuring the safety of the troops against local contagious diseases, and so he wants up-to-date information on what health conditions to expect. Some of these data are available in the open domain, but part of the military action is apt to take place in a remote jungle where few Western medical experts have traveled. The commander needs to know what inoculations and other precautions are necessary to keep his troops free of disease, and he needs to know immediately. His civilian counterparts who will be dealing with humanitarian aid have the same concerns, as their workers must also be protected from indigenous health risks.

- The president has just read a technothriller about a member of a Middle East terrorist faction who leases a Twin Otter airplane from a small airport in the Virginia countryside, heads for Washington, D.C., and drops a fine rain of anthrax spores out the window from a suitcase while flying at low altitude along the Smithsonian Mall in the nation's capital. In the novel, the attack proves fatal within forty-eight hours to almost everyone inside the Washington Beltway. The president wants to know how farfetched this plot is, along with a full report on anthrax and other biological materials that could kill Americans targeted by a terrorist attack. He also wants to know what can be done to guard against such contingencies, as well as the history of international agreements controlling biological substances. He charges the Department of Defense and the Federal Emergency Management Agency to determine whether the U.S. government is working to develop easily available antidotes in case of a terrorist strike using disease-inducing substances. These agencies in turn request from the intelligence community a full report on the threat of biological terrorism.[18]

- The secretary of state is expected to attend a worldwide conference addressing the health dangers to citizens and military combatants when environments are destroyed as a by-product of warfare. Of interest to the conferees is likely to be the health effects of toxic gases released in the aftermath of damage inflicted on the environment during warfare, as occurred during the Persian Gulf conflict in 1991. She requests an immediate intelligence report on the subject.[19]

- The secretary of defense wants to know if his counterpart in a certain Asian nation is mentally unstable, as rumored, or if in fact the man is someone with whom the secretary can work. He wants, in other words, a psychological profile of the foreign minister of defense, prepared before the secretary's meeting with him scheduled in a fortnight. For this mental health information, the secretary of defense has no place to go except to America's secret agencies.[20]

- A White House science adviser informs the president that North Korea is probably developing biological weapons, most likely using smallpox, a disease thought to have been responsible for the deaths of at least 300 million people in the twentieth century alone and more people through the ages than any other infectious disease (including the Black Death of the Middle Ages).[21] The adviser suggests that the leaders of North Korea, known to have resorted in the past to risky acts of brinkmanship in their dealings with other nations, may have in mind loading a missile with hundreds of small bomblets filled with smallpox virus and firing the projectile at the United States. At least some of the bomblets would likely slip through any missile-defense program the United States might develop in the near future, and the disease would be disseminated over a wide area. After considering this nightmare, the president orders the DCI Nonproliferation Center to prepare a report on the credibility of the adviser's prediction.[22]

One does not have to be a Chicken Little to have some concern about scenarios like these (though some are less likely and immediate than others). After all, when an outbreak of the Ebola virus in Zaire killed 240 people in 1985, American officials were properly alarmed at the potential of the disease for wider dissemination and, in 1989, even feared that

Ebola might gain a foothold in the United States as a result of diseased monkeys housed in a medical facility at Reston, Virginia.[23] And in 1997, an outbreak of "bird flu" in Hong Kong stirred anxieties over its possible global reach.[24]

Researchers have pointed to the relationship between a nation's health and its political stability. With respect to the AIDS pandemic, for instance, Garrett found that as early as 1988, economists envisioned the creation of "a global underclass" and "an economic disaster" in Africa because of "the direct costs of AIDS care, HIV-testing costs, a year's supply of condoms, AZT (azidothymine) and other drugs for opportunistic infections (where such pharmaceuticals were at all available); and loss of net industrial and agricultural productivity due to deceased work force."[25]

A chemical or biological weapons attack against the United States by a rogue nation or a terrorist group is also increasingly possible. Drawing on a U.S. government study, two correspondents reported that three nations—Iraq, North Korea, and Russia—are almost certainly hiding unauthorized caches of the smallpox virus, and another fourteen are "suspected of having or trying to acquire germ weapons."[26] Former Soviet scientist Kanatjan Kalibekov, now using the Americanized name Ken Alibek, defected from the Russian military in 1992 and brought with him to America reports that Moscow had made tons of smallpox virus during the cold war. According to Alibek, the USSR had also designed special warheads to deliver the lethal scourge to the United States in long-range missiles, should a shooting war break out between the superpowers.[27]

The chairman of the National Intelligence Council agrees that the peril of chemical and biological terrorist operations against the United States is rising, and former DCI James Woolsey views biological terrorism as "the single most dangerous threat to our national security in the foreseeable future."[28] President Clinton recently confirmed that it was "highly likely" that a terrorist group would try a chemical or biological attack against this nation within the next few years.[29]

Experts consider smallpox the greatest biological threat facing the United States, since 42 percent of the American public have never been vaccinated against the disease. Next in the hierarchy of dangers is an anthrax attack, which at least has the virtue of not being contagious[30] (a fact of small comfort to those in the attack area). Some specialists look upon germs like smallpox as even "far more deadly than a nuclear weapon . . . because most people are no longer vaccinated and hence have lost their immunity to the virus."[31]

Bioweapons present an acute problem for intelligence detection, since the manufacture of such armaments is "easily disguised as peaceful research."[32] As the director of the DCI Nonproliferation Center explained, "The overlap between BW [biological weapons] agents and vaccines, and between nerve agents and pesticides is considerable; the technologies used to prolong our lives and improve our standard of living can quite easily be used to cause mass casualties."[33]

Policymakers understand that relying on media reports alone for information on global disease conditions is insufficient. Foreign governments sometimes try to conceal health dangers from media correspondents, as witnessed recently in the cover-up by Chinese military leaders and Communist Party officials of an AIDS-contaminated blood product (serum albumin) produced by a military-run factory in China.[34] The purpose of clandestine intelligence collection by secret agencies is to help ferret out the facts behind such subterfuge.

## Monitoring Global Health Concerns

Policy officials want the secret agencies to assess health conditions in both regions and individual countries. Some U.S. officials believe, for example, that Russia's greatest challenge now is not so much economic or military reform but the health of its citizens. As one result of their copious consumption of vodka, Russia's male population has a very short life expectancy. Some observers even predict that rampant alcoholism may prevent Russia from ever achieving the economic and political reforms to which it aspires.[35]

Long before the debate over a New Intelligence Agenda emerged in the aftermath of the cold war, the secret agencies had completed scores of studies on country, regional, and global health trends, supplementing UN, CDC, and other public reporting with information from all-source collection (both open and clandestine). Once again, as with economic and environmental matters, one of the intelligence analysts' most important contributions is their skillful blending of open information about global health conditions with facts and insights from espionage channels, something no one else is in a position to do.

Separating the wheat from the chaff in the open information can be an enormously valuable (but often difficult) task in itself, confirming from the reports of intelligence assets on location whether the public record is reliable. Is a particular city in the Balkans actually under siege, as reported (let us say) by a European correspondent? What is an accurate population estimate for the city, taking into account the waves of refugees pouring in, so that the amount of humanitarian aid airlifted into the city will fulfill its needs without oversupplying it and creating a black market? The number of refugees descending on a city may be particularly important to know, since the movement of great masses of people is often associated with outbreaks of dangerous epidemics. What is the quality of the city's drinking water? Are newspaper reports accurate about an outbreak of cholera in the main hospital? How much and what kinds of medicines are available in the hospital and in smaller clinics throughout the city?

On the list of health topics analyzed by the U.S. intelligence community in the past are studies on the access of people in developing countries to safe drinking water and adequate sanitation. The underlying assumption is that a populace whose physical and mental well-being is under stress is vulnerable to radical political movements and other manifestations of social and political unrest that can shake the stability of its government and possibly affect America's interests. Another topic of growing concern is the spread of HIV in foreign countries, which is so extensive already that it may well have already begun to undermine the stability of some regimes. In Janeiro, Zaire, for instance, 23 percent of the babies born in 1990 reportedly were HIV positive.[36] In Zimbabwe, some segments of society are recording 25 percent HIV infection rates and still higher rates of TB (which is currently the leading infectious cause of death worldwide, killing 3 million people each year).[37]

American intelligence units have also gathered information from around the world on medical concerns related to peacekeeping and humanitarian operations and have shared these data with UN and NATO officials. Of recent special concern to intelligence analysts are the incidence and effects of HIV and AIDS on UN and NATO military forces with whom the United States has worked shoulder-to-shoulder in combat zones. Similarly, analysts have studied the possible hazards to American soldiers from having to handle HIV-infected prisoners of war or to American civilians involved in the humanitarian aspects of peacekeeping missions in regions where AIDS is prevalent.[38]

The secret agencies also keep tabs on environmental health dangers. The accident that occurred in 1986 at the Chernobyl nuclear plant, located in the Soviet Ukraine, is an example. In the region near the stricken plant, cancer cases have doubled and calves have been born without heads and limbs. Radioactive particles from the Chernobyl meltdown have been tracked as far away as Scandinavia and, as noted in the preceding chapter, even in more distant California. One ranking UN official estimated that "up to 40 potential Chernobyls are waiting to happen in the former Soviet Union and Central Europe."[39] What if there was another Chernobyl? What would be the health implications for U.S. personnel and citizens traveling or living in Europe and for America's allies in that part of the world? And as the 1999 nuclear accident in Japan proves, these dangers are hardly limited to the poorly maintained nuclear reactors of the former Soviet republics.

A related concern is the use of chemical and biological agents against American troops on foreign battlefields. While beyond the scope of this analysis, the federal government is well aware of the serious risks faced by U.S. troops abroad as a result of chemical and biological warfare. "Reversing earlier opposition, the nation's military chiefs have endorsed a plan to vaccinate all U.S. forces against anthrax in what would be the Pentagon's first regular inoculation program against a germ warfare agent," reported the *Washington Post* in 1996.

> The about-face . . . reflects heightened Pentagon concern about the prospect of biological attack. Iraq, Russia and as many as ten other countries are said by U.S. officials to have at least the capability to load spores of anthrax into weapons, although no country is known is have released the bacteria on a battlefield.[40]

While a wealth of information on global health threats can be found in the public library and on the Internet, someone has to find it in obscure documents, databases, and archives (sometimes in difficult foreign languages), and collate it into a readable—ideally, an eye-catching—

format that will attract and hold the attention of busy policymakers. Just as important, someone must ensure that the information on global health addresses the immediate demands of the most prominent officials in Washington. The UN does not do this for Washington officialdom. Neither does the CDC or the Carter Center, the government's VA hospitals, the Library of Congress, the Brookings Institution, RAND, the Heritage Foundation, the Cato Institute, the Aspen Institute, or the American Enterprise Institute. So when the information is needed, the intelligence community is expected to have it, and it must be accurate, timely, and focused on the latest health danger or crisis.

## Resources for Public Health Intelligence

Despite all the excitement over the New Intelligence Agenda, global health concerns have received only limited support in Washington, D.C. The efforts of America's elected representatives to balance the federal budget have been misdirected. Rather than cutting the costs of large and expensive satellites, budget officials have significantly reduced the number of U.S. intelligence personnel overseas and closed many installations, especially in Africa, where many of the worst infectious diseases originate. The United States in the post-Communist era has shifted from a condition of "global presence," with eyes and ears in every country, to one of "global reach" in which collection resources must be mobilized from different parts of the world and "surged" against targets of imminent concern.

In a time of budget restraint with respect to most government programs (if not for the ongoing infatuation with surveillance satellites and reconnaissance airplanes, none of which can discern the spread of an infectious disease), health is low on the list of intelligence priorities for Washington decision makers. Nonetheless, by 1996 the CIA had established its Conflict Issues Division within the Intelligence Directorate's newly established Office of Transnational Issues (OTI). Here a dozen analysts track health and humanitarian issues, from the spread of global diseases to the (sometimes related) movement of refugees.[41]

At times the open media do report accurately on global health issues, as when Reuters documented that during the summer of 1994, hundreds of Rwandan Hutu refugees in eastern Zaire died each day of cholera.[42] Often, though, media correspondents are not in the right place at the right time, or they may fail to report fully (if at all) the health side of a story and its implications for U.S. security interests. Then the secret agencies' intelligence collection and analysis become especially valuable.

The U.S. Army Medical Research Institute for Infectious Diseases (USAMRIID), the Armed Forces Medical Intelligence Center (AFMIC), and the United States Army Medical Research and Material Command (USAMRMC) also monitor global health conditions that may affect peacekeeping, humanitarian, and rescue missions, as well as other American military operations abroad (either alone or in coalition with UN or NATO forces).[43] Their primary responsibilities are to identify health threats to American soldiers abroad, although sometimes their expertise is sought as well to counter disease threats inside the United States.[44] Their funding is modest and the degree to which they are integrated into the communitywide intelligence process is inadequate, particularly in regard to the collection and the subsequent sharing of information for the production of all-source reports. While efforts have been made to elevate the intelligence community's attention to issues of health security, sometimes the left hand has been unaware of what the right hand is doing—a persistent problem facing the vast and loosely connected bureaucracies spread out around Washington (a theme that runs through this book and elsewhere).[45]

## The Future of Public Health Intelligence

In recognition of the more complicated nature of world affairs since the end of the cold war, the secret agencies have begun to concentrate more on global and multilateral issues, including health concerns. The new national intelligence officer for global affairs has health-related topics in her oversized portfolio of duties, and the National Intelligence Council has produced from time to time national intelligence estimates on world health issues.[46]

In the grand scheme of things, though, public health intelligence is a far less important focus for the intelligence community than traditional military, political, and economic collection requirements. Foreign diseases, it is true, can infect American soldiers, but Russia continues to be able to level the cities of the United States with nuclear missiles. Moreover, a resumption of fighting in the Balkans or some other foreign locale would again require extensive tactical intelligence for U.S. forces. Around the world, terrorists attack civilian as well as military targets. Political unrest in Mexico can result in additional waves of immigrants fleeing across the Rio Grande. International economic conditions in Thailand can directly affect the living standards of Americans. For the time being, these perils are of more immediate concern to the U.S. government than tuberculosis or malaria.

Still, health risks to American soldiers serving overseas can hardly be dismissed out of hand, nor would prudent policymakers ignore the other global health concerns discussed in this chapter, even if the limitations of available resources prohibited a full coverage of every possible risk to Americans' well-being. The need to keep public health intelligence in proper perspective, neither ignoring its obvious importance nor becoming hysterical about the dangers of global disease, leads to this central conclusion: in an era in which citizens are appropriately skeptical of government spending, it is nonetheless important to preserve the current levels of funding for public health intelligence (as the Aspin-Brown commission concluded, however elliptically).

## Taking Global Disease Surveillance Seriously

Moreover, and on this point the Aspin-Brown commission was silent, without appreciable cost, some steps can be taken to provide better information about global health risks to policymakers. This will require the cooperation of groups unaccustomed to working together—or even being in the same room. First, the CIA and its companion agencies must take the health portfolio more seriously. Global health reports to policymakers based on open sources of information are currently inadequate. As one physician emphasized, "Never before has the world more desperately needed a system of early warning stations [on global disease] distributed about the most likely sources of emergence that would alert us to the first sign of danger," adding that WHO's surveillance capabilities are now "fragmented and sadly neglected" and other disease watchdogs (like the Rockefeller Foundation) have also cut back their monitoring capacities. The end result is that the world is "less prepared in terms of [global health] surveillance than it was even in the sixties and seventies."[47]

As a means for improving the quality of information on global health issues disseminated to policymakers, the CIA's Directorate of Operations should report more regularly and systematically from the field on country and regional health conditions that might not be picked up by CDC and WHO monitors (some of the possibilities were mentioned in the scenarios discussed earlier in this chapter). Such information is presently neglected in the cable traffic sent back to CIA headquarters by DO case officers.[48] In addition, case officers should pay closer attention to the spread of infectious diseases among specific foreign military, political, and economic elites.

The Operations Directorate cannot cover the international health beat alone, however. Since the FBI is to increase its presence overseas to fight international crime,[49] it should be called upon as well to tap bureau assets for information regarding global health concerns, including information on the physical and mental status of foreign elites. This would represent an expansion of the FBI's traditional investigative mandate, yet only in the narrow sense of passing along intelligence on foreign health matters to the CIA as it is picked up by bureau assets abroad in the course of their anticrime activities. Is this likely to happen? Not without the insistence of both the DCI and the FBI director. Although these activities should be only a secondary interest of the collectors, such information could well be important to the national interest and so should be given more attention.

## Improving Health Surveillance Methods

The proper threshold for triggering collection on health matters—whether global, regional, national, group, or individual in focus—should be refined. The system now is too haphazard. Intelligence managers have yet to work out explicit and systematic triggering criteria that would indicate when a health issue had reached the level of national security significance, say, by virtue of disease lethality, proximity to U.S. interests, or communicability. As with every intelligence topic, analysts and managers throughout the intelligence community must redouble their efforts to learn what types of global health issues most concern policymakers.

Clandestine reporting and open-source material on world health conditions are currently not well integrated. Since a considerable amount of health data surfaces in the public domain, the intelligence analyst's first step must be to satisfy the policymaker's request for information quickly by way of rapid open-source data searches. Then clandestine findings can be added to the materials found through open-source searching.

In the case of certain public health threats, WHO and the CDC already serve as centers for indications and warning (I&W), that is, a quick alert to threatening health conditions. The intelligence community must monitor more closely the published reports of WHO, the CDC, and other health entities with a global focus, turning to its own clandestine collection capabilities only for those topics insufficiently reported by the public agencies (such as the health of specific foreign leaders, the presence of disease in potential battlefields, or the threat of bioterrorism).[50] In addition, those officials in the intelligence community who are responsible for tracking open-source information should search more carefully the databanks and eyewitness accounts of individuals who work on health-related missions abroad for nongovernmental organizations (NGOs) and private volunteer organizations. Just as for a missile attack, the rapid dissemination of accurate information about global health threats—a kind of "viral telemetry"—is essential.

The community's relationship to private groups must be handled carefully. As one FAS scientist stressed, "We are in communication with DoD [Department of Defense] officials and are, of course, aware of the value of disease surveillance data to the intelligence community. We—and they—recognize that any overt involvement by DoD or intelligence [in the data-collection activities of civilian groups] would kill [our] effort to monitor effectively."[51]

The intelligence community's databank on global health topics is deficient. The CIA's sophisticated in-house computer system charged with scanning the open literature (known as ROSE, for Rich Open Source Environment) does not have among its machine-readable subscription lists many of the key specialized publications from private and international governmental organizations dealing with health and medical subjects. For very little money, the ROSE system could be enriched with open-source global disease data useful for both early warning and a more complete understanding of international health threats.

## Sharpening the Focus on Chemical-Biological Dangers

The secret agencies need to shift some resources from intelligence collection regarding conventional military targets to the more probable danger facing the United States of a terrorist attack employing chemical or biological weapons. Given the current resource bias favoring technical intelligence over human intelligence, too few assets are currently exploring the chemical-biological warfare capabilities and intentions of foreign nations and factions (and, in the case of FBI intelligence, for comparable threats at home).[52] More research on antidotes and their quick dissemination in times of emergency is necessary, with private industry, the Department of Defense, and the secret agencies working in tandem (as they have done so well over the years in the development of satellites and reconnaissance airplanes). "Our ultimate goal," stated a recent White House report, "is to foster the creation of a worldwide disease surveillance and response network."[53] This laudable objective warrants resources to match the rhetoric.

## Organizing for Health Security

The collection tasking and analytic integration of health intelligence cry out for better coordination. Several federal agencies have given some attention to public health intelligence, but it has not been well coordinated. The FBI, FEMA, and the U.S. Public Health Service, for example, have put together a crisis-management plan to cope with a chemical or biological terrorist attack, but "there has been relatively little emphasis on devising practical measures for protecting public health in the event of such an attack."[54]

The current fragmentation of efforts could be mitigated by the creation of a task force on global disease surveillance and analysis, under the auspices of the DCI. The task force would be expected to convene at least twice a year to review current world health issues and to determine how well the intelligence community and relevant open agencies have cooperated in the collection, data analysis, and dissemination of global health data and assessments.

Members of the task force should include

- The NIO for global issues (who would chair the panel and report directly to the DCI).
- A representative from the CIA's Directorate of Operations with knowledge of clandestine collection methods related to public health intelligence.
- A global health analyst from the CIA's Directorate of Intelligence.
- Representatives from the National Security Agency and the Defense Intelligence Agency.
- A representative from the State Department.
- A representative from the FBI.
- A representative from the U.S. Customs Service.
- Representatives from the Armed Forces Medical Intelligence Center, the U.S. Army Medical Institute for Infectious Diseases, and the U.S. Army Medical Research and Material Command.
- A representative from FEMA.
- A representative from the U.S. Public Health Service.
- A physician/researcher from the CDC.
- An academic medical expert with extensive international experience.
- The NSC staff aide responsible for global health issues.

The task force would also need to establish a close working relationship with WHO and appropriate NGOs.

One of the task force's key issues to consider would be who needs to know what and when about potential disease threats, especially when the territory of the United States itself is threatened. The intelligence agencies must do a better job of informing policymakers about health dangers that have been uncovered by agents in the field, and they must keep them better informed as well about new analytic reports prepared by the community on global health issues. At present, often the wrong or unneeded information is gathered because of inadequate communications between the consumers of intelligence and its producers. One part of the government is frequently unaware of what another, related part is doing on health security, even at high echelons. One recent senior NSC staffer had never met the key national intelligence officer dealing with global health issues, even though both individuals had been in their respective positions for almost a year. Furthermore, while the United States already has procedures in place to deal with health threats when the warning comes from public sources, less adequately planned is the manner in which clandestinely derived disease warnings should be disseminated to the civilian population in times of an emergency involving a health danger (such as a terrorist attack employing biological substances).

## Winning the War against Disease

Those who guide American foreign policy will continue to concentrate on traditional balance-of-power issues with respect to the world's major military forces. As always since the advent of nation-states, this is a sensible, prudent concern. International affairs, though, have become more complicated in recent years. The Clinton administration's first secretary of state, Warren Christopher, was on the mark when he warned in 1996 that the greatest future threat to America's national security is apt to come from a host of "transnational issues," among them environmental stress, population growth, narcotics flows, and infectious diseases.[55]

While continuing to monitor the whereabouts of weapons systems that can cause the United States great harm, this nation's secret agencies must expand their responsibilities to include more serious attention to the New Intelligence Agenda. The first line of defense against the outbreak of infectious disease is the global surveillance of health conditions, and America's intelligence organizations can contribute to this defense. To be successful, however, they must receive the necessary encouragement and support for such initiatives, through a more efficient organization and the shifting of some funds away from profligate spending on gold-plated collection platforms.

# PART II

# Strategic Intelligence

*Fissures in the First Line of Defense*

# FIVE

# The DCI and the
# Eight-Hundred-Pound Gorilla

What has been gathered will be dispersed.
—Buddhist saying

The jack of hearts has a major liability: he has only one eye. America's directors of Central Intelligence have longed for perfect vision with respect to the foreign threats discussed in the first part of this book, yet they too have suffered from partial blindness. This malady is inescapable in one sense, because no one—not even vast and expensive espionage organizations—can know all there is to know about world events, especially when adversaries are determined to hide their activities. This vision impairment can, however, be corrected to some extent, for in part it reflects both bureaucratic rivalries and an imbalance of missions among the nation's intelligence agencies. The inability of DCIs to give presidents a consistently integrated perspective on global affairs creates a major disconnection between the challenges presented earlier in this volume and the capacity of the intelligence agencies always to respond effectively.

## A Season of Change

The mid-1990s were meant to be a period of change for America's intelligence organizations. An array of reform-minded commissions and study groups, inside and outside the government, scrutinized the state of U.S. intelligence, found it wanting, and offered a variety of correctives.[1] But on even the most fundamental points of how the secret agencies should be organized and what their missions should entail, the various panels of inquiry often disagreed with one another.

This lack of consensus came as no surprise to those who had tracked the intelligence community's troubled history during the cold war. A series of controversial missteps, including the domestic spy scandals uncovered in 1974–75, had raised questions about the state of American intelligence. Worrisome, too, was the CIA's use of extreme covert actions, even the recruitment of Mafia hit men to assassinate Cuba's Fidel Castro (revealed in 1975). Then in the 1980s came the excesses of the Iran-contra affair and the failure to anticipate the sudden collapse of the Soviet empire. In the inquiries that followed, some critics called for sweeping reforms, even the abolition of the CIA, but others seemed content to leave the secret agencies to their own devices.[2]

Further evidence that a movement for intelligence reform would not be easy could be found in the testimony and management decisions of recent DCIs. Some directors readily expressed their dismay that the intelligence community was so resistant to supervision by the director's office. Admiral Stansfield Turner, DCI from 1977 to 1981, claimed that running the CIA was "like operating a power plant from a control room with a wall containing many impressive levers that, on the other side of the wall, had been disconnected."[3] Turner's response was to accelerate the downsizing of the CIA's subdivision most resistant to higher management: the Directorate of Operations (DO), home of the Agency's spy handlers. This reduction in personnel had begun four years earlier by order of DCI James R. Schlesinger (1973), who for his efforts came to be known inside headquarters as "the most unpopular director in CIA's history."[4] Similarly, Admiral Turner's tenure is viewed by insiders as a dark chapter in the Agency's history. First an academic (Schlesinger) and then not long after a navy man (Turner)—both intelligence outsiders, or "irregulars," not bound to a specific career service[5]—had dared to interfere with the Agency's sacrosanct internal structure.

One of Turner's successors recalls how the CIA had intentionally obstructed the admiral's efforts to gain control of the permanent intelligence bureaucracy. "I had learned a valuable lesson working for him," writes Robert M. Gates, a career CIA officer. "I now knew that I never wanted to be DCI—anyone who wanted the job clearly didn't understand it."[6] Although Gates eventually did become director (1991–93) despite these misgivings, his memoirs recall his frustrations as the nation's spymaster. Even with this career "regular" at the helm, the intelligence bureaucracy—again, most notably the Operations Directorate—resisted change mandated from the management suites on the seventh floor at Langley Headquarters. Had Gates come up through the ranks in the Operations Directorate, rather than the Intelligence Directorate, he no doubt would have been more palatable to DO personnel.

Downsizing the CIA and the other secret agencies has not been the only reform pursued by DCIs. On the contrary, for the directors during the 1980s, the answer to a more effective intelligence community was an expansion of its programs. The new growth took place within each of the intelligence agencies, with little attention to how their work might be most effectively integrated. The result of this approach was the creation of large, fragmented systems, which are ideal climates for the pursuit of parochial interests by individual program directors. As one authority of bureaucracies has noted, "This involves seeking higher salaries, better perquisites, greater reputations, and more power; dispensing more patronage; increasing programmatic outputs; and it adds up to immense pressures to expand organizations and increase budgets."[7] The various agency directors throughout the intelligence community have acted accordingly, and their combined budgets ballooned from $20 billion annually at the end of the Carter administration to $30 billion annually during the Reagan and Bush administrations.[8]

### Organizational Dilemmas Facing the Intelligence Community

The intelligence community reflects the organizational complexity of American government with its many agencies, differing cultural perspectives, and various modi operandi. The community's centrifugal forces raise a pertinent issue of governance: is it possible to integrate the secret agencies more closely in order to give U.S. policymakers a more comprehensive and cohesive understanding of global threats and opportunities? One thing is certain: the simple redrawing of boxes on an organizational diagram is unlikely to help. Writing about intelligence, a leading academic expert on bureaucracy has wisely cautioned that it is "difficult to achieve a given outcome by changing an organizational chart."[9] Before exploring possible ways of better integrating intelligence, we should first look at the extent of fragmentation within the community. A starting place is to examine the CIA's own considerable internal disaggregation.

## CIA Structural Divisions

The CIA has within its walls five major organizational divisions: the Directorate of Intelligence (DI), the Directorate of Operations (DO), the Directorate of Administration (DA), the Directorate of Science and Technology (DS&T), and the Office of the Director of Central Intelligence, each with an elaborate set of subsidiaries (see figure 2). More significant still in trying to understand the difficulties of governing just this agency alone (the other dozen aside) is its multitude of cultural keeps. These informal cultural fissures add to the formal divisions in producing, for intelligence directors and policymakers alike, a dismaying institutional fragmentation.

## Cultural Divides

The CIA's internal cultures reflect the divergent training and outlook of each of the directorates' intelligence officers. The members of each directorate usually share basic values and practices that distinguish them from those that staff the rest of the Agency. Among the cultural groupings are scholarly analysts with expertise in foreign political, military and economic systems, located in the Directorate of Intelligence; scientists, in the Directorate of Science and Technology; case officers, propagandists, paramilitary officers, and counterintelligence specialists, in the Directorate of Operations; administrators and security officers, in the Directorate of Administration; and managers, attorneys, inspectors, arms control specialists, and legislative liaison personnel, in the Office of the DCI.

## The Analysts

The analysts are the CIA's scholars, usually Ph.D.s and area specialists. During the CIA's early days, the stereotypical analyst was an Ivy League professor replete with elbow-patched tweed jacket complemented by the mandatory button-down collar and regimental striped tie, but today

**Figure 2.** The Office of the Director of Central Intelligence and the CIA

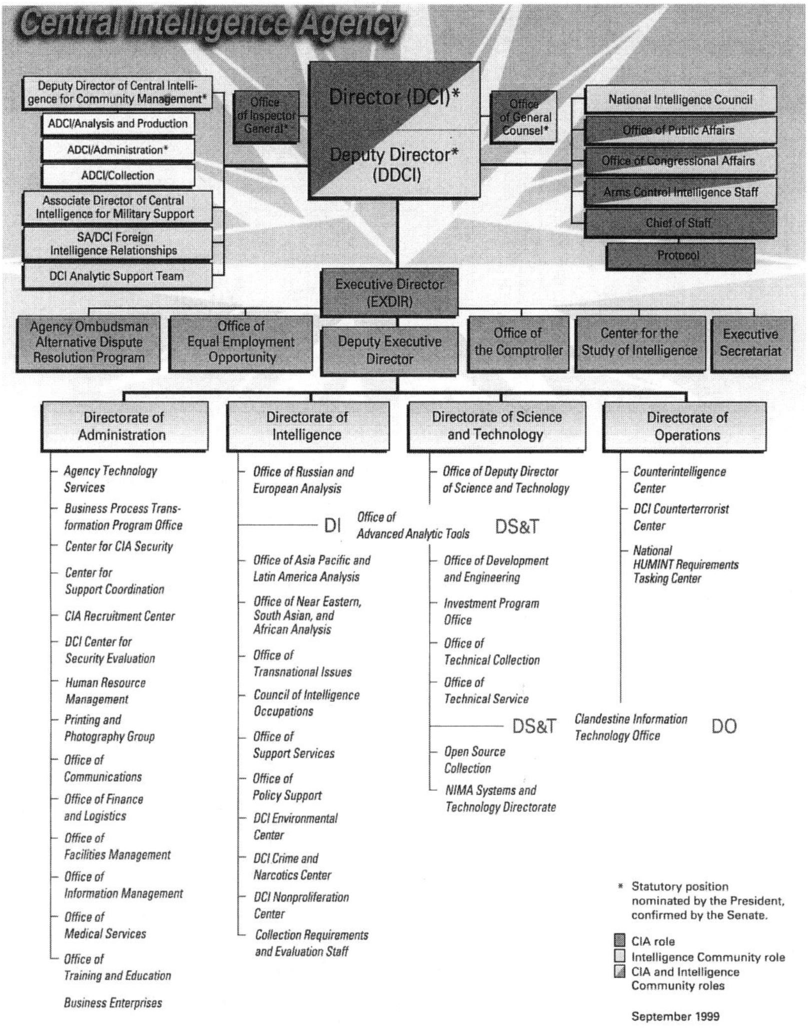

## Central Intelligence Agency

**Director (DCI)***

**Deputy Director* (DDCI)**

Deputy Director of Central Intelligence for Community Management*
- ADCI/Analysis and Production
- ADCI/Administration*
- ADCI/Collection
- Associate Director of Central Intelligence for Military Support
- SA/DCI Foreign Intelligence Relationships
- DCI Analytic Support Team

Office of Inspector General*

Office of General Counsel*

- National Intelligence Council
- Office of Public Affairs
- Office of Congressional Affairs
- Arms Control Intelligence Staff
- Chief of Staff
- Protocol

**Executive Director (EXDIR)**

| Agency Ombudsman Alternative Dispute Resolution Program | Office of Equal Employment Opportunity | Deputy Executive Director | Office of the Comptroller | Center for the Study of Intelligence | Executive Secretariat |

### Directorate of Administration
- Agency Technology Services
- Business Process Transformation Program Office
- Center for CIA Security
- Center for Support Coordination
- CIA Recruitment Center
- DCI Center for Security Evaluation
- Human Resource Management
- Printing and Photography Group
- Office of Communications
- Office of Finance and Logistics
- Office of Facilities Management
- Office of Information Management
- Office of Medical Services
- Office of Training and Education
- Business Enterprises

### Directorate of Intelligence — DI
- Office of Russian and European Analysis
- Office of Advanced Analytic Tools
- Office of Asia Pacific and Latin America Analysis
- Office of Near Eastern, South Asian, and African Analysis
- Office of Transnational Issues
- Council of Intelligence Occupations
- Office of Support Services
- Office of Policy Support
- DCI Environmental Center
- DCI Crime and Narcotics Center
- DCI Nonproliferation Center
- Collection Requirements and Evaluation Staff

### Directorate of Science and Technology — DS&T
- Office of Deputy Director of Science and Technology
- Office of Development and Engineering
- Investment Program Office
- Office of Technical Collection
- Office of Technical Service — DS&T
- Open Source Collection
- NIMA Systems and Technology Directorate

### Directorate of Operations — DO
- Counterintelligence Center
- DCI Counterterrorist Center
- National HUMINT Requirements Tasking Center
- Clandestine Information Technology Office

\* Statutory position nominated by the President, confirmed by the Senate.

■ CIA role
□ Intelligence Community role
▨ CIA and Intelligence Community roles

September 1999

*Source:* A Consumer's Guide to Intelligence, Central Intelligence Agency, 1999.

they are generally less tweedy and come from colleges outside the Ivy League. Nonetheless many are educated in the nation's top private schools, and most have an academic air about them. Their job is to sift through secret information procured abroad, blend it with information in the public domain ("open source"), and prepare short, up-to-date reports ("current intelligence") or longer "estimates" ("research intelligence") on world conditions for consideration by the president and other policy officials. Analysts are meant to be—and usually are—thoughtful, unbiased, and empirical, with a sharp eye for nuance and the academician's training to consider every perspective. The milieu of the analyst is the library, increasingly the virtual one inside a word processor, aided by the ongoing development of ties with colleagues through a secure computer network across the intelligence community (called Intelink). The ethos—in theory at least and usually in practice—is objectivity, and the goal is to provide decision makers with accurate, timely, and relevant information and insight, free of policy spin or bureaucratic parochialism.

*The Case Officer*

Although in the same building as the Directorate of Intelligence, the Directorate of Operations is another world, largely sealed off from the rest of the CIA. (In an attempt to overcome this separation, a recent experiment in "co-location" has seated a small percentage of DO and DI personnel together, although some DO officers have already skittered away from the project, as if on the rim of a vortex.) Some of its personnel, known as case or operations officers, live abroad and are responsible for recruiting and handling native agents or "assets" who, if they are both prick eared and well positioned, can collect useful information in their respective countries, from sources both open (Iraqi newspapers) and closed (military documents in a safe at the intelligence headquarters of the Iraqi government).

The successful case officer, typically a gregarious sort, completes a tour of duty overseas having recruited a stable of new agents. Indeed, the criterion of success for CIA case officers was once the number of assets that he or she had recruited.[10] Recruitment is still very important, but promotion boards now take other skills into account as well. Whereas analysts are trained to value "all-source" intelligence—data drawn from all of America's spy machines and espionage assets (blended with open sources)—case officers are aficionados of old-fashioned human spying or, in their terminology, HUMINT. This, in their opinion, is ground truth; their assets, with whom they frequently develop close personal relations, are (ideally) in the enemy's secret councils or at least have access to someone who is. The case officer spends most of his or her career abroad and believes that this experience provides a better sense of the target country than that held by the narrowly specialized Ph.D. analyst—Rodin's *The Thinker* stuck behind a desk at Langley and venturing overseas only occasionally.

These differing perspectives can lead to disagreements and sometimes even hostility between the two cultures. Until a truce ("partnership") was signed in 1995, DI personnel could not even enter the DO's suite of offices at headquarters, barred by special combination locks that kept out all but the elite cadre of the "real" intelligence officers, those who learned the lessons of espionage during their overseas assignments. According to a former senior CIA official, as recently as the Reagan administration DO officers refused even to tell the DCI's intelligence community staff "what was going on overseas."[11]

### Covert Action Specialists

Within the Directorate of Operations is the Covert Action Staff (CAS), always the most controversial of the Agency's subsidiaries—and the most cosseted. This unit plans and manages operations designed to influence (and sometimes to overthrow) foreign governments through the use of propaganda, political and economic manipulation, and paramilitary (PM) or warlike activities.

One wing of the CAS suite of offices resembles those of a metropolitan newspaper, with "journalists" writing articles for placement in foreign media. Another buzzes with political campaign activities, as specialists produce everything from bumper stickers and brochures to political pins and leaflets meant to benefit pro-U.S. candidates in foreign elections. In still other offices, economic experts concoct schemes to disrupt an adversary's monetary system or to mine harbors as a means for disrupting the enemy's maritime commerce. Although the art form has declined since the end of the cold war, most of the clandestine operations during the struggle against Communism took the form of propaganda, particularly the use of articles placed in foreign newspapers and magazines to discredit the leaders of the USSR.

One of the CAS offices has the Latin phrase *Actiones Praecipuae* above the entrance, indicating the site of the Special Activities Division, home of the paramilitary cadre—macho war fighters sporting blue-tinted aviation glasses and rolled shirt sleeves and displaying a certain swagger that comes from having faced danger abroad. These intelligence officers relish the peril of unmarked air flights behind enemy lines and the command of speedboats in hostile waters. Given the choice, they would prefer (at least in the lingering and overdrawn Rambo cartoon image from the cold war days, which CAS officers are not above nurturing) to scale enemy walls in the dead of night, knife between the teeth, rather than fret over analytic nuances in a report destined for the president.

During the cold war, CAS officers frequented the world's hot spots, blowing up bridges in Vietnam and Laos and concocting assassination plots against pro-Soviet leaders in the developing world ("terminate with extreme prejudice," the order would read). Their involvement in these primordial pursuits earned them the monikers "knuckle-draggers" and "snake eaters," evoking the image of men crawling on their bellies through foreign jungles. (Some journalists labeled them "The Gang That Couldn't Shoot Straight," since none of the assassination plots succeeded.) "The analysts are a bunch of academics," summed up a former DCI, "while the DO types would be entirely comfortable in the Marine Corps."[12]

### The Counterintelligence Corps

Farther down the hall in the DO are the CIA's counterintelligence specialists, another breed unto themselves. Counterintelligence (CI) is the art of thwarting hostile intelligence operations directed against the United States. In these suites, paranoia is paramount: a distrust of everyone, for perhaps even one's best friend might be a Russian or Chinese "mole."

Some CI officers possess the countenance of Talmudic scholars poring over faded intelligence archives in search of clues to which foreign intelligence officer may be susceptible to recruitment (the best way of discovering what operations the enemy is running against the United States is to penetrate its foreign intelligence service with a mole of one's own). Other CI officers are cut from quite different cloth: muscular security guards who check safes to ensure they are properly locked at the close of business and monitor the internal CIA computer databanks to guard against personnel surfing outside the narrow province of one's "need-to-know." They also keep an eye on CIA officers overseas, say, during happy hour at local watering holes, in order to warn them away from socializing with individuals who may be hostile intelligence officers or their "cut-outs" (intermediaries).

When James Angleton ran the CIA Counterintelligence Staff within the DO (1954–74), it resembled Arthur Conan Doyle's *Lost World*: remote, unchartered, mysterious. Angleton personally carried out aggressive penetration operations against foreign targets, often without the knowledge of the U.S. ambassador, the DCI, or even his most immediate supervisor, the deputy director for operations (DDO). His charge was to catch foreign spies, especially those run by the Soviet intelligence services; how he did it was up to him—or so he decided.[13]

### The Techies

In another domain all their own are the scientists of the S&T Directorate, the technological wizards—"techies" or "techno-weenies"—made famous for moviegoers by Major Boothroyd (aka "Q") in the James Bond films. In the early days, they helped the air force build airplane and satellite surveillance "platforms" (most famously, the U-2), now a task shared by the National Reconnaissance Office and the air force. The scientists in DS&T design and manufacture state-of-the-art espionage devices, from tools for picking locks and burglary ("black-bag" or "second-story job") to clandestine communications facilities and disguises that can utterly transform an agent's physiognomy. In the most notorious intervals of their history, DS&T scientists have crafted exotic killing instruments for assassination plots (including a highly efficient poison dart gun or "nondiscernible microbioinoculator"), conducted LSD experiments on unwitting personnel (among them one of their own scientists, who subsequently committed suicide), and provided wig disguises for Watergate conspirators (though without knowing their criminal political intentions). Just as every university campus is culturally divided between "hard" scientists and other faculty members, so is there some distance between the CIA's scientists and the rest of the organization. The CIA's techies are essentially a lab-based support service, often driven by a stronger interest in pure research than in the traditional concerns of spy agencies.

### The Admin

The Directorate of Administration keeps the Agency's floors mopped and its cafeterias well stocked with food and drink. Yet it, too, has its pockets of insularity, especially the dreaded "admin" inspectors and the Office of Personnel Security. These intelligence officers are the cause of periodic dyspepsia inside the CIA, because of their marmoreal demeanor and officious enforcement of security regulations: everything from correctly wearing one's identification badge to never leaving a classified document out of its safe at night. The admin also descend from time to time on the CIA's embassy-based offices abroad ("stations"), conducting detailed audits and white-glove inspections.

The DA also administers the Agency's lie-detector or polygraph tests to prospective employees and, at least every five years (a rule honored more in the breach than in the commission), to career intelligence officers as a check on their loyalty. Taking a lie detector test is always stressful and can also be a demeaning experience. In some instances, the polygraph unfairly casts doubt on the test taker's integrity, without confirming evidence. The machine is far from infallible. It failed to uncover Aldrich H. Ames, Wu-Tai Chin, and other traitors inside the intelligence community. Now and then, though, the lie detector has proved to be a useful security device for uncovering foreign espionage agents (CIA traitor Harold Nicholson became a suspect after failing a routine polygraph test in 1995), as well as for catching thieves and even, on one occasion, a murderer who confessed to killing his wife. But whatever the polygraph's merits or demerits,[14] it nonetheless contributes to the cultural tensions between an element within the DA and the rest of the Agency, as does a concern (however unfounded) among some CIA officers that financial and medical information acquired by security personnel might be misused to harm an individual's career.

### The Seventh Floor

The CIA's intelligence managers, the DCI and his immediate entourage of deputy and executive directors and their retinue of aides, reside on the seventh floor. At this level, personnel are forced into a less parochial perspective, as their job descriptions require them to plan for the entire community, however resistant the individual agencies may be to central guidance.

Depending on the particular objectives of individual DCIs (some are more community oriented than others), this management group does try to improve cooperation in intelligence collection and analysis. The goal is to overcome turf battles between the agencies, focusing instead on producing the best possible analysis for the decision makers. To this end, the DCI tries to behave as a genuine director of *central* intelligence, not just the director of the Central Intelligence Agency. If most of the other units inside the CIA's building are centrifugal or fragmenting in their organizational effect, the DCI and his staff represent a degree of centripetal or centralizing influence both within the CIA and throughout the wider community.

The extent of this centralization has been modest over the years, however. Even those employees on the seventh floor meant to assist the DCI in communitywide activities can yield to narrower interests. The DCI's legal counselors, legislative liaison team, arms control experts, and the inspector general, for instance, are chiefly concerned with (respectively) legalisms, the congressional perspective, arms-accord monitoring, and accountability. These professional interests may or may not help the DCI's quest for greater community integration—if, in fact, that is even the director's goal. As a result of this internal fragmentation throughout the CIA, from the labyrinth of basement corridors to the seventh floor, DCIs have found their hands full with the task of leading the CIA—let alone all the other agencies in the community.

## The DCI's First Job: Running the CIA

No DCI has successfully negotiated the straits between the Scylla of the CIA and the Charybdis of the intelligence community. Managing the Agency is obviously a less daunting challenge for a DCI than guiding the entire community (which is essentially a dozen other CIAs—indeed, some many times larger), yet none has managed to grasp even the CIA's reins tightly in hand. Admiral Turner described the leadership dilemma as he saw it during the Carter years:

> These differing outlooks [of the CIA's internal directorates] give rise to a lot of pushing and pulling on what position the Agency as a whole should take on specific questions. In any other organization such disputes would be brought to the person at the top, who would have to adjudicate them. Not so at the CIA. There, the branch heads go a very long way to compromise with each other rather than let an issue reach the DCI for resolution. The last thing [the directorates] want is for the

DCI to become a strong central authority. In adjudicating between them he might favor one or the other, and the others would lose some of their traditional freedom.[15]

The admiral attributed the independence of the CIA's operating directorates to a combination of three influences: their initial separateness at the beginning of the Agency's history in 1947, each with distinctive and (in his view) "haphazard" evolutionary arcs; the philosophy of a need-to-know compartmentalization (or what the CIA refers to as "compartmentation") of activities that, for security reasons, fractures the sharing of information along directorate and even office lines; and their differing responsibilities (collection, analysis, and technical support). In what manner does the CIA's professional intelligence bureaucracy want the DCI to govern? In Turner's opinion, by leaving the CIA alone and concentrating on outside political battles with the White House, the Congress, and the public—a blend of public relations and Washington infighting to protect Agency budgets and programs.

Admiral Turner was not willing to tolerate this degree of internal autonomy, believing that in order to combat foreign threats more effectively, information had to be shared more equitably, both inside the CIA and across the community. Moreover, excessive internal discretion in the past had led, he was convinced, to the intelligence abuses documented by White House and congressional investigators in 1975. Yet try as he might, Turner conceded that he had little success in overcoming the centrifugal forces at Langley, and his experience in attempting to discipline improper behavior by two renegade CIA officers in the Operations Directorate illustrates the point. Rather than support his efforts, the Agency closed ranks against him, sharply resisting intrusion by this outside military man and his uniformed aides (quickly dubbed "the Navy mafia" by inside regulars). As Turner recalled, "Not one CIA professional concurred with my instant reaction to fire the two men."[16]

President Bill Clinton's first DCI, R. James Woolsey (another irregular), had a similar experience in 1994. When cracking down on the lax security that allowed DO officer Ames to sell secrets to the Kremlin, he found to his amazement and chagrin that the Directorate's own leaders had chosen to confer medals on the very individuals he was attempting to punish, clearly a signal from the DO regulars to back off their turf. Apparently intimidated, Woolsey ignored the recommendations of the CIA's inspector general (Frederick P. Hitz) in favor of dismissals and other tough sanctions, deciding instead merely to reprimand eleven senior DO managers. When Woolsey's successor, John Deutch (also an irregular, a former MIT chemistry professor and provost), sought to discipline DO officers for improper activities in Guatemala, he became the first director ever booed by senior intelligence officers assembled in "the Bubble," the Agency's main auditorium.[17]

### The DCI's Second Challenge: Running the Community

Admiral Turner also did not have much success in leading the wider community, but none of the other DCIs that followed him has done much better. Turner's immediate successor, the controversial outsider William J. Casey (1981–87), devoted little attention to issues of community integration (although he did take an active interest in national intelligence estimates, detailed reports based on communitywide sources). Indeed, he bypassed altogether the Agency's normal procedures and the community during the centerpiece operation of his tenure, the Iran-contra affair.

Another outsider, former FBI director William H. Webster (1987–91), followed by insider Gates, both achieved some success in integrating the intelligence community based on the creation of interagency intelligence "fusion" centers and task forces. Although the next DCI, Woolsey (1993–95), built some bridges between the CIA and the Pentagon (where he had once served), his role as a community leader was modest as well.

Subsequently, DCI Deutch (1995–96), who had also served in the Defense Department, further tightened the ties between the Agency and the Pentagon and strengthened the feeble Community Management Staff in his search for better interagency coordination. In addition, both Woolsey and Deutch enriched the DCI's top board of analysts, the National Intelligence Council, by drawing in more communitywide personnel, and responding to Washington's budget-cutting pressures, they experimented with pooling a communitywide legislative liaison staff. But all these efforts represented only piecemeal attempts to integrate the secret agencies, despite Deutch's euphoric hope to "orchestrate the symphony" of the community's component parts.[18]

*Fusion Centers*

"The basic themes of American governmental institutions are distrust and disaggregation," notes a political scientist.[19] Nothing so exemplifies this phenomenon as the intelligence community. In response to the centrifugal tendencies both within the CIA and—more pronounced still— throughout the community, recent DCIs have experimented with fusion centers that concentrate on specific intelligence problems. These fusion centers include the Center for CIA Security, the Center for Support Coordination, the DCI Center for Security Evaluation, the DCI Nonproliferation Center (NPC), the DCI Counterterrorist Center (CTC), the Counterintelligence Center, the National HUMINT Requirements Tasking Center, the DCI Crime and Narcotics Center (CNC), and the DCI Environmental Center (DEC).

These centers offer planning, research, analysis, technical support, and operations all in one place ("one-stop shopping," officials in the centers boast), bringing together community experts to focus on specific threats to the United States. They encourage the sharing of information across agencies, in contrast to the more traditional emphasis on separate agency hierarchies, competition, and the hoarding of knowledge. Seated in the same suite of offices within easy conversational reach are CIA, Federal Bureau of Investigation (FBI), and other intelligence officers with common specialties (such as counterterrorism). Currently, each center is housed in, and dominated by, the CIA, yet the number of communitywide experts participating in several of the centers is steadily increasing, and the organizations are becoming more truly all-source integrators of information, analysis, and operations.

*Task Forces*

In another effort to overcome internal CIA and communitywide fragmentation, recent intelligence directors have experimented with using special task forces to deal with specific problems. Some dozen in number, they have addressed such matters as covert action, information management, and future planning. Director Woolsey put together one of the most successful task forces to monitor intelligence needs for UN and

NATO forces in Bosnia. Field commanders and Washington policymakers alike commended this communitywide team for its exemplary all-source ethos and reporting of timely, useful information from the Balkans. A comparable team also performed with merit during the war in Kosovo in 1999.

Centers and task forces notwithstanding, disaggregation remains the order of the day for the intelligence community. The community resembles nothing so much as a byzantine mosaic—or, in the apt description of one observer, "a Hobbesian state of nature."[20] This fragmentation poses a staggering leadership challenge for any DCI who hopes to piece together, on behalf of the president, all-source intelligence products from all parts of the community. Little wonder that a deputy DCI once threw up his hands in despair and declared the community nothing more than a "tribal federation."[21] The movement toward centrism has gained some momentum, albeit at a glacial pace, and this description remains close to the mark.

## The Eight-Hundred-Pound Gorilla

A major obstacle confronting any DCI who seeks to establish a true intelligence *community* has been what CIA officers refer to as the "eight-hundred-pound gorilla" that resides in the Pentagon: the secretary of defense. Of the approximately $27 billion currently spent each year on intelligence, the secretary of defense controls about 85 percent of the total.[22] Moreover, the nation's military intelligence agencies (including the largest, the NSA, and the most expensive, the NRO) are tied directly to both the Department of Defense and the Office of the DCI (see figure 1).

A result of a hasty compromise in 1947 between the founders of the CIA and entrenched military intelligence leaders anxious about threats to their domain, these blurred lines of authority created conditions ripe for bureaucratic conflict in which the DCI holds a poor hand. The secretary of defense enjoys much higher status in the government; he, not the DCI, is a statutory member of the National Security Council (NSC). Moreover, the secretary of defense (known before 1947 as the secretary of war) has stood at the top of the cabinet's pecking order—along with the secretaries of state and treasury—since the beginning of the nation's history. The DCI, in contrast, is not a member of the cabinet. President Reagan did make William Casey a member, but since then no other DCI has served in this capacity. The DCI may be the formal head of the intelligence community, but in terms of genuine clout in the high circles of government, he has minimal leverage over people like the secretary of defense.

Moreover, the defense secretary is only one of several powerful figures in the government who preside over intelligence agencies within their own departments. The secretary of state can have considerable bureaucratic influence in the White House and on Capitol Hill and is quite capable of deflecting unwanted DCI control over the State Department's Bureau of Intelligence Research (INR).

The director of the FBI, too, is not exactly a lightweight in Washington circles. This point is obvious with respect to the legendary J. Edgar Hoover, director of the bureau between 1924 and 1972, who refused even to talk to DCI Richard Helms (1966–73) during a CIA-FBI squabble over counterintelligence jurisdictions. More recent FBI directors— and certainly the current incumbent, Louis J. Freeh—also have had minds of their own, close ties to the Hill, and a manifest capacity to thwart DCI "interference" in bureau affairs. Despite the DCI's initial opposition, Freeh successfully expanded the presence of the FBI overseas to fight international crime, a move viewed with alarm by some senior officials in the CIA as an exercise in global empire building by the bureau at the expense of Agency billets in U.S. embassies abroad. Moreover, lamented a recently retired CIA official, "The FBI is absorbing all of the Agency's counterintelligence responsibilities."[23]

The less well known "program managers" who head up the other intelligence agencies (such as the director of the NSA) are also expert at shielding their operations from the DCI and at building alliances in the White House and in Congress. Furthermore, whereas the CIA is an independent, nonpolicy agency that serves the president directly (through the DCI), all the other intelligence agencies report to their *policy* department secretaries (whether civilian or military) as well as to the DCI. Not surprisingly, the directors of these agencies are quick to run to their departmental secretaries for protection should a DCI become too aggressive in trying to shape their programs and budgets.

The DCI cannot depend on the president's national security adviser as a reliable ally in the White House. The reason is that the security adviser's views may contradict the information brought to the Oval Office by the intelligence director, and the security adviser has the considerable advantage of a suite in the West Wing and frequent access to the president.

The position of DCI, then, is not at all what it appears to be on the standard organizational diagrams: a colossus standing astride the secret agencies and driving them forward in his chosen direction, as if they were so many horses in a wagon train. Rather, the director is primarily the titular head of the community and must depend heavily on personal bargaining skills, support in Congress, friendship ties with key departmental secretaries and program managers, and—vital to success—the president's backing. In this sense, the Office of the DCI is reminiscent of the view of the presidency as a position of persuasion, not command,[24] although the DCI lacks the resources of funding, staff, and authority enjoyed by the president and other senior figures in the national security apparatus.

The DCI does have a few face cards in the game of political persuasion that characterizes American government. Depending on the chemistry between the two, the director sometimes has a close relationship with the president. William J. Casey was a long-time friend and confidant of President Reagan, and Robert Gates also benefited from strong ties to President Bush. In addition, the DCI has ready access to the CIA's storehouse of information gathered overseas by agents recruited by the Operations Directorate, as well as to the reports prepared by the thousands of analysts in the Intelligence Directorate (who, free of affiliation with a cabinet department, enjoy a reputation for policy neutrality).

The secretaries of state and defense have their wellsprings of information, too, of course, from open sources as well as from their own departmental intelligence services, but sometimes the CIA can provide the DCI with unique data and assessments, especially on global political and economic matters. In the truism, information is power and the DCI can use Agency information to gain standing in the government, particularly if the president values intelligence and regularly seeks briefings from the DCI.

Military versus Civilian Intelligence

The dilemma faced by the DCI in governing the intelligence community can be seen in the current tug of war over "support to military operations" (SMO in the inevitable Pentagon acronym). As Operation Desert Shield gathered momentum in 1990, Congress heatedly debated for four days the wisdom of intervention to halt Iraqi aggression against its neighbor, Kuwait. Senator Sam Nunn (D, Georgia) agonized over the risk of high U.S. casualties that might result from the military action. Backed by former chairman of the Joint Chiefs of Staff Admiral William J. Crowe Jr., Nunn argued forcefully in favor of economic sanctions to punish Iraq rather than the use of an American invasion force in the heart of the Middle East.

Nunn lost the debate, but as it turned out, the ensuing fatalities on the U.S. side numbered fewer than two hundred. One of the main reasons for this outcome was the transparency of the battlefield for American war fighters, a result of saturating the region with intelligence surveillance platforms. The possibility in the future of ever greater battlefield transparency, allowing for still fewer body bags, has understandably whetted appetites in the Pentagon for acquiring additional intelligence resources to support the war fighters. As a consequence, "SMO" has become a popular bureaucratic battle cry inside the Pentagon among those who prepare the secretary of defense for annual intelligence budget negotiations with the DCI.

Naturally, DCIs also favor the reduction of U.S. casualties as far as possible during warfare; however, they have the added responsibility of reporting to the president and other policy officials on intelligence related to foreign political, economic, and societal—not just military—matters. Given the Pentagon's control already over 85 percent of the intelligence dollar, further erosion in the direction of the SMO mission would drastically reduce the budget for intelligence on these other global threats. As the staff director of the House Intelligence Committee has put it, "There is a need to rebuild a strategic, or what we sometimes call the national, capability to end what has been an absolute and total fixation on near-term, tactical [military] intelligence."[25]

Sometimes the bargaining over resources between the intelligence chief and the secretary of defense has been cordial. Indeed, Woolsey's and Deutch's ties to the defense secretary were too cozy in the opinion of some CIA officers, who feared that both men were selling out to the Pentagon's dreams of perfect battlefield transparency. Often, though, the relationship has been distant, like, in the words of a former CIA officer, "ships passing in the night."[26] In the Carter administration, Secretary of Defense Harold Brown and DCI Turner rarely saw eye to eye. In those infrequent cases when disagreements between the secretary of defense and the DCI are pushed into the Oval Office for arbitration, presidents have been disinclined to oppose the military. And even if the secretary of defense were to lose in the White House, the Pentagon's powerful allies on the Armed Services Committees in Congress are likely to enter the ring on the military's side.

The Office of the DCI is thus an incongruous leadership post, with major responsibilities for guiding national intelligence but without concomitant authority, jostled on all sides by muscular rivals and torn by deep historical and cultural divisions even within the director's own immediate home agency, the CIA. As one intelligence specialist put it, "For all the talk about community, the reality is different."[27] Indeed, it is unlikely that even James Madison (the father of institutional disaggregation in America's government) could have imagined the hyperpluralism that characterizes the intelligence community today. Agency autonomy is the guiding norm even within the subdivisions of the secret organizations.

The end result of this institutional fragmentation has been a steady drift away from the centrism that Harry S Truman endorsed with his creation of a more *central* intelligence. Some recent steps have been taken to reverse the powerful centrifugal forces emanating from the separate departments and agencies that deal with intelligence, but they have met fierce resistance, especially from the guardians of military intelligence in the Pentagon. Even the DCI is nervous about seeking more authority. "Every time you try to give me new authority," George Tenet has remarked, "you get me in a fight with a building much bigger than mine [that is, the Pentagon]."[28]

## The Elusive Quest for Intelligence Centrism

In 1996, the Aspin-Brown commission attempted to overcome some of the institutional fragmentation in the community by recommending that the DCI be given more authority.[29] When Congress addressed these and related reform proposals in the Intelligence Authorization Act of FY 1997, it gave the director some extra governing leverage, including a special Committee on Foreign Intelligence (CFI) lodged in the NSC.[30] The new CFI is chaired by the president's national security adviser, and its members include the DCI, the secretary of defense, and the secretary of state. Although the intention of this reform was to provide more focus to intelligence issues at a high level, it achieved little more than to create still another layer in the NSC's increasingly encumbered bureaucracy.

The Aspin-Brown commission (and subsequently Congress) embraced the creation of even another new NSC committee, this one entitled the Committee on Transnational Threats. Again chaired by the national security adviser, its membership included the DCI, the secretary of defense, the secretary of state, and the attorney general—in short, the CFI plus one. The catchall phrase "transnational threats" is meant to include global crime, narcotics flows, and weapons proliferation, as if the NSC had somehow overlooked these menaces in the past.

Finally, Congress created in this same statute one deputy director and three assistant directors to support the DCI. The deputy director for Central Intelligence (DDCI, already in existence) is supposed to help manage the CIA. The new deputy director of Central Intelligence for community management (DDCI/CM) is meant to help manage the wider community. The assistant directors of Central Intelligence (ADCIs) are positions designed to aid the DCI and the DDCI/CM in the communitywide coordination of three core activities: administration (ADCI/A), intelligence collection (ADCI/C), and analysis and production (ADCI/A&P). With respect to the spending powers, Congress recoiled from the notion of a stronger DCI. According to the language of the 1997 Intelligence Authorization Act, the director would be allowed only to "facilitate the development of annual budget for intelligence" (as he already does, insofar as the secretary of defense lets him).

The DCI's most notable success in the 1997 legislation, however modest, came in the realm of selected appointment powers. That is, the secretary of defense must seek the "concurrence" of the DCI before appointing the program directors for the NSA, the NRO, and the National Imagery and Mapping Agency (NIMA). If the DCI did not concur, the secretary of defense could then take the case to the president or select another nominee. For other key appointments, including the heads of the Defense Intelligence Agency (DIA), State's INR, and the FBI, the intelligence director would only have to be "consulted" by the secretary of defense, the secretary of state, and the attorney general, respectively; no concurrence would be necessary—another victory for institutional autonomy.

## Toward a Protean Centrism

Should the nation embrace the Hamiltonian impulse to strengthen the Office of the DCI, as recommended by some reformers (including the Aspin-Brown commission)? Or in light of the political realities discussed here, would one be better off (in the British expression) to save one's breath to cool one's porridge? The presence of a strong secretary of defense and a large portion of the intelligence budget dedicated to military needs are facts of life unlikely to change. Nor should they, since most observers agree that America's defense requirements must remain preeminent in this nation's hierarchy of foreign policy priorities. Nonetheless, reformers point to the unbridled centrifugal forces that dominate the intelligence community. They argue that America's secret agencies will continue to fall short in their duty to provide the president with cohesive civilian and military information until greater centrism is achieved (as Truman sought five decades ago) through an increase in the DCI's authority.[31]

The goal of the centrists, as one observer has astutely put it, is to achieve "the efficiencies of a 'department of intelligence' without performing major surgery."[32] Major surgery is unlikely, as the secretary of defense and the Pentagon's congressional allies are unwilling to allow the creation of a countervailing eight-hundred-pound DCI. Moreover, the antigovernment mood in the United States and ongoing concerns about excessive federal spending present an unfavorable climate for the creation of a Department of Intelligence, even if that were a smart idea. The most centrists can now hope for is some modest strengthening of the DCI and a concomitant consolidation of the intelligence community.[33]

Former representative Lee Hamilton (D, Indiana), an experienced intelligence overseer, clearly stated the core objective of those reformers who seek greater centrism, namely, a more prominent role for the DCI in interagency coordination, which would also tilt the community away from the Department of Defense and toward a richer reporting of civilian intelligence:

> We don't really have a Director of Central Intelligence. There is no such thing. The DCI at CIA controls only a very small portion of the assets of the Intelligence Community, and there are so many entities you don't have any Director. There is not a Director of Intelligence in the American system, and I think we have to create one.[34]

The current chairman of the House Intelligence Committee agrees. "The DCI needs greater capability, since he is the chief intelligence architect," argues Porter Goss (R, Florida). "We have a management problem designed for failure, and it's amazing it works as well as it does. We need more comprehensive management."[35] The chief source of the problem, in his view, is lodging the intelligence budget in the Department of Defense. The staff director for the House Permanent Select Committee on Intelligence articulated the case for a strengthened DCI:

> There is still no management of the intelligence community. The intelligence agencies are each managed, but there is no one in a position to make the tradeoffs within the intelligence community that will make a coherent, efficient organization that will function as a whole. So, we end up doing it on Capitol Hill. And I've got to tell you, if you are depending on Capitol Hill to do something as important as this, you're in trouble.[36]

A first step in remaking the DCI would be to give the office added stature, not in an unrealistic attempt to match that of the secretary of defense, but at least to raise the profile of the intelligence director in the national security establishment. To this end, amending the National Security Act of 1947 to make the DCI a full statutory member of the NSC (along with the president, vice president, secretary of state, and secretary of defense), and not merely an adviser to the panel, is likely to be more important than the superfluous NSC committees created by the Intelligence Authorization Act of 1997 (which place the DCI in a subordinate role to the national security adviser). Such a law would have to state clearly, however, that the DCI would serve on the NSC strictly in a non-policy capacity, only to provide information and analysis and not policy pronouncements that would contradict his role as a neutral presenter of facts and insights.

In addition, the DCI's approval of the appointment of *all* intelligence program directors would make the various agency chiefs more responsive to the individual supposedly in charge of the entire community. The DCI's role in preparing the annual intelligence budget could be strengthened as well, again not to have the intelligence director replace the secretary of defense, but to remind the Pentagon and others that the nation's civilian intelligence needs are important, too. Except in times of war, 25 percent of the annual intelligence budget should be turned over to the DCI for civilian intelligence purposes, such as the collection of information on global political and economic matters.

In regard to consolidating the community, some important measures have been adopted since the end of the cold war, such as the development of centers and task forces. Useful too is a new joint system set up by the CIA and the Pentagon to keep track of clandestine operations involving agents abroad, what the DCI's assistant director for administration calls "an excellent first step" and a concept "we need now to extend . . . throughout the community."[37] The melding of dispersed space reconnaissance activities under NIMA's direction is another example of consolidation. Some CIA officers worry, though, that this new organization was simply a ploy by the Defense Department to take away photo-reconnaissance and imagery interpretation from the Agency.

The nation's National Photographic Interpretation Center (NPIC) was indeed once sheltered in the CIA's DS&T Directorate, and its shift into the NIMA was, in this sense, a "militarization" of this important function. Still, logic was on the side of fusing communitywide imagery and mapping components for the common task of researching global geographic details and taking note of any changes that might have strategic significance for the United States (just as signals intelligence is concentrated in another disciplinary "stovepipe," the NSA). The DCI has full access to the imagery analyses prepared by photo interpreters in the new NIMA. Nonetheless, the most important power over imagery is the ability to direct satellite and airplane cameras toward the targets of one's choice in the first place (a decision called "tasking"). This is another place where the DCI and the secretary of defense have often bumped heads, since NIMA is basically a combat support agency and belongs to the Department of Defense.[38]

An expansion of the program to rotate officers through different agencies as part of their career progression and a greater emphasis on common security badges, training, and the sharing of facilities would lead to better interagency cooperation.[39] Pooling recruitment data would be sensible, too. Seymour Hersh reported that U.S. Naval Intelligence recruited Jonathan Pollard, who eventually became an American spy for Israeli intelligence, without knowing that he had already flunked the CIA's recruitment tests on security grounds.[40] The CIA's recent efforts at co-location for DO and DI officers in order to increase the interaction between intelligence collectors and analysts could also be replicated among the specialties inside other agencies. The desired outcome is to build bridges that will enable people in different cultures to collaborate on assignments that cut across agency boundaries.

The organizational objective of most intelligence reformers is to build a community that is lean, flexible, and synergistic, with each agency integrated with the others and all led by a DCI with more effective management control. It is driven by a centrist vision. Reformers propose not a simple-minded model of centrism, however, headed by a potentially dangerous intelligence czar but, rather, a more fluid model that draws together different strands of the community for different tasks. This model envisions concentrating communitywide resources into the Counterterrorist Center to deal with that specific threat, or into an all-source task force for, say, an intense focus on ethnic strife in central Africa, or into a collection discipline (such as HUMINT) to blend the results of that approach to information gathering.

The model envisions a DCI with the authority to redirect community resources wherever they are necessary in future contingencies—in some instances, a rapid shifting ("surging") of capabilities from one nation or region to another. For such enduring interests as terrorism or international narcotics flows, the DCI would order a more permanent concentration of resources into new fusion centers. Increasingly, centrism would become more a matter of setting up secure electronic networks for communications among intelligence specialists throughout the community than establishing physical sites at Langley or elsewhere. These virtual fusion centers, according to a senior intelligence officer, have "made cross-cultural linkages [within the community] easier."[41] Temporary teams of visiting experts could be brought in to assist the intelligence community (for example, the nation's leading academic experts on Sudan should a crisis occur there). According to this perspective, the DCI would have a continuum of coordinating strategies—a protean centrism—to focus the community's efforts on the limited number of targets where the secret agencies could contribute to the already available public knowledge on foreign events and conditions.

## Balancing Unity and Diversity

The main purpose of America's intelligence establishment is to provide the president and other officials with the best possible information about and insights into global events. Since the end of World War II, presidents have generally supported the idea of a more central intelligence in place of the extreme institutional fragmentation that characterized U.S. intelligence before and during the war against the Axis powers.

Yet despite the creation of a CIA and a DCI in 1947, institutional disaggregation has remained the hallmark of American intelligence, as units within the policy departments (civilian and military) have resisted the movement toward centrism as a threat to their own authority. Unable to stop the establishment of a CIA and a DCI, the existing agencies reverted to the next line of defense: retaining as much of their original autonomy as possible within the new, more centrist framework. Although DCIs have managed to increase somewhat their control over all the intelligence agencies, the intelligence "community" remains essentially a confederation of disparate elements. At the other extreme, excessive intelligence aggregation would not be desirable, since each government department and agency has unique informational needs that a single organization would probably not be able to fulfill.

The problem, as always in government, is how to balance unity and diversity. The American Constitution is grounded in a theory of governance that favors institutional diversity, a disaggregation of power to ensure liberty or ambition counteracting ambition, in Madison's conception. Modern presidents and DCIs, in contrast, worry about efficiency, having the right information at the right time and getting things done. They seek to harness the intelligence agencies to gather and interpret worldwide information in a timely, holistic fashion, with a good balance between civilian and military reporting.

"In unity lies strategic direction and clarity," remarks an expert on America's executive branch of government. While on the one hand commending the National Security Council for exhibiting this attribute, he praises on the other hand the value of diversity displayed by the Department of State, noting that diversity encourages "sensitivity to implementation and to nuance."[42] Likewise for intelligence, greater centrism would permit the White House (through the DCI) to derive better insights from the enormous inflow of global information gathered separately by the various intelligence agencies. But if the United States were to concentrate all of its intelligence resources into a single intelligence department or perhaps a committee of the NSC, the result would be an erosion of diversity, agility, and the responsiveness that allows each intelligence element in the existing cabinet departments to respond to the needs of their individual secretaries, especially the tactical intelligence requirements of the secretary of defense.

Furthermore, excessive centrism would discourage competition among the secret agencies, which currently offer to the president (although not always) a range of views rather than a single, homogenized common denominator. In addition, as an intelligence expert observed, "Competition is essential for innovation."[43] Diversity of structure and a division of power in the intelligence community can lead to a healthy debate over the meaning of world events, a "competitive analysis" that is a valuable (if more complicated) precondition to thoughtful presidential decisions.

Just as the homogeneity of excessive centrism would be a mistake for the intelligence community, so would a system that was too diverse and unwieldy and no longer served the president's needs for reliable, timely, and cohesive information—Truman's lament. Over the years, the agencies of the intelligence community have largely eschewed unity in favor of functional diversity, protected as they are by their department secretaries against centrism in the form of a strong DCI.

The recent growth of interagency task forces and centers suggests some movement toward greater centrism. Whether this trend will continue depends ultimately on the leadership of future presidents. If, like Truman, they believe that greater intelligence unity is necessary, the centrist trend will continue. The adversarial, individualistic culture of the intelligence community may begin to approach the greater analytical integration exhibited in the British system. Even then, however, the secretary of defense will likely fight for the autonomy of military intelligence, the secretary of state for intelligence (support to diplomatic operations or SDO), the FBI director for the bureau's perceived prerogatives in the war against international criminals, and on down the line.

Given what is likely, on the one hand, to be the policymaker's growing interest in quick, integrated information from the intelligence community on civilian and military developments around the world and, on the other hand, the enduring desire for autonomy among the intelligence agencies, we can anticipate the struggles between the values of unity and diversity to continue in the national security establishment. In light of the relatively rapid turnover of presidents and the more permanent nature of the intelligence bureaucracy, it would probably take an intelligence failure of Pearl Harbor proportions to shock the American people and their chief executive into demanding the greater efficiencies of centrism.

However imperfectly the intelligence community is now organized, presidents and other top officials continue to rely on the secret agencies and spend a king's ransom each year for the information, insight, and other services they provide. These costs of intelligence are explored next.

# SIX

# Spending for Spies

I have little doubt that half this huge [intelligence] budget is
wasted. Trouble is, I'm not sure which half!
—Harry Howe Ransom, "Reflections on Forty Years
of Spy-Watching," 1994

Perhaps no topic is more central to an understanding of politics than budgeting, for in the annual allocation of funds is the ultimate outcome of the struggle over finite resources among government agencies—the "who gets, what, when, and how" of a famous definition of politics reduced to cold, hard numbers.[1] This chapter looks into the funding of America's intelligence agencies in an effort to shed light on the politics of spending for spies since the end of the cold war.

The study of U.S. intelligence spending confronts some unique research barriers, foremost the secrecy in which budgeting for the hidden side of government is shrouded. The public record yields a fair amount of reliable information on this subject, however, and coupled with interviews with intelligence officials, it is possible to piece together an accurate portrayal of budgets and politics even in this shadow land. Regardless of the methodological difficulties, this topic warrants more attention than it has been given in the past. After all, the intelligence agencies attract a large slice of the annual tax revenues in the United States, by all accounts more than $26 billion to $30 billion in recent years, a sizable sum compared with what other nations spend on intelligence (though equivalent to only about 12 percent of the total U.S. defense budget).[2] These monies are sometimes used for highly controversial purposes, including the overthrow of foreign governments (a form of covert action), highly intrusive collection operations like the economic espionage conducted in Paris by the CIA in 1995 that resulted in an embarrassing diplomatic flap between France and the United States, and the U.S. espionage caper against Germany in 1997 that went awry.[3]

## The Budget Process for Intelligence

The government's review of the intelligence budget has three steps. First, the heads of the thirteen agencies in the intelligence community determine their funding requests. Second, the DCI and staff in the Office of Management and Budget (OMB) review and create an overall budget. Third, the secretary of defense incorporates the intelligence budget into the rest of the budget for the Department of Defense, which is then included in the president's annual budget for presentation to Congress.

Although this process is similar in many respects to the one employed by other government agencies, some aspects of the intelligence budget are unique. First, the DCI has no line authority over the requests of the individual agency heads whose budgets he is responsible for reviewing. The directors of the principal military intelligence agencies—the National Security Agency (NSA), the National Reconnaissance Office (NRO), the National Imagery and Mapping Agency (NIMA), the Defense Intelligence Agency (DIA), and the intelligence units in each of the four military services—all report to the secretary of defense. As mentioned in the previous chapter, this funding accounts for about 85 percent of the money spent annually on U.S. intelligence[4] (see figure 3).

Each of the military intelligence chiefs is appointed and promoted by the secretary of defense. Through a "cross-walk" process of meetings and exchanges of memoranda, the DCI and the Department of Defense work together to draw up the annual intelligence budget. The DCI is expected to compile the budgets for all the agencies in the intelligence community, and he also is blamed if the agencies perform poorly. Even so, the director has only partial control over their management and funding practices, except for the CIA. The DCI has complete authority over its activities and budget, which partially explains why DCIs have traditionally paid more attention to the CIA than to their broader communitywide responsibilities.

Further handicapping the DCI is the fact that he does not have an independent staff to review the programs and budgets presented by the

*Figure 3.* The Dominance of Military Agencies over Total Intelligence Funding

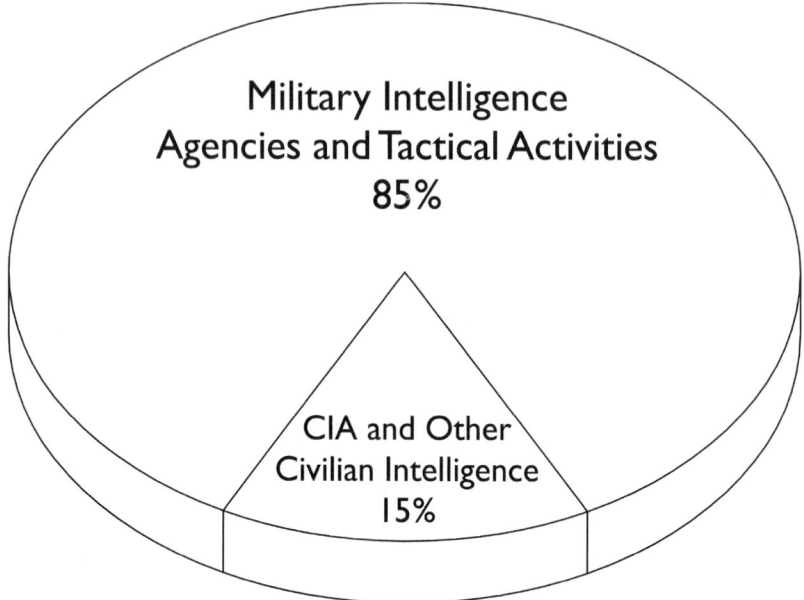

*Note:* Military intelligence agencies include the National Security Agency, the National Reconnaissance Office, the Defense Intelligence Agency, and the tactical intelligence activities of the military services. Other civilian intelligence activities include the FBI's foreign counterintelligence activities, the State Department's Bureau of Intelligence and Research, the Intelligence Community Management Account, and small offices in the Energy and Treasury Departments.

other agency heads. The staff that is available to him—about seventy professionals making up his Community Management Staff (CMS)—are for the most part on temporary assignment from the agencies they are expected to oversee. Clearly, when the parent agency pays the salary of a staff person, approves his or her promotion, and determines where the staffer's next assignment will be, the chance that this person will carry out a careful, objective examination of the "home" agency's budgets and performance is dubious. While not the intent of this staff arrangement—at least from the DCI's point of view—it has usually been the practice in most years since the creation of the DCI's office in 1947.

Finally, and perhaps the most telling indication of the DCI's tenuous central control over the intelligence community, he lacks a common database to tell him what he is paying for in each of the agencies. The director runs the largest enterprise in the history of the world for the collection and analysis of global information, yet he does so partly blindly, another aspect of the one-eyed jack phenomenon discussed in the preceding chapter.

When previous directors have attempted to create a communitywide database, their requests to the agencies have largely been ignored. It is little wonder that DCI R. James Woolsey (1991–94) appeared ill informed on C-SPAN in 1994 when explaining the details of the NRO's exorbitant $300 million headquarters building in the Virginia countryside. The funding for the building had been tucked away under the innocuous category "Mission Support," essentially lost in the NRO's top-secret budget document.[5]

## Act 1: Early Budget Estimates

The bureaucratic process of deciding how much to spend on spying and for what end is an obscure, secretive ritual. The opening act of the intelligence budget review, as bewildering to most Americans as Japanese kabuki theater, begins in the spring of each year when the government's secret agencies estimate the amount of funding they will need for the coming year. In a rather unscientific manner, each agency's offices, divisions, and directorates use their previous year's budget to determine how much more money they will need to cover inflation, payroll increases, rises in operational expenses, and new or expanded missions. The managers of each agency and their respective budget shops also weigh operational risks against potential payoffs in new intelligence, estimate the costs of addressing new intelligence targets, plan infrastructure improvements, and review staffing levels. In each agency, this process is usually dominated by the directorate that is responsible for the line function. At the CIA, for example, the Directorate of Operations (which, recall, collects intelligence abroad by means of HUMINT assets) is at the top of the budget review.

During the 1980s, when intelligence funding increased much faster than even Defense Department spending (see figure 4),[6] this initial phase of internal agency review emphasized how best to spend "new money" rather than whether or not the way an agency spent the previous year's funds was having the desired payoff. The intelligence agencies institutionalized this practice by assuming that 75 to 85 percent of their budget constituted the "base" program that would be required to keep the agency running at current levels of activity. The remaining 25 to 15 percent consisted of new spending and drew the attention of those overseeing the budget. As a result, what the agencies presented to the DCI at the end of each summer was a detailed description of how they would spend additional funding, but with little to no analysis of what they were doing with the bulk of their funds. The DCI had limited insight into each agency's "base" activities, since he had neither an adequate independent staff to check each agency's estimates nor a comprehensive budget database that covered the entire intelligence community.

Not surprisingly, what was new spending one year soon became part of the review-free "base program" in subsequent years. Thus the bulk of intelligence funding receives little scrutiny, as the agency heads, the DCI, and others in oversight positions focus on marginal issues loosely referred to in the community as "shortfalls" or funding "gaps." As increases in the community's budget began to taper off (temporarily) after 1989 with the end of the cold war, the intelligence agencies had fewer opportunities to propose new activities. This led the DCI, the White House, and Congress to look more closely at the activities being funded in the previously review-free "base." The community's individual bureaucracies have fought the exposure of the agencies' base budgets, resulting in a great deal of frustration for the DCI, the OMB, and the two congressional oversight committees (the Senate Select Committee on Intelligence and the House Permanent Select Committee on Intelligence).

The practice of focusing on the margin is common in the federal budget process, certainly for defense budgeting, and has been immortalized in the phrase "marginal incrementalism," the widely accepted description of how budgets are drawn up at the federal level in the United States.[7] What the intelligence community calls its "base program" is what civilian agencies refer to as their "current services" budget. In each case, the bureaucracy's intent is to focus the attention of those in oversight positions on new spending rather than on the full program.

This approach is not necessarily a ruse, for most of what is in the "base" (or is funded through "current services") will be required if an agency is to continue functioning, including payments for salaries, building construction, electricity, water, computers, and telephones. None-

*Figure 4.* Percentage Increase in Intelligence versus Defense
Spending since 1980

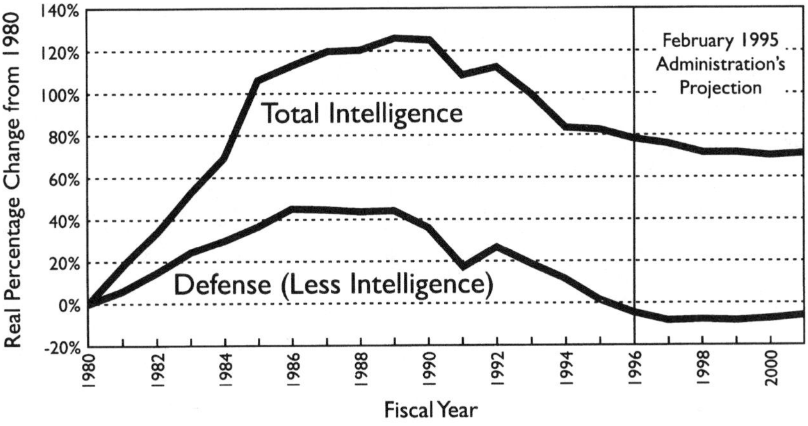

Note: Constant 1996 dollars used to plot change. The figure compares total intelligence (national, defensewide, tactical) spending with DoD's military spending, less intelligence.

Source: Report of the Commission on the Roles and Capabilities of the United States Intelligence Community (Aspin-Brown commission), *Preparing for the 21st Century: An Appraisal of U.S. Intelligence* (Washington, D.C.: U.S. Government Printing Office, March 1, 1996), 131.

theless, if an activity in the base is no longer required to achieve the agency's mission, the funds are usually diverted to other activities, such as the construction of new facilities or allowances for more liberal travel. An additional problem—and one starkly apparent in the intelligence community—is that programs that were a high priority one year continue long after they have diminished in importance. For instance, intelligence programs once targeted on the former Soviet Union are now justified (or marketed) for countering drug trafficking or weapons proliferation. Hence, the radar operator who once looked for Bear bombers coming over the North Pole is now searching for propeller-driven Cessnas carrying drugs from Colombia, a case of cold war elephant guns being used for hunting ducks.

## Act 2: DCI and OMB Budget Reviews

The second act of this drama begins in the fall, typically September, when the DCI and the OMB are given the budgets prepared by the individual agencies. At the same time, the director's staff and the OMB staff weigh the competing requests of the various agencies and formulate a consolidated intelligence program for the government. The DCI's lack of a truly independent budget staff to examine and challenge the requests developed by the agencies have left him seriously disadvantaged. Rarely, if ever, has the analysis performed by an intelligence agency or the DCI's personnel on the CMS identified possible savings. In contrast, the OMB staff assigned to review the intelligence budget, though composed of only five people, is at least independent and can often point out to the DCI and OMB management where savings might be realized. Although these suggestions are sometimes adopted, the process remains dominated by the Pentagon.

### Act 3: Integration with the Defense Budget

By mid-December, the final act of the intelligence budget cycle is performed when the DCI discusses projected funding levels with the secretary of defense, the most crucial of all the dialogues in this elaborate sequence. Before this, two parallel and concurrent budget processes were conducted simultaneously (the "cross walking" referred to earlier), in which the DCI's Community Management Staff and the Department of Defense's intelligence budget officials compare notes and numbers at all levels as they move toward the summit meeting with the DCI and the secretary of defense.

At the end of this sequence, the secretary of defense has discussed the status of the Department of Defense's budget with persons in the Executive Office of the President, including the director of OMB, White House officials, and (if the secretary wishes) the president himself. Thus, the secretary of defense has an understanding of the current politics that drives budgets beneath the surface and so knows whether the Department of Defense faces budget reductions, increases, or a continuation of the status quo. If budget reductions are on the horizon, the DCI and the secretary of defense negotiate where they can cut the funding, if at all, for the intelligence community. These discussions usually take place over lunch at the end of a National Security Council (NSC) meeting, in the secretary of defense's office at the Pentagon or simply over a secure telephone.

In these negotiations, the DCI knows who is in charge. His budget goals hover around $28 billion, a fraction of the Department of Defense's budget. The secretary of defense is the eight-hundred-pound gorilla, and the DCI is the organ-grinder's monkey, tin cup in hand. Not even the largest intelligence agencies—the NSA, the NRO, and the DIA—need the DCI's representation, even though they are officially part of the intelligence community. Rather, these military intelligence agencies are part of the Pentagon, and so they benefit from a strong protector and advocate in their other and more senior boss, the secretary of defense. This is not to say that the secretary of defense simply rubber-stamps these agencies' initial intelligence budget proposals; on the contrary, the secretary can wield his own budget scalpel. It is to say, though, that the military intelligence agencies are inclined to be more attentive to the spending priorities of their boss in the Pentagon than those of their boss at Langley.

## Myths Surrounding the Intelligence Budget

Beyond these facts of life the DCI faces with respect to the intelligence budget process, he also must contend with a number of myths about intelligence spending that further complicate his responsibilities.

### Myth 1: The Intelligence Budget Must Be Classified

During the cold war, concern about exposing the amount of funding the United States was spending on security made some sense. The Soviet Union would have been able to determine when the budget was expanding and then could direct its own intelligence agencies (the KGB and the GRU) to redouble their efforts to uncover the new programs and institute countermeasures. Especially when the amount of money spent on intelligence was small and directed toward clandestine operations, an adversary like the USSR might have drawn some valid conclusions about America's espionage priorities.

Now, however, a dollar spent on intelligence goes toward feeding a sprawling bureaucratic infrastructure with domestic and overseas facilities staffed by tens of thousands. As the Aspin-Brown commission emphasized, disclosure to the public of what is spent on this infrastructure each year would not damage the national security (as those who wish to retain the "secret" classification for the aggregate budget continue to insist); rather, it would simply allow the public to know at least broadly what they are spending on intelligence and force the intelligence community to justify this expense.[8]

Sensitive clandestine operations, the names of spies, and the capabilities of space reconnaissance satellites should remain classified, of course, so as not to jeopardize foreign agents who act on behalf of the United States or to undermine delicate technological advantages. Nonetheless, the intelligence establishment (just like other government agencies) should have to be questioned and challenged by taxpayers through their representatives in Congress. These agencies should be evaluated each year on the merits of their overall spending plans, in the same way that stockholders periodically hold the feet of private corporate bureaucracies to the fire.

This logic—and, perhaps more important, rising political pressure (including a lawsuit filed by the Federation of American Scientists)—finally led the DCI to release the aggregate spending figure for its 1998 budget: $26.6 billion.[9] The following year, however, the director balked at releasing the comparable figure, arguing that intelligence spending had increased significantly in the interim and disclosing the new budget figure might tip off America's enemies to U.S. intelligence plans and operations. "Because the 1998 appropriation represented approximately a $3.1 billion increase—or less than a 0.4 percent change—over the 1997 appropriation," the DCI stated, "I concluded that release of the 1998 appropriation could not reasonably be expected to cause damage to the national security, and so I released the 1998 appropriation."[10] The larger figure the next year—a "bump in the snake," according to the director—caused him to reconsider disclosing the next annual budget number.

Although his decision was supported by a U.S. district judge who heard a complaint filed by the Federation of American Scientists (disclosure would provide, according to the judge, "too much trend information and too great a basis for comparison and analysis for our adversaries"),[11] it remained hard for outside observers to imagine how the release of a single aggregate figure each year would reveal much to America's adversaries about specific intelligence activities. What it would provide is some sense of accountability. The DCI's real fear seemed to be that the release of this figure would somehow lead to the media's demand for disclosing more detailed budget figures, as if officials in the intelligence community were likely to forget how to say "no" to reporters on the specifics of intelligence operations.

### Myth 2: The Spy Budget Receives Careful Oversight

The reality, it bears repeating, is that the DCI does not have a sufficient independent staff to review, challenge, and question the budgets submitted by the various intelligence agencies. Recall that members of the CMS staff are primarily "detailees" from various parts of the community on temporary assignment. Often they are most interested in defending their own home agency's turf and are not always the best people for the DCI to consult for an objective perspective on budgeting. And the White House/OMB staff of five assigned to examine the intelligence budget is obviously stretched thin. By contrast, the OMB has thirty-one examiners who review the same amount of money in the Departments of State, Treasury, Interior, and Commerce.

The General Accounting Office (GAO), whose staff of 3,700 seek to improve government by exposing poor management and wasteful spending, has been shut out by the DCI and the secretary of defense from almost all access to the CIA, the NSA, the NIMA, and the NRO. Furthermore, the Department of Defense's inspector general concentrates on relatively minor issues—building leases, parking allocation, and personnel processes, for instance—without questioning such matters as the mishandling of NRO funds.

The House Permanent Select Committee on Intelligence (HPSCI) and the Senate Select Committee on Intelligence (SSCI) do engage in some meaningful oversight with respect to intelligence funding.[12] Yet each of these two committees uses only a few staffers for this task (in some years the figure has been four or five, in other years around a dozen). Moreover, these overseers are sometimes denied access to the basic information necessary to analyze the budget. That the review of intelligence programs by Congress is uneven is illustrated by an exception to the rule: the relatively effective legislative monitoring of the CIA's Reserve for Contingencies. This special fund for the rapid financing of unanticipated expenditures, including covert actions, is fenced off from the CIA's regular budget. In times of emergency, this reserve gives the president some flexibility to spend money without going through the formal appropriations process. The only requirement is that the president notify the congressional oversight committees. The reserve fund is closely watched by the legislative committees, and the money can be released only with the OMB's approval, another important check on possible misuse of these funds.

As a result, even though the Reserve for Contingencies is held to exceptional accountability, it contains only a relatively small amount of money. The huge sums of money spent on the NRO headquarters buildings and on satellite programs is, in contrast, subject to more limited accountability. The procedures for the Contingencies Reserve to the contrary notwithstanding, oversight of the intelligence community's budget is woefully inadequate, even if it is better monitored now than before 1976 (before the congressional oversight panels were created).

### Myth 3: The Intelligence Agencies Form a "Community"

As argued in the previous chapter, only a Yugoslavian definition of "community" could apply to the U.S. intelligence community. These agencies have very little in common, primarily because they perform such different functions. Moreover, they evolved in an era when interagency—or even intra-agency—sharing of information, talent, or know-how would disregard the cold war mentality of sealing off ("compartmenting") all these resources from one another in order to improve security. A further complication was that the NSA employee who enjoyed solving an encryption puzzle was sometimes at odds with the CIA employee who relished a late-night rendezvous with an agent in a foreign capital, another manifestation of the "cultural divides" described in chapter 5.

The DCI lacks the authority to mitigate these inherent differences of temperament and "tradecraft" (the bag of espionage tricks used by the various secret agencies). He does not have the sole right to appoint the heads of the dozen agencies outside the CIA, all of which are part of the National Foreign Intelligence Program (NFIP) and therefore theoretically within the director's ambit of authority. So while the DCI is supposedly in charge of formulating and defending these agencies' budgets, the funds for intelligence are ultimately appropriated to their parent departments, Defense, State, Energy, or Justice. And while the DCI officially has the authority to transfer funds from one agency to another, in reality the various agency managers throughout the community have successfully blocked any attempts to exercise this authority without their prior approval.

Even though executive order 12333, signed by President Ronald Reagan in 1981, formally acknowledges the existence of an intelligence community, the assemblage is still only a loose confederation of agencies. Each takes advantage of having two masters, the DCI and a department secretary, and often plays one off against the other to advantage. Most departments in the federal government are a collection of disparate agencies. Within the Commerce Department, for example, are the Patent Office, the National Oceanographic and Atmospheric Administration, and the Bureau of the Census, among others. Yet unlike the DCI, their departmental secretaries have clear authority over the heads of these agencies. Furthermore, each secretary has an independent staff to manage his or her department and its budgets. But to manage the intelligence community, the DCI has little more than the Community Management Staff, with its mixed loyalties and limited authority.

For some policies—particularly counterterrorism, counterproliferation, counterintelligence, and counternarcotics—the "fusion centers" located inside the CIA represent an attempt to help increase interagency comity. The results have been uneven, however, and most of the other agencies complain that the CIA has too much control over these centers.

## Myth 4: Intelligence Is a "Force Multiplier"

Some officials have argued that in the post–cold war era, a dollar spent on intelligence saves many dollars in defense. This concept of intelligence as a so-called force multiplier is derived from the notion that in a more transparent world, the United States can focus its "smart" weapons more efficiently against predetermined targets. Fewer weapons will be necessary because their value will be multiplied by their greater intelligence-guided accuracy.

When intelligence funds are dedicated to purely clandestine collection operations, they can indeed yield information of special value.[13] Today, however, most of each intelligence dollar goes to support a massive bureaucracy rather than field operations. The more efficient tooth-to-tail ratio exhibited by the secret agencies in the early stages of the cold war has been lost. Today, the agencies employee tens of thousands of people, with thousands of additional personnel under government contract. The number of civilian personnel at the CIA, the NSA, and the DIA is 33 percent higher now than in 1980, despite the end of the cold war, reductions through attrition, and voluntary buyouts mandated by Congress.[14]

The intelligence community's physical facilities around Washington and worldwide account for more than 15 million square feet of office space—dwarfing even that legendary behemoth, the Pentagon. Little of this investment, however, actually results in new information about America's foreign adversaries, the main reason for having an intelligence community in the first place. The computers, the communications facilities, heating and cooling equipment, support staffs, cars, trucks, airplanes, satellites, and related costs all add up to one of the largest bureaucracies ever. In order to believe that a dollar spent on intelligence really saves dollars in defense, we would have to forget that the care and feeding of these agencies siphons away most of the hoped-for "profit" of valuable information on foreign events and military targets.

## Influences on Intelligence Funding

Like any major decision in democratic governments, the annual intelligence budget is the result of many interacting influences, international, national, and individual. A close look at each level should show what the end of the cold war meant for intelligence funding, once viewed as crucial to the struggle against global communism.

### The International Level

#### *The Perceived Magnitude of Threat*

Intelligence funding, like America's budget making generally, tends to remain static. From year to year, if the budget changes at all, it is not in any sweeping fashion but at the margins. For intelligence funding, the exception to this rule during the cold war occurred in the Reagan administration. Under President Reagan, the intelligence budget rose by $10 billion (a 50 percent increase), driven by the strong anti-Soviet ideology of the president and his advisers. But what happened when the cold war ended? Did this startling change in world affairs lead to major redirections for U.S. intelligence spending? With America's nemesis in tatters and an exponential growth in the U.S. national debt wreaking havoc on the U.S. economy, did the budget makers toss marginal incrementalism to the winds and cut back sharply on spending for all government agencies, including intelligence?

When the USSR dissolved, the funding for intelligence might have been expected to be cut, since the international "threat environment" began to appear more benign. The reasonable hypothesis would be that if a nation faces a well-armed and belligerent adversary, it will be more inclined to increase funding for intelligence as a "first line of defense" against attack.[15] Conversely, with the disappearance of such an adversary, intelligence funding might be expected to decline. After all, if an adversary has the capacity to strike the United States with a devastating military blow from which (at the extreme) this nation might be unable to recover—say, a massive Soviet first strike during the cold war—policymakers might be inclined to spend large amounts of public funds to increase the warning time for an impending attack. The objective would be no surprises like Pearl Harbor (or worse).

Put another way, a nation that finds itself vulnerable to a "nuclear decapitation"[16] or some other form of lethal assault from abroad will probably prefer low risk-taking behavior, manifested by an increase in capabilities for information gathering, especially a search for early-warning indicators of an imminent attack. Intelligence serves as useful insurance, and this low-risk behavior requires a larger intelligence budget, as depicted in figure 5. Since the prospect of annihilation seemed much greater for this nation at crisis points during the cold war (the Cuban missile crisis, for instance) than it does now, the United States might be expected to have spent larger sums of money on intelligence during the cold war than since the fall of the Soviet Union.

### The Question of Threat Uncertainty

Another line of reasoning is compelling as well. At the end of the cold war, the United States faced an uncertain world. Almost overnight, its leaders shifted from having to cope with an often tense standoff between the two superpowers to a situation of relative global dominance enjoyed by the United States. Before the euphoria of dominance could

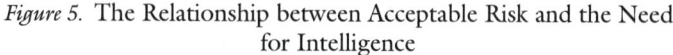

*Figure 5.* The Relationship between Acceptable Risk and the Need for Intelligence

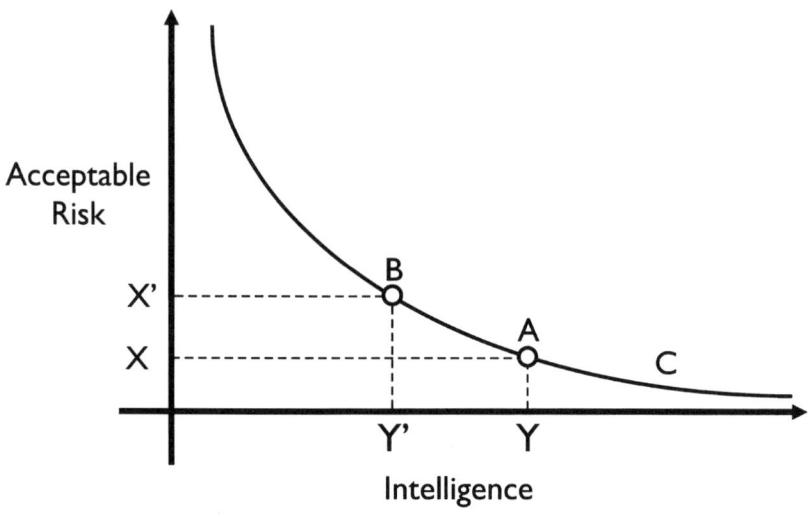

be savored, however, the emergence of smaller—albeit highly aggressive—state and nonstate actors on the world scene challenged what the first post–cold war U.S. president, George Bush, hoped would be a "new world order."

In this new, uncharted international environment, a variety of seemingly less perilous dangers began to add up to an overall threat that (at least to some observers) seemed as unsettling as the former superpower rivalry. Iraq, Iran, North Korea, Serbia, and other "rogue" or "outlaw" states—a few with accelerated programs of weapons of mass destruction—focused the attention of U.S. national security officials and required their shifting intelligence resources toward targets once considered to have a much lower priority. The situation was the same for televised humanitarian crises, like those in Somalia, Rwanda, Bosnia, Kosovo, and East Timor. During the cold war, such threats seemed to pale in comparison to the USSR's capacity to reduce American civilization to rubble in half an hour. Intelligence spending was thus concentrated against the Soviet target, with a timely warning of attack foremost in mind.

An observer of American society notes, though, that "the collapse of the Communist threat has, paradoxically, made it harder, not easier, for the United States to draw the line [on national-security interests]."[17] While threats to this nation may have become less lethal than the prospect of Soviet rockets, they continue to exist and are more globally dispersed. Or, at any rate, policymakers are prepared now to focus more on pockets of international strife once largely overlooked during the cold war. Consequently, from this point of view, the United States should in fact spend *more* money on intelligence in the post-Communist era if its leaders are to prepare themselves properly for these diffuse new dangers. Remember DCI Woolsey's admonition that the several "poisonous snakes" of the new international setting might well turn out to be as dangerous as the old Soviet "dragon."[18] Indeed, it is arguable that the continuation of the cold war would have prevented the emergence of a number of these hot spots in the developing world that have come to weigh so heavily in U.S. military and intelligence planning. If so, the end of the U.S.-Soviet rivalry may have actually led to a greater sense of insecurity and an increased need for global intelligence.

### The Influence of the Military Establishment

A third argument also grows from the change in international affairs since the Soviet demise. During the cold war, armed conflict between the United States and the Soviet Union could well have escalated into World War III, which quite likely would be an Armageddon. Facing this extreme danger, both sides usually acted prudently. The Cuban missile crisis was the most conspicuous exception, a highly dangerous and sobering event that caused both sides to draw back from the nuclear abyss with a heightened desire to avoid risks.

With the dissolution of the USSR, though, the United States has found it more feasible to venture forth—frequently with armed combat units—in the defense of perceived security interests. American intervention in the Persian Gulf would have been considered highly risky, and probably would never have been undertaken, had the USSR not been so preoccupied at the time with its own severe economic problems and internal political upheaval. In 1991, as the Soviet Union fell apart, the United States carried out a massive counterattack against Iraq with only minimal debate in Washington. Subsequently, the Bush administration dispatched American troops to Somalia, and the Clinton administration followed suit in Haiti, Rwanda, and Bosnia, and U.S. aircraft relentlessly attacked Serbian targets during the Kosovo War of 1999. These last two interventions would have been especially perilous and unlikely during the cold war.

Thus, with the United States' greater global dominance in this new world has come its more frequent use of military force abroad. This in turn has brought demands from the Pentagon for more extensive intelligence regarding areas unfamiliar to U.S. military leaders. It understandably seeks up-to-date street maps of Mogadishu, Tuzla, Pristina, and Rwanda, not the topography of the Fulda Gap in Germany.

In the Pentagon, a new military doctrine has evolved since the end of the cold war that corresponds to the more fragmented world we now face, with its tendency toward brushfire wars and ethnic bloodletting. This doctrine is known as the "two-war strategy." According to this view—clearly the prevailing paradigm in the Department of Defense, even if repudiated by critics like former member of the Joint Chiefs of Staff, General Merrill McPeak,[19]—the United States must be prepared to wage two major regional conflicts simultaneously, say, one war on the Korean peninsula and another in the Middle East or the Balkans. Regardless of how valid or realistic this doctrine may be, it obviously has a clear implication for intelligence spending. Whereas technical and human-agent collection was once focused on the gathering of information about the Soviet Union, today's military wants high-quality, instantaneous information from around the globe, an expensive proposition.

The declaration "Support to Military Operations!" (SMOs in Pentagonese), examined in the preceding chapter, has become a budgetary battle cry in the halls of Department of Defense for those who negotiate intelligence budgets. The spending emphasis should be on tactical battlefield support, runs the argument of military leaders, and not so much on the production of "national" intelligence for the president's enlightenment with respect to global political and economic affairs. The SMO emphasis is on winning wars with minimal U.S. casualties, which translates into increased spending for intelligence to illuminate battlefields around the world.

## The National Level of Analysis

### *Domestic Economic Stress*

At the national level—that is, in Washington, where the nation's global security decisions are made—three additional influences impinge on intelligence-spending decisions in the post–cold war era. The first has to do with the state of the U.S. domestic economy. The argument is that a nation facing economic distress at home is apt to turn to belt-tightening corrections, even to the detriment of existing legitimate programs; therefore, after the cold war, serious budget deficits in the United States would have been likely to push national leaders toward budget-balancing measures, including a reduction in spending on intelligence.

In the wake of the cold war, the United States felt the pangs of domestic economic problems. Experts warned of dire consequences unless the federal budget were restored to some semblance of balance following the runaway spending spree of the Reagan years. Budget-slashing lawmakers gained national prominence; the GOP swept the House and the Senate in 1994 on platforms to ax government expenditures and enact a constitutional amendment to balance the budget; and citizens groups like the Concord Coalition opened chapters across the country in support of measures to reduce the deficit.

### *The GOP's Pro–Defense Spending Agenda*

Two additional arguments point to influences working against a budget-reform agenda. The first stems, ironically, from the success of cost-cutting Republicans in gaining control of the House and the Senate in 1994. Their budget-balancing campaign rhetoric did indeed take the form of legislative proposals designed to dismantle portions of the government, most notably the welfare system. However, many Republicans—a party with a long tradition of supporting military programs—drew the line at defense and intelligence cuts. Slice spending on welfare and health care, yes, but not the B-2 bomber, the Seawolf attack submarine, or the Comanche helicopter—all better suited, perhaps, to fight the old Soviet military, but important jobs programs for constituents back home nonetheless.[20] Similarly, the Republican Party has had a stronger pro-intelligence orientation than the Democratic Party in roll-call voting and legislative hearings during and since the end of the cold war.[21] Thus, one might surmise that GOP dominance in Congress would lead to legislative initiatives in support of robust intelligence funding.

### The Intelligence "Iron Triangle"

Any discussion of spending at the federal level must also consider the question of lobbying influence. In intelligence policy, the concept of "iron triangles" and "issue networks" is alive and well, just as in the rest of the government. According to the venerable theory of iron triangles (and the more nuanced and realistic issues-network derivative), interest groups, agencies in the executive branch, and congressional committees form an alliance around policy domains for their mutual benefit.

In the last few years, the private sector has lobbied much more aggressively for contracts to build costly intelligence hardware, chiefly reconnaissance satellites and low-flying drone aircraft. Industry receives government funding; intelligence bureaucrats benefit from new programs; and legislators win the votes of constituents employed by the industries and the intelligence agencies.[22] Reinforcing this triangulation is the widely noted propensity for bureaucracies to perpetuate themselves. When the cold war ended, the CIA and its companion agencies were likely to seek other intelligence missions to replace their concentration on the Soviet Union. Consequently, one might reasonably anticipate the growth of policy alliances among industry, executive agencies, and legislative committees dealing with intelligence policy to result in added pressures to increase intelligence spending.

## The Individual Level of Analysis

### The Influence of Leadership

At the individual level of analysis, researchers probe the likely views and behavior of key decision makers. For the topic of intelligence (as for most policy domains), these individuals include at a minimum a core group of elected officials: the president, the Speaker of the House, the Senate Majority Leader, and the chairs of the intelligence committees on Capitol Hill. Added to this list is a group of foreign policy elites appointed by the president: the secretaries of state and defense, the chairman of the Joint Chiefs of Staff, the DCI, and the president's national security adviser. Among the central questions we would want answered about these policymakers are, To what extent are they isolationists or internationalists? Of the same or different political parties? Risk takers or risk avoiders? Budget balancers or spenders? Impressed by intelligence or skeptical about its usefulness?

It is difficult to generalize about individuals as diverse as Speakers J. Dennis Hastert (R, Illinois) and, preceding him, Newt Gingrich (R, Georgia); Majority Leader Trent Lott (R, Mississippi), and, preceding him, Bob Dole, (R, Kansas); and President Bill Clinton. Nevertheless, based on their public pronouncements on the subject, it is safe to say that none has sought a reduction in spending on intelligence, despite the end of the cold war.

Moreover, some of them—most vocally, Speaker Gingrich and HPSCI chairman Goss (as well as his predecessor, Larry Combest, R, Texas)—have been enthusiastic about an *increase* in intelligence funding. "We have hollowed out our intelligence capability dangerously," Goss argued. "This is what motivates me every day."[23] Their public comments indicate an acceptance of the force-multiplier perspective, in which intelligence can be counted on to offset the cutbacks in military spending sought by some budget balancers in Congress. When an American pilot accidentally bombed the Chinese embassy in Belgrade during the Kosovo war, Representative Goss concluded that the error was "a reaping of the harvest of the underinvestment in our intelligence capabilities."[24] As if an accurate map of Belgrade were that expensive or hard to find—it costs 28 Yugoslav dinars ($2.80) at a local kiosk in the city!

Goss's counterpart in the Senate, Richard Shelby (R, Alabama), agreed with him. "We've been doing defense, which intelligence is part and parcel of, on the cheap for about thirteen straight years," he opined, "and now you're seeing the fruits of it."[25] The lawmakers vowed to seek a 9 percent spending increase for intelligence in the FY 2000 budget.

In the waning days of his speakership in 1998, Newt Gingrich telephoned DCI George Tenet and said, "How would you spend an extra billion dollars if I could arrange that?" Like any good bureaucratic chief, the director had no trouble coming up with a quick wish list, and the Speaker—by now the CIA's favorite Corinthian on Capitol Hill—folded the added funding into the defense budget for use by the DCI.[26] Gingrich was also reportedly behind successful efforts in 1998 to increase covert action funding for Iraqi dissidents by $97 million, despite the view of Marine General Anthony C. Zinni, commander of U.S. forces in the Middle East, that this approach was ineffective and unrealistic.[27]

An examination of leadership views on intelligence might lead us to suppose that the current constellation of national security officials, like their predecessors during the cold war, generally agree on the need for preserving—even raising—the level of intelligence funding. Indeed, it seems likely that those Washington policymakers responsible for foreign policy usually are inclined to protect the funding for those agencies that give the United States an early warning of threats from abroad. According to this perspective, given the prominence of these officials in policy-making and budgeting, spending on intelligence would be unlikely to decrease even with the disappearance of America's archenemy, the USSR

## The Post–Cold War Intelligence Budget

In light of these various possibilities, what has actually happened to the intelligence budget since the end of the cold war? It began to decline in 1989 (adjusting for inflation), the year in which the Berlin Wall fell, and continued to drop until flattening out in 1994 at 21 percent below 1989 levels (see figure 4). Despite this modest decline, the funding levels for intelligence remained robust, fully 80 percent above 1980 levels, compared with a Department of Defense budget (excluding intelligence) that was 4 percent below its 1980 level.[28] As a recent official review of intelligence spending concluded, "Reductions taken in the intelligence budget since 1989 have been at a rate to allow intelligence agencies to continue most of their basic activities."[29] Rather than a precipitous drop after the cold war, then, the budget cuts for intelligence were gentle, incremental, and short-lived, rapidly leveling out and beginning to rise again in 1998 (as is the case for the overall defense budget, driven in part by expenditures for UN and then NATO military operations against Serbia).

From among the various arguments presented earlier, which are most useful for understanding what happened to funding for intelligence after the cold war? Interviews with individuals close to intelligence spending decisions in Washington indicate that funding levels in this new era are a result of many commingling influences, as is almost always the case with major government decisions. The fact that the USSR had suddenly vanished did make the world seem somewhat less threatening to most policy officials, despite DCI Woolsey's warning about poisonous snakes loose on the globe. Had the Soviet Union remained an adversary, a decline in intelligence spending (however temporary) would have been unlikely. Thus the magnitude of the foreign threat is a compelling consideration for policymakers who address spending decisions.

With the dramatic change in international politics brought about by the dissolution of the Soviet empire, the intelligence budget—and the larger defense budget—may well have yielded a "peace dividend" had not policymakers been concerned about the imponderables of the new world and its rogue states. The sudden prominence of Iraq, Somalia, Rwanda, Haiti, Bosnia, and Serbia, and other "flavors of the month" that demanded U.S. military attention gave pause to policymakers who had hoped for a new world order in which America could trim back its global defenses and focus more on domestic needs. "When you get away from L.A. and New York, the rest of the country loves us," declares a senior CIA official. "They want us to catch the bad guys, and they don't care about budgets."[30]

In this sense, Woolsey was correct in the early months of this new era: even though the Soviet dragon had died, the world remained in flux and required ongoing intelligence gathering to guard against untoward surprises from abroad. In advancing this argument to the OMB and congressional budgeteers, Woolsey and his successor John Deutch were successful in resisting more accelerated and deeper spending cuts urged by those in Washington worried about the domestic economy and budget imbalances.

Woolsey and Deutch found strong allies in the Pentagon (from which both had come before serving as DCI) who were adamantly in favor of increased support for military operations—the SMO mantra. Not only was the world an uncertain place, but the United States military would be called on to fight in remote locales about which policymakers and Pentagon brass had little knowledge. A peace dividend derived from a reduced intelligence budget would have to wait; money would be needed to improve the flow of war-fighting intelligence to U.S. commanders in once-ignored locations like Bosnia and Kosovo.

Each of these arguments relating to the international setting provides an explanatory insight. The end of the cold war might have led to intelligence spending cuts had not new problems immediately arisen in places like Somalia, Iraq, and Kosovo. The quest for SMO has been a prime driver toward maintaining cold war levels of intelligence spending. In budget-drafting councils, the need for improved intelligence to help protect U.S. troops in harm's way overseas has been a persuasive argument blocking deeper cuts in post–cold war intelligence budgets. Furthermore, the United States was at the end of a generation of IMINT and SIGINT satellites that needed to be updated and replaced, an expensive undertaking.

Similarly, at the national and individual levels of analysis, each of the arguments outlined earlier contributes to an overall understanding of the budget outcome for intelligence. The political ethos in the United States favoring a balanced budget—dramatically displayed in the rhetoric of the 1992 and 1994 federal elections—did encourage a reduction in government spending across the board, including that for defense and (briefly) for intelligence. Once more, however, this trend was offset by countervailing domestic influences, chiefly a Congress dominated by pro-defense Republicans, an iron triangle that supported a perpetuation of the intelligence establishment at cold war levels, and individual leaders responsible for the nation's security—particularly Speaker Gingrich and Representative Goss—who expressed little to no inclination toward cutbacks in intelligence (or most defense) spending.[31]

In the wake of the cold war, domestic pressures for budget balancing pushed the government toward trimming intelligence funding, but other influences at home ensured that the trimming stayed just that, rather than turn into more substantial reductions. Among these national and individual influences, one in particular exercised special sway over a few key legislators: the component of the "iron triangle" related to jobs for constituents. Selected members of Congress with large intelligence agencies in their states or districts, or with industrial plants manufacturing satellites and other spy hardware, were inclined to trim intelligence budgets only slightly if at all.

Senator John Warner (R, Virginia) is a good example. In 1994, he spearheaded the creation of a special panel of inquiry on intelligence (which eventually became the Aspin-Brown commission) for one main reason: to head off the movement after the cold war in Washington favoring a cutback in the spy budget and perhaps even the abolition of the

CIA. Most of the people who work for the CIA (and many of the other intelligence agencies) live—and vote—in Virginia. After a year of study, the Aspin-Brown commission had found no reason to reduce the intelligence budget (even though its vice chairman, Warren Rudman, served as a member and cofounder of the Concord Coalition, whose raison d'être is a reduction in national spending and the accumulated debt). Senator Warner looked upon the commission as a way to cool down overheated rhetoric in favor of dismantling the CIA and other elements of the intelligence community. Another influential commission member was Representative Norman D. Dicks (D) of the Seattle area, home of Boeing, which has a substantial interest in manufacturing expensive intelligence equipment (especially satellites). He also did not favor cutting the intelligence budget.

## Toward a More Sensible Intelligence Budget

At the end of the cold war, the intelligence budget did decline, as might have been anticipated with the removal of America's major international threat and, at the same time, a growing concern at home for excessive government spending. The downturn was, however, both limited and short-lived. Fortunately for President Clinton and the nation, a robust economy permitted the government to balance the national budget without major surgery on existing programs.

In 1998, Congress and the White House approved the largest spending increase for intelligence in fifteen years, a 7 percent rise to about $29 billion, which almost matched the cold war peak of $30 billion in the middle of the Reagan years.[32] This happened because of the successful domestic economy and, even more important, a realization that the world posed new threats to U.S. security interests (the prospect of renewed efforts by Iraq to gain dominance over Middle East oil, for instance, and Serbian expansion in the Balkans). In response, influential national security officials—especially those in the Pentagon—insisted on greater funding for intelligence to support military operations in the Middle East, the Balkans, and elsewhere. The intelligence bureaucracies, their allies in industry, and, most especially, key legislators in Congress fought reductions that would undermine spy missions, erode private-sector contracts, and eliminate constituent jobs.

In addition, the new DCI, George Tenet, vowed to restore the CIA to its cold war strength and "to mount increasingly complex and expensive operations."[33] His goals included building up the CIA's clandestine espionage service, opening more overseas Agency stations, undertaking more covert actions, hiring more in-house experts, buying faster and more sophisticated computers, and bringing in a new generation of recruits.

However promising it may have seemed for reformers in 1989–91 to achieve a substantial peace dividend and balance the budget in light of the less dangerous international environment the United States faced, their hopes were soon dashed by the exigencies of unforeseen peace-keeping missions abroad, politics-as-usual at home, and a sea change in intelligence community personnel (as senior officers reached retirement age) that warranted a large number of new hires. Of course, savings from reductions in the intelligence community's $30 billion budget would have contributed only modestly toward the goal of reaching a balanced budget, but nonetheless the secret agencies could have made a contribution along with all the other departments and agencies in the government, and without cutting into muscle.

The uncertainties of a fragmented world and its host of ethnic wars, however, persuaded Washington officials to support intelligence operations at almost full cold war levels. The United States had to know more about regions of the globe that had been relatively ignored during the cold war, but that now posed threats to U.S. interests abroad. So the argument went. At the same time, it seemed possible to cut back on big-ticket military weapons systems in this time of brushfire warfare. Thus, intelligence budgets remained relatively flat and defense budgets declined until both started moving back up in 1998. This concern about an uncertain and still hostile international setting was reinforced by the desire of a few important legislators to protect the interests of their constituents by maintaining the intelligence bureaucracies in their districts.

Has the intelligence community struck the correct spending posture since the end of the cold war? Generally, yes, although some important adjustments could be made and substantial savings accrued. Excessive support for winning wars by focusing the intelligence community's attention on support for military operations detracts from attention to *avoiding* wars in the first place by providing broader intelligence support to the president and the diplomatic corps.

Moreover, beyond maintaining a better balance between war-fighting and war-avoiding capabilities, the budget process could be improved. Spending would become a much more rational enterprise if the DCI had greater control over the formulation of the entire intelligence budget. As things stand now, the centripetal forces in the community place critical budget decisions into the hands of the various "program managers" such as the directors of the NSA and the DIA. With a stronger community staff for budget drafting, the DCI would have a better chance at drawing the budget strings together. Under DCIs Deutch and Tenet, the Community Management Staff has strengthened its role in the funding process by hiring a few independently minded budget specialists to help the director sift through the various initiatives pursued by agencies throughout the intelligence community; but more needs to be done to broaden this base for independent budget analysis carried out on behalf of the DCI.

To give the DCI greater authority in negotiations with the secretary of defense, it should be made clear that the director will have *all* intelligence funding appropriated to him, not to the heads of the individual agencies within the community. The DCI should have the responsibility for dispersing these funds and should be held accountable for how they are spent.

The director of Central Intelligence will never have more authority than the secretary of defense, nor should he (or, one day, she). Nevertheless, in the negotiations between the two over the annual intelligence budget, a strengthened community staff under the DCI's direction—along with a stronger legal and congressional affairs staff to present the DCI's budget on the Hill—would permit the director to enter into negotiations with the secretary of defense carrying more than a tin cup. He or she could come armed with a well-considered set of numbers that made sense for the entire community—an integrated intelligence budget in place of the current patchwork quilt. This would also give the DCI a chance to make trade-offs within the intelligence community where necessary, say, reducing spending on airplane reconnaissance in favor of increased HUMINT and the hiring of more and better qualified analysts. (At the present time, only about 1 percent of the total intelligence budget is spent on analysis.) [34]

"America's intelligence should be more like the British model," an experienced intelligence officer contends, "smaller, more efficient, a few good—very good—spies, a small budget, and some military gear."[35] Many of the so-called New Intelligence Agenda targets in the post-Communist world (examined in part I of this volume) require classic espionage with human agents, not airplanes and satellites—neither of which can infiltrate terrorist cells or narcotics cartels or divine evil intent among foreign leaders. Human agents are relatively cost effective, too (even though many of their reports prove to be inaccurate)—and they do not have microchips that fail, as happened with a group of U.S. image-collecting satellites over most of the New Year's holiday weekend in 1999 and with the NSA's data-processing computers in January 2000. The salaries for spies are tiny compared with the costs of building enormous and heavy spy satellites and then launching them into space. During the cold war, the spending ratio between technically based intelligence collection (TECHINT) and HUMINT was approximately seven-to-one, roughly what it remains today.[36]

So classic espionage is not only the best, and sometimes the only, way to acquire certain kinds of information valuable to America's security interests—such as the trade-negotiating strategies of foreign economic rivals (often best detected through a combination of HUMINT and SIGINT). Reductions in spending on technical intelligence in favor of human spies has the added virtue of reducing a bloated intelligence budget.[37] Such trade-offs must be pursued cautiously, though, because satellites and other hardware have demonstrated their enormous value in monitoring Russian missiles and other threats (real and potential). They cannot be indiscriminately eliminated, even in the unlikely event that their political constituencies were no longer there to defend them.

Finally, much can be done to save money in the intelligence domain. As the Aspin-Brown commission pointed out, even as the CIA seeks an upgraded HUMINT capability, some of the intelligence agencies should undergo additional personnel reductions, especially from the NSA, where staff salaries are choking off funds that are badly needed for research and development (at one time this agency's strong suit).[38] The intelligence agencies could also further consolidate many of their operations, from counterintelligence to legislative liaison.

The large number of collection systems—the reconnaissance airplanes, satellites, and other mechanical "platforms" that account for the overwhelming proportion of the intelligence budget—could have much smaller budgets than the Aspin-Brown commission recommended. Too much redundancy is built into these systems, with satellites, airplanes, and unmanned aerial vehicles (UAVs) often staring down at the same location.[39] Moreover, many of the satellites are Cadillac de Ville models, with all the latest accessories. They could be replaced with less expensive, smaller satellites (Chevies). The smaller the satellite, the less expense involved in positioning them in space (since launch costs are linear with weight).[40] Happily, the new NRO director seems willing to replace some of America's Battleship Galacticas with smaller satellites having more specific missions.[41]

Consolidating and streamlining the large intelligence agencies and moving away from emphasizing expensive technical collection toward cheaper—and, for some tasks, more effective—human assets could reduce intelligence spending by 20 percent over the next five years (based on staff estimates of the recent Aspin-Brown commission on Intelligence).[42] If the often-reported aggregate annual spending figure of $26 billion to $30 billion for intelligence remains accurate, that would mean a savings of some $26 billion to $30 billion over five years, all without damage to the national security or any significant diminution in mission coverage. In this manner, the New Intelligence Agenda can be addressed while at the same time the DCI acquires a more efficient intelligence community and helps cut back the size of the federal government and Washington spending. These savings could be used to reduce the national debt, support social security, provide a tax cut, or whatever other measure leaders in the executive and legislative branches deem appropriate.

Naturally, cuts in the intelligence budget are not in themselves going to eliminate the national debt, save social security, or lead to much of a tax cut, but the secret agencies can nonetheless contribute to such worthy goals and grow more agile at the same time. This is an objective that should unite budget balancers and all but the most diehard Pentagon planners, with their quixotic and costly visions of transparent battlefields in every corner of the globe.

# SEVEN

# Sharing the
# Intelligence Burden

The main effect [of intelligence cooperation between nations]
is to make national systems more productive than they would
otherwise be, with more data and the technical advantages of
dialogue with others. Governments get better views of the
world at cut prices.
　　　—Michael Herman, *Intelligence Power in Peace and War*

Nations exist in a world of threats and opportunities. If their leaders are
responsible, they seek knowledge—ideally, foreknowledge—about these
conditions. The more accurate their understanding of global affairs is,
the more likely they will be able to protect and advance their national interests. The goal of global awareness can be achieved only through the
painstaking collection and assessment of information (from both open
and concealed sources) about key events, circumstances, and personalities around the world. This gathering and analysis of information is the
essence of intelligence.

This chapter focuses on the ways in which the United States has
sought intelligence relations with other nations (usually close allies)and
with international organizations to help collect and analyze information
about common adversaries and problems. To illustrate, this chapter uses
the experience of American-German intelligence ties during the second
half of the cold war, a relationship largely overlooked in the literature on
this subject.[1]

Liaison relationships can vary from quite close (America's ties with
Great Britain, New Zealand, Canada, and Australia) to rather weak
(American and Russian cooperation on environmental intelligence).

Germany falls toward the close end of the spectrum, though short of the long-standing bonds between American and British intelligence. The U.S.-U.K. model, perhaps the most exhaustively researched foreign intelligence relationship, is a special case with an extensive, intertwined history between two enduring democracies that share a common language and culture. The U.S.-German case is closer to the norm, however, and therefore more instructive, marked as it has been by less wholehearted cooperation on both sides.

From time to time, Germany and the United States have joined in intelligence operations against the Soviet Union, the one foe that could bring about the sudden demise of their societies under a storm of nuclear missiles.[2] This chapter explores the main issues involved in the efforts of officials in Bonn and Washington to work together against this common target and other threats through the sharing of espionage responsibilities.

## The Raison d'Être of Intelligence Cooperation

The development of a human and technical spy network is expensive, especially if the host nation is a world power, or aspires to be one. Even when a nation's focus is a single adversary, resource investments can be high when the target is geographically large and well protected, as was the USSR. A number of nations, the United States and Great Britain among them, spend about 10 percent of their total defense expenditures on intelligence activities. At the end of the cold war, the United States was spending about $30 billion per year on intelligence and West Germany about $550 million.[3] Particularly expensive are the spy satellites, which can be as large as a bus and cost a fortune just to propel into space, not to mention the expense of their design, construction, and management.

Costs are not the only limitation on a nation's ability to fashion an extensive intelligence network. Particular skills also are required and can take a long time to refine. Human intelligence requires experience in recruiting foreign agents, which in turn rests on a sound knowledge of the language and culture of other countries. Some nations, like Great Britain and France, have a long and successful record of espionage going back to the Middle Ages. In contrast, U.S. intelligence remains in its infancy, with a modern organization dating back only to the creation of the CIA in 1947. Technical intelligence requires sophisticated skills, including scientists with advanced research knowledge, elaborate management teams to build and deploy the spy machines, and highly trained operators.

Geography is important, too. The United States remained largely uninvolved with the rest of the world until the twentieth century. Even then, the Atlantic and Pacific Oceans kept Americans relatively isolated from most of the world. Only in the second decade of the twentieth century were American soldiers finally drawn into the vortex of war in Europe, followed twenty years later by another war in Europe and the Pacific and, later, two more in Asia (Korea and Indochina). Whatever advantages this remoteness may have offered the United States (and they were considerable), it failed to motivate an interest in creating an international spy network, as developed by other leading powers that often had contiguous—or at least nearby—enemies. Then came the Japanese attack on the U.S. Pacific fleet at Pearl Harbor, Hawaii, in 1941, a startling wake-up call. In this, the hard way, the United States learned the importance of developing a worldwide intelligence capability in an age of increasing vulnerability.

No nation, not even those with a long history of intelligence activity, has all the requisite resources—money, experience, scientific skills, a dispersed array of mechanical eyes and ears—for perfect or even near-perfect global coverage. As a consequence, every nation has some interest in working with allies to share the burden of intelligence costs and thereby compensate for gaps in its own spy network. Indeed, intelligence "burden sharing" is the phrase often used in the United States to describe cooperation with foreign intelligence services. More formally, these ties are referred to as "intelligence liaisons."

## Intelligence Liaisons

America's intelligence activities include the cultivation of "an immense network of multiple liaison relationships," notes an intelligence expert, that includes the sharing of information and insights on global affairs and cooperation in training and support, access to facilities, and even collaborative operations.[4] The most common and important form of cooperation is information sharing. Throughout the cold war, the United States and West Germany, for example, had much to offer each other. The Americans had the advantage of technical intelligence. From its constellation of space satellites that engaged in both photography (imagery intelligence or IMINT) and electronic listening (signals intelligence or SIGINT), the United States knew the location of Soviet armies, tanks, warships, and missiles, as well as their state of readiness—the most important military data one would want as a member of the Western alliance.

West Germany had no spy satellites of its own, but it did have first-rate human intelligence.[5] The West German foreign intelligence service, the Bundesnachrichtendienst (BND), had a stable of agents in East Germany and elsewhere throughout the Soviet sphere of influence who served as a sometimes helpful complement to the efforts of the CIA, which also had a network of spies but often with less language proficiency and European cultural understanding.

The West Germans also had the advantage of geography. The Federal Republic of Germany provided an ideal base for U.S. intelligence operations directed against the Soviets. West Germany's eastern border was the longest contiguous boundary between the Western alliance and the Warsaw Pact and thus was a splendid launching pad for America's U-2 and other aerial reconnaissance flights over Eastern Europe and the USSR, as well as for the eastward infiltration of spy teams and propaganda materials. Moreover, both Berlin and Bonn were important centers of diplomatic activity and thus were infested with spies pursuing diplomats in hopes of acquiring useful information. What better place for the CIA (with the help of the BND) to recruit disaffected and avaricious officials from the Soviet Union and its allies posted in West Germany?

The West Germans and the Americans had other reasons to cooperate on intelligence operations. West Germany had some aerial reconnaissance capabilities and was willing to share the information it obtained. The BND gathered additional information through the use of wiretaps and other ground-based, technical means, The West Germans also helped break foreign diplomatic and spy codes, a science heavily dependent on advanced mathematical and computer skills in which Germans have traditionally excelled.

As a source of espionage information—on Soviet weapons systems located in East Germany, for instance—and as a base for operations, West Germany thus contributed crucial resources to Western intelligence. On a strategic level, however, the Federal Republic could not offer much that the CIA did not already know from America's more powerful surveillance platforms in space; but on such matters as the details of Soviet conventional weaponry throughout Eastern Europe, BND agents were able to contribute to the Agency's intelligence estimates.

Bonn had every reason to seek cooperation with the West, even despite the forced "partnership" that followed Germany's defeat in World War II. For one thing, the CIA had a few well-positioned agents in the Soviet bloc whose information was of continuing interest to Bonn. Moreover, the United States had vital satellite data to share, in particular, strategic "warning intelligence" if a tank blitzkrieg or missile attack from the east was imminent. Washington officials were also in a good position to help West German leaders achieve their broader political and economic objectives. The political quid from Washington for the intelligence quo from Bonn would further legitimize the rise of West German political and economic power in the European community. Intelligence cooperation, then, was yet another means that Bonn used to ingratiate itself with the United States (and other Western powers with whom it formed comparable liaison relationships), in return for its growing integration into the Western alliance. Intelligence goodwill would beget political goodwill, or so Bonn hoped.

The United States also stood to benefit from winning the allegiance of West Germany to the West in the tug-of-war with Moscow over world alignments. In this sense, intelligence was essentially an instrument for expanding U.S. power and influence abroad, what some might view as American imperialism. Or this use of liaison could be seen more benignly as simply a smart way to compensate for the United States' own intelligence weaknesses and to save money (economy through synergism) while at the same time forging bonds of political friendship within the pro-democracy Atlantic alliance.

The sharing of information and a base of operations were only two of many opportunities for U.S.-West German intelligence cooperation. Counterintelligence, thwarting hostile operations carried out against the West by the secret services of the Communist nations, also was important. At the end of World War II, Western intelligence agencies aggressively sought to acquire the espionage records of the Third Reich—a huge repository of information about possible agent recruitments in Eastern Europe and the Soviet Union. Even former Nazi intelligence officers with records of despicable war crimes were quietly spirited out of postwar Germany and absorbed into the ranks of the CIA and other Allied intelligence agencies to tap into expertise and contacts that would be useful from a counterintelligence perspective in the new cold war against Communism.[6]

The most valued CIA counterintelligence technique is penetrating the enemy's secret service by planting a mole at the center of his operations, someone who can warn of clandestine schemes directed against the United States ("the gift that keeps on giving," joke CI specialists). Because the Third Reich had just fought the USSR, former Nazi intelligence officers arrested by Allied powers in the western sectors of Germany after the war held obvious potential for assisting Western penetration operations against the East. Naturally, these officers touted—not to say exaggerated—their own value to avoid the gallows or long imprisonment. Even in the latter stages of the cold war, this old knowledge (and some new findings) of BND intelligence officers and their agents about Eastern Europe and the USSR occasionally proved useful to the CIA (which, after the war, handpicked and groomed BND officials and otherwise shaped the organization in its own image).[7]

Covert action was yet another intelligence discipline in which the CIA and the BND cooperated. Covert action is the secret attempt to influence the affairs of other countries through the use of propaganda and political, economic, and, at the extreme, paramilitary activities. The classic illustration of CIA-BND solidarity in this domain during the cold war was the use of covert propaganda espousing pro-West and anti-Communist views. The two intelligence agencies joined in fashioning propaganda themes and, of greatest value, in devising methods to infiltrate the propaganda into the Soviet camp (including such means as smugglers, balloons lofted over the Iron Curtain, and, most effectively, radio transmissions).

Radio Free Europe and Radio Liberty (Radio Liberation, in the 1950s) were two important channels of propaganda. Beginning in 1949, the CIA operated both radio transmitters out of Munich throughout the cold war with assistance from the BND (whose headquarters is located in a shabby, eerie building seemingly untouched since its days as a Nazi interrogation facility on a military base in Pullach, a Munich suburb).[8] During the first few years of transmission, the American and West German governments frequently clashed over issues of policy and communications, but these tensions gradually relaxed as relations between Bonn and Washington settled into a routine. When the CIA connection to the radio stations was exposed in 1971, Congress began funding the broadcasts openly and created a small agency called the Board for International Broadcasting to supervise the propaganda transmissions.[9]

A final—but unspoken—reason for intelligence liaison is that it may enable a country to spy on its own partner. CIA liaison officers might be able to learn about West Germany's foreign policy and intelligence objectives, another source of information on the direction of German and European affairs that the CIA could put into its reports for Washington policymakers. The same, of course, was true for BND liaison officers who visited the CIA (and other U.S. intelligence agencies) and no doubt kept their eyes and ears open for extracurricular information.

## The Risks of Liaison

However useful in some respects, intelligence liaison inevitably engenders an attitude of ambivalence in both parties, whether West Germany and the United States or even the close wartime allies, Great Britain and the United States. Lord Palmerston explained why some distance would always exist between friendly nations. "We have no eternal allies, and we have no perpetual enemies," he remarked. "Our interests are eternal and perpetual, and those interests it is our duty to follow."[10]

The foreign policy objectives of West Germany and the United States were often similar during the cold war, but they were never precisely congruent, any more than those of the British and the Americans have been. Both have a double agenda: cooperation combined with a chance to learn more about the partner's global intentions and capabilities. As a savvy *New York Times* reporter has observed, "When spies from two countries shake hands, they are often trying to pick one another's pockets."[11] At the extreme, this could mean even attempting to recruit an intelligence officer from the ranks of the ally's secret service, perhaps someone on the liaison team itself. This is a highly risky venture, though, and is rarely undertaken because of the potential for destroying ongoing intelligence cooperation and even higher government-to-government relations.

Ambivalence characterizes liaison partnerships for yet another reason: concern that the allied intelligence service may have been penetrated by a common adversary. During the 1960s, the CIA's chief of counterintelligence, James Angleton, wined and dined the visiting British liaison officer, the suave and witty Harold "Kim" Philby, for months in Georgetown's finest restaurants, sharing with him closely held CIA views on how best to battle the KGB and the GRU—only to discover at the time of Philby's defection to Moscow in 1963 that his clubby British counterintelligence companion had been in the service of the KGB since his student days at Cambridge University.[12] This taught Angleton a memorable lesson and henceforth made him doubly suspicious—some would say paranoid—of virtually everyone.

The Israeli recruitment of a U.S. Navy civilian intelligence analyst, Jonathan Jay Pollard (arrested by the FBI in 1985 and sentenced to life in prison two years later), taught the lesson anew in the 1980s. Pollard claimed he was simply passing on information that had been unfairly denied by Washington to a trusted American ally. Beyond their disgust at Pollard's treachery, intelligence officials in the United States feared that Israel's intelligence service (Mossad) may have been penetrated by the KGB, and as a result, Pollard's acquisitions for Israel—thousands of top-secret U.S. intelligence documents for which he was secretly paid—could have benefited the Soviet Union as well. Or perhaps ordinary Israeli officials and Mossad officers might simply trade away America's secrets in their own negotiations with Moscow and the KGB.

In a effort to promote peace between Palestinians and Jews in the Middle East, President Clinton considered the Israeli prime minister's request in 1998 that Pollard be pardoned as part of the negotiation package. The president reportedly weighed this appeal seriously, but his DCI, George Tenet, threatened to resign if he approved the pardon. Evidently Tenet, having never served as a career intelligence officer himself, thought he would lose credibility throughout the intelligence community if Pollard were freed from prison. Pollard's release might also have undermined the DCI's efforts to boost the morale of CIA employees in the wake of a more disastrous spy scandal, the discovery in 1994 of

Agency officer Aldrich Ames's treason on behalf of the Soviet Union. The president accordingly backed away from the controversy.[13]

Like every other nation, West Germany was vulnerable to penetration during the cold war by foreign agents, Communist or otherwise. Some moles were indeed discovered, and although some traitors have been found, others may still be in place unrevealed.[14] One U.S. intelligence officer asserts that the BND has had "a history of penetration, and the truth is we have never really taken them too seriously as an intelligence organization."[15] It is a refrain that one hears privately expressed by U.S. intelligence officers with respect to most of America's allies (except for the British).

In 1998, the chief of German counterintelligence, Volker Foertsch (alias "Fleming"), came under suspicion as a long-time Moscow mole in the heart of German intelligence operations. According to a newspaper report, "C.I.A. officials have been left to wonder if German intelligence, which was often compromised by Communist agents during the cold war, is again being infiltrated by Moscow."[16] German authorities investigated Foertsch, exonerated him, and returned the counterintelligence chief to his sensitive position. His backers believe that he had been the victim of a Russian disinformation operation designed to harass German intelligence. Still, U.S. intelligence officials remain uneasy over the possibility of Russian agents in the BND, even if access to the dossiers of the old East German intelligence service (Staatssicherheitsdienst, or Stasi) has at least allowed the CIA and the BND to root out the former Communist moles in Germany.[17]

Thus mindful of the ever possible presence of a mole inside the partner's intelligence service, a liaison team never reveals its most sensitive secrets to another country, even a close ally. If the CIA had shared its intelligence fully during the cold war, a penetration of the BND run by Moscow would have been tantamount to a penetration of the CIA. Moreover, America's intelligence agencies have suffered Soviet penetrations of their own, thereby reminding the BND of the risks to its agents of cooperating with the United States. In a word, every liaison relationship is marked by suspicion.[18]

The details of tradecraft—the methods of espionage—also induce liaison ambivalence. While understanding and enjoying the benefits of sharing, both sides are careful to protect both their own intelligence sources (the names and locations of agents) and methods (the specifics of their most advanced espionage techniques). This is particularly true with respect to America's desire to maintain an edge in satellite and other technical surveillance. Rarely does the United States disclose its very best (that is, highest-resolution) satellite imagery, even to close allies, for fear of revealing to other intelligence services—penetrated as they may be by an enemy agent—just how capable its spy cameras are. If this technical information were made known to the enemy, it could devise more effective methods for evading the camera's eye. Even liaison disclosures of tradecraft on miniature surveillance devices could aid the enemy or put the liaison partner on alert for methods that America's intelligence agencies might want to use against it one day, should the friendship disintegrate.

## Threat as a Cohesive Force for Liaison Relationships

The most important reason for countries to share their intelligence information is the threat felt by the sharing partners with respect to a common adversary and a belief that by combining their resources, both parties may better understand the dangers they face (even if the threat assessment of both parties does not always prove entirely congruent). The fear of a Soviet attack against the West gave birth to the NATO alliance in 1949 and nurtured intelligence liaison relationships among its members. Nothing is more important than this fact in understanding the burden sharing of the CIA and the BND during the cold war, especially in its early stages.[19]

Threats and the perception of their imminence change with time. Today, the CIA views Germany as less a staging area for espionage operations against Eastern Europe than as a convenient place to work against Middle East and North African targets like Iran, Iraq, Libya, and Sudan. At the beginning of the cold war, however, the Soviet threat seemed real enough for the United States to adopt special liaison measures in the battle against Communism—even recruiting venal Nazi intelligence officers who might prove helpful in debriefing German POWs from the eastern war zone, in comprehending the organization and operations of the KGB and GRU, and in mounting an intelligence offensive against Russia and its puppet states.

By 1969, East-West relations had changed significantly. Under the leadership of Chancellor Willy Brandt (1969–74) and a coalition government composed of the Social Democratic Party and the Free Democratic Party, West Germany reached tentatively toward the East in search of improved relations through a policy known as Ostpolitik (eastern politics). This policy both reflected and encouraged further efforts in the West to relax tensions with the Soviet Union. Known as détente, this approach resulted from the growing sense that the Soviet threat had diminished significantly since both the days of Joseph Stalin and even the East-West confrontations of the 1960s (epitomized by the Berlin and Cuban missile crises). Both the United States and Europe began to worry more about political and economic disparities instead of remaining fixated on the Kremlin's military machinations.[20] In addition, West Germany was beginning to become more assertive in economic and political affairs, buoyed by a strong GDP and a new self-confidence gained from its role in helping make détente a reality.[21]

The preoccupation of the United States with the Vietnam War gave further credence to Bonn's belief that Europe would have to look out more for itself as American forces became bogged down in the jungles of Southeast Asia. A former U.S. ambassador to West Germany recalled: "The drift of Brandt's thinking [on Ostpolitik] was not unwelcome in Lyndon Johnson's Washington, but as the president became progressively more obsessed by Vietnam, he could not provide the kind of sustained pressure required to get things moving."[22] The Soviet invasion of Prague in 1968 further checked President Johnson's hopes to pursue détente with Moscow.

The 1970s and 1980s were a critical period during which West German political leaders and other members of the Western alliance questioned the basic U.S. cold war principles of containment and strategic deterrence.[23] Even though Brandt's personal relationship with President Richard M. Nixon was cordial,[24] during the 1970s it became clear that "American and West-European interests were no longer as congruent as they appeared to be in the immediate postwar period. . . . In addition to differing interpretations of the meaning and results of détente, a series of U.S.-German disagreements over economic and monetary matters occurred in the 1970s."[25]

During Helmut Schmidt's chancellorship (1974–82), U.S.-German relations were further strained because of personal differences between him and President Jimmy Carter. Schmidt, having respected both presidents Nixon and Gerald R. Ford as level-headed statesmen and able diplomats, complained about Carter's (and later Ronald Reagan's) naive and moralistic approach to questions of international security.[26] Distrusting his own intelligence officers, whom he repeatedly accused of collecting nothing but irrelevant or outdated information, Schmidt was reportedly even less willing to base his political decisions on information provided by American intelligence sources.[27] In addition, Schmidt held that West Germany should be a "critical partner" to the United States, addressing not only common interests but also disagreements and differences.[28]

When Germany elected a Christian Democratic Union (CDU) majority to the Bundestag in 1982, the Reagan administration expected a relaxation of U.S.-German tensions and an increased willingness to cooperate. Yet American hopes were not fully realized under the resulting administration of the conservative Chancellor Helmut Kohl (1982–98), and the continuing growth of German political self-confidence prevented a return to the post–World War II levels of German submission to U.S. leadership in intelligence and other affairs. Nevertheless, the stability and pro-West outlook of the Kohl government helped the long-term efforts at cooperation between the two nations, as did Kohl's political ideology, which aligned well with the Reagan—continuing into the Bush and even, to some extent, the Clinton—administration's.[29]

The ups-and-downs of foreign policy priorities on both sides of the Atlantic had only minimal effects on CIA-BND liaison ties. Despite experimentation with Ostpolitik and détente, West Germany remained firmly rooted in the Western alliance and closely attuned to leadership from Washington on most security policies, though not so much on political and economic initiatives. Even with the Soviet threat in decline (at least until rejuvenated by President Reagan with his "evil empire" rhetoric aimed at the Kremlin during his administration's middle years), Bonn and Washington found other common threats that encouraged an ongoing liaison relationship.[30]

Chief among these threats was the specter of terrorism, which had risen in West Germany during the 1960s in the form of the Baader-Meinhof gang and other violence-prone rebellions against the established order. This was a target the CIA and the BND could readily agree on as a danger to both nations, and the two intelligence services' sharing of information accelerated, especially after 1985 when global terrorism became more widespread.[31] Beyond intelligence sharing, West Germany's counterterrorism units also gained a reputation for considerable skill and courage. Indeed, the CIA and other NATO intelligence services turned to them frequently for short-notice paramilitary operations against skyjackers and other terrorists.[32]

Terrorism continues to be a problem that prompts intelligence services to cooperate. A senior CIA counterterrorist official concluded that the greatest chance for thwarting terrorism lay in the "long-term disruption of the activities of terrorist organizations," adding

> I'm talking here not about foiling specific plots, but rather about impeding the day-to-day work of terrorist groups—the recruitment, the cell-building, the moving of men, money and matériel, and the mere maintaining of a presence in a foreign country—all of the things that a group needs to be able to conduct terrorist operations in a given area. For us, this task involves regular cooperation with many foreign policy, intelligence, and security services around the world.[33]

Additional threats encouraged liaison during the Kohl years. In rough descending order of cooperation among intelligence services, after terrorism came the danger of narcotics trafficking in West Germany and the United States. Much of this illegal drug trade originated in Latin America, and therefore the United States had useful information to share with the BND about Colombian and other drug cartels. In return, the BND had data to share regarding U.S.-bound heroin stemming from poppy fields in Turkey and elsewhere in the Middle East. During and after the cold war, Bonn and Washington have had a further common interest in halting the proliferation of weapons of mass destruction. Information collected by the CIA and the NSA enabled U.S. government officials to alert German authorities to illegal private exports from Germany, such as equipment for poison gas plants shipped to Iraq and Libya in the late 1980s.[34] Since German law prohibits the BND from collecting information that might incriminate German citizens, help from foreign intelligence services (including the CIA) was—and remains—invaluable to

German law enforcement in its efforts to track down the sources of illegal exports.[35] The CIA and the BND continued their efforts to monitor military events in the Soviet Union, and near the end of the cold war, the activities of unpredictable "rogue states" have concerned both nations, particularly Iraq's aggressiveness and the destabilizing ethnic wars in the Balkans at the end of the century.

Even after the collapse of the Warsaw Pact in 1989–91 and the subsequent reunification of the two German states, the CIA and the BND have continued to cooperate, sustained by the threats of terrorism, narcotics, weapons proliferation, and rogue states. Events and personalities in Moscow have remained a common concern as well, especially the future of democracy there, where Washington—and, even more, Bonn—has invested large sums of money to support a more open and free Russian society. Above all, German intelligence officials have been interested in joint BND-CIA counterterrorist activities.[36]

The U.S. intelligence community has also concentrated on improving its relations with foreign intelligence liaison services in the domain of counterintelligence, as indicated by the creation of the DCI Counterterrorist Center (CTC) at the CIA. "Before CTC was formed," remembers a senior official in the center, "when a liaison officer came to town, he had to knock at about ten doors. Now he can come to one single pegpoint. This has smoothed our relations and led to a greater exchange of information and a greater level of success in terms of tracking the terrorist target." The official emphasized, though, that "of course, nobody ever tells the complete truth."[37]

Thus, despite the diminishing ability of the cold war in its latter stages to bind together West Germany and the United States, the Soviet threat remained potent enough to encourage ongoing CIA-BND liaison ties. The Euromissile crisis of the Carter and Reagan administrations—when the Soviet Union placed SS-20 missiles in Eastern Europe as a counter to the U.S. Pershing IIs in Western Europe—produced a fourth-quarter irritation between the West Germans and the Americans during the cold war, relieved by ratification of the Intermediate-Range Nuclear Forces (INF) Treaty in 1988. Finally, bureaucratic inertia no doubt has helped preserve the liaison ties, as "[intelligence] interdependencies become habitual and systemic, for good and for ill."[38]

## Ambivalence and Continuity

In 1991, the cold war ended, and a foreign policy specialist predicted that it would "be an uphill struggle to keep this [German-American] bilateral security relationship intact and of central importance to the two countries."[39] Scholars have emphasized the tension inherent in Germany's situation, as Chancellor Kohl and his successor Gerhard Schroeder pushed their nation further to integrate with the rest of Europe while at the same time remaining committed to Washington's leadership of the Western alliance. From an American perspective, the future of the security relationship depends on the German government's continuing willingness to cooperate with the United States, eschewing a narrow German nationalist agenda.[40]

Strains between the CIA and the BND have also arisen since the end of the cold war. A wrestling match over access to information in the newly available Stasi files is one example.[41] Another is the Germans' feeling that because the cold war is now over, America's intelligence services should reduce their presence on their country, a view that gained popularity when German counterintelligence discovered in 1997 that a CIA officer had tried to recruit a German government official in Bonn as an American spy.[42] Again in 1999, the German government (now relocated in Berlin) expelled three CIA officers for spying against their country.[43] At a higher level of government, disagreement over the possible introduction of ground combat troops into Kosovo (America for and Germany against) caused friction between the two nations in 1999. Despite such aggravations, however, a leading German scholar is surely correct that "Germany is committed to strengthening emerging European security structure within the framework of the Atlantic alliance."[44] Cooperation is likely to endure between the two nations, regardless of occasional discord over military, political, economic, and intelligence issues. Not only is there an extensive overlap between the current worldviews of Berlin and Washington, but over the years the two nations' trade and cultural connections have tightened.[45] This relationship, like all intelligence liaisons, will remain ambivalent, constrained as always by the limits of sovereignty, a fear of espionage penetration, divergent policy interests and perspectives, and the need for secrecy, in short, by the distrust endemic to the current system of nation-states.

## Liaison's Slippery Slope toward Policy

One of the fundamental tenets of intelligence is that practitioners of the trade must remain objective. The goal is to provide policymakers with facts, along with an objective analysis of the meaning of those facts. All personal bias and spin must be wrung out of intelligence reports, to the extent humanly possible. Sometimes this cardinal intelligence rule is violated. Intelligence officers—from beginning analysts to DCIs—have been known to let their own policy views color their work, although instances of this lack of professionalism are few and far between. Indeed, this emphasis on objectivity is as strong among intelligence analysts as it is among reputable journalists and academics.

In 1998, a liaison relationship—rarely discussed in the media—thus became a matter of open concern for those worried about preserving the traditional line between intelligence and policy. When the Clinton administration entered into peace negotiations as an honest broker between Israel and Palestine, the president asked the CIA to play a role. For years before this peace initiative, the Agency had maintained liaison relationships with the secret services of both the Israeli government and the Palestinian Authority, particularly for joint operations against terrorists. With offices in the cities of Hebron, Ramallah, and Nablus on the West Bank and also one in the Gaza Strip, the CIA has for some time been helping train Palestinian security forces and has assisted Israeli intelligence with sophisticated border-control devices.[46]

Trusted by security officials on both sides, the CIA has become a conduit of information and advice between Jews and Palestinians in the region. As DCI George Tenet stated,

> We have also tried to improve communications between the two sides on security matters as well as to improve the professionalism of security forces on the West Bank and Gaza. Just as important, we have tried to bolster confidence among all responsible parties that appropriate steps are being taken to end violence.

He concluded that there was "nothing new in this role for the CIA,"[47] and he revealed that the CIA has been asked in the past to support other Middle East agreements, to monitor U.S.-Soviet arms control pacts, and to intercede to ease tension between India and Pakistan. As a global agency with security contacts in all corners of the world, the CIA (Tenet implicitly argued) is sometimes well positioned to provide a helping hand in peace negotiations. "The CIA is not making policy," the DCI emphasized, "but helping to carry it out. This is consistent with the agency's history of fighting terrorism and helping friends and allies in the region live together peacefully and safely."[48]

Other administration officials joined in the effort to defuse the controversy over whether the CIA's role in the Middle East had ventured too far in the direction of involvement in questions of policy. The Agency's role was "to try to deal with these issues without being personally involved," Secretary of State Madeleine K. Albright said.[49] National security adviser Samuel R. Berger reassured the public that the CIA would just "help to facilitate cooperation," not enforce the provisions of the peace accord.[50] Specifically, the CIA would sit on a security committee (with Israeli and Palestinian intelligence leaders) in the role of judge, reviewing Israeli charges against suspected terrorists involved in attacks against Israelis, some of whom were thought to be members of the Palestine police. The Agency would study the cases and determine which Palestinians should be jailed and tried, though in Palestinian courts.

A former chair of the Senate Select Committee on Intelligence, David Boren, found it "entirely appropriate to use our intelligence assets to promote stability and peace in the world."[51] Former DCI R. James Woolsey fretted, however, over the possibility that some policymakers might inappropriately draw the Agency away from its primary responsibility of collecting intelligence and providing unbiased assessments.[52] A prominent American intelligence scholar expressed deep reservations. "The problem is that the agency can become committed to policy, thereby compromising its ability to objectively report on the facts of the situation and the viability of the policy," reasoned Harry Howe Ransom. "United States intelligence history includes numerous examples—including the Bay of Pigs and the fall of the Shah of Iran—of major intelligence failures that resulted from its commitment to carrying out a wrongheaded policy."[53]

Others worried that the heightened visibility of CIA operatives could compromise the Agency's sources and methods, not to mention placing its officers in a risky political cross fire between Israeli and Palestinian officials. "Enmeshing the CIA in this is a serious, serious mistake," grumbled a former Pentagon official from the Reagan administration. "The CIA is essentially getting involved as an umpire. If anything goes wrong in the Middle East, guess who gets blamed?"[54] "The agency will have to guard against taking sides," warned the *New York Times*, "or becoming involved in punitive actions that make the United States a protagonist rather than a mediator in the conflict." But if it can maintain its strict policy neutrality, "it can make an important contribution."[55] On balance, the CIA would have been better off leaving diplomacy to the diplomats and concerning itself with its traditional duty of gathering intelligence and providing independent assessments about world affairs.

## Liaison with International Organizations

Since the end of the cold war, international organizations, especially the United Nations and the North Atlantic Treaty Organization, have played an important part in America's foreign policy. During the Persian Gulf War, the United States relied heavily on the UN as a framework in which to build a coalition of forces to drive the Iraqi army out of Kuwait, and the U.S. intelligence community shared information and assessments with coalition members as the war unfolded. In fact, even before the end of the cold war, the United States had been sharing intelligence with NATO members "for many years on a classified basis, albeit within established limits."[56]

As a larger organization with less well formulated security procedures (and with some members hostile to America), the UN has received less information from the U.S. intelligence community over the years than has NATO, although according to the Aspin-Brown commission, the United States still provides most of the information the UN uses to support its activities (contrary to a CIA officer's claim to a reporter that "we don't get involved with international organizations").[57] When UN and NATO missions overlap, as they did in Bosnia in the early 1990s, the intelligence community provides one level of classified information to NATO participants and a less detailed version to UN participants.

Most of the U.S. intelligence shared with the United Nations has quite a low classification, a special category of "UN Use Only," not to be distributed to the media or anyone else outside the United Nations. This means that the information can go to 185 nations, including a number of America's adversaries. As a result, the information is unlikely to stay secret. With this in mind, the intelligence community gives to the UN what one of its representatives calls "vanilla" information: somewhat bland, highly sanitized documents which, after various interagency "predissemination reviews," are usually less than timely in their arrival to consumers at the United Nations. Nevertheless, the information is still considered useful by UN officials, for often it is the only reliable source of analysis on some global issues.[58]

If asked, the United States sometimes supplies information on specific topics of interest to the United Nations at a somewhat higher level of classification than normal, although still carefully vetted to remove clues to sources and methods before being passed along. One example is an analysis of military, political, and economic developments in a war-torn developing nation. As a rule, the United States does not provide classified documents to the UN, with the occasional exception of tactical battlefield information for the UN's "blue helmet" troops in times of crisis.

Another kind of "information sharing" (the term the UN prefers to "intelligence") and one that avoids giving sensitive documents to the United Nations is the timely oral briefing. When the intelligence community determines that the blue helmets are in jeopardy, a member of the U.S. mission to the United Nations presents, with clearance from the Department of State, valuable battlefield information orally to the appropriate UN officials, possibly saving lives and without leaving any documents behind.

Sharing intelligence with international organizations is a complex procedure that depends on the kind of organization (its size and whether its members are U.S. allies, for example) and America's experience with that organization. Whoever the recipient is, the United States shares information following precise procedures. Usually the intelligence is given in a highly diluted fashion; when more sensitive information is disseminated, it is to only a small group of consumers. There have been mishaps. In Somalia, UN officials ineptly handled U.S. intelligence documents and, worse still, left some behind during their withdrawal in 1994.[59] Subsequent inquiries into this case revealed that the documents were less sensitive than initially feared; nevertheless, and as a result of this experience, UN administrators have tightened their security procedures.

Whenever the United States shares information with the United Nations, its purpose is to advance America's national security interests, not to create goodwill toward Washington. Information that uncovers transgressions by Saddam Hussein, protects peacekeepers in Bosnia, provides a realistic picture of events in Rwanda, or confirms acts of atrocity by Serbian or Albanian soldiers benefits the United States as well as the United Nations. In general, America's best interests are served when the United Nations has accurate information about world affairs. In many cases, however, UN officials are already well informed. As a result of their diplomatic contacts, world travel, and familiarity with the standard sources of public information, most officials do not need secret information (except for tactical military intelligence when blue helmets are under fire). These officials like, nonetheless, to receive from reliable member states more studies produced by their individual intelligence agencies on the issue of human rights, as well as on such broad topics as world population growth and global food supply.

The extent of U.S. liaisons with international organizations raises the question of whether Washington's secret agencies undermine their credibility by making them appear as lackeys of American foreign policy. This possibility was brought to the public's attention in 1999 when news reports revealed that the CIA and the NSA had assisted the UN Special Commission (known as UNSCOM) in eavesdropping operations against some of Iraq's most sensitive communications. In this case, the United States had decided to go far beyond its normally low-level intelligence activities with respect to the United Nations.

The UN commissioned UNSCOM, a team of arms inspectors, to monitor Iraqi compliance with a 1991 cease-fire agreement requiring it to dismantle its program for strategic weapons. The team was nothing less than what one reporter called "an international intelligence service for the new world order . . . the first of its kind," adding that "more than 7,000 weapons inspectors from around the world served UNSCOM over seven years, spying on Iraq, surveying its military and industrial plants, trying to do what smart bombs could not: destroy nuclear, biological, chemical and missile programs hidden by Saddam Hussein."[60] For instance, Germany provided helicopters to UNSCOM with special radar to penetrate Iraqi sand dunes in search of buried weapons; Britain contributed sensitive scanners to intercept Iraqi military communications;

and the United States lent U-2 spy planes and even navy divers to probe Iraqi lakes and rivers for submerged weapons.[61] According to another reporter, "The spirit of post–Cold War cooperation promised a miracle: UNSCOM, operating on behalf of the U.N. Security Council, would utilize the secret intelligence agencies of its members states, Communist and non-Communist alike, to investigate the Iraqi arsenal."[62]

Information acquired by the NSA, which has the capacity to unscramble encrypted telephone conversations between Saddam and his aides, could help the UN search for weapons of mass destruction inside Iraq. At the same time, UNSCOM could be used by the U.S. intelligence community for its own purposes, namely, ridding the world of Saddam Hussein. Under the cover of UNSCOM, the NSA apparently had even wired a UN microwave transmission system (without the knowledge of UN officials), which allowed the eavesdropping agency to monitor a wide range of secret Iraqi military communications.[63]

"The UN cannot be party to an operation to overthrow one of its member states," complained a confidant to UN Secretary-General Kofi Annan, when the United States' intelligence ties to UNSCOM became a matter of public knowledge. "In the most fundamental way, that is what's wrong with the UNSCOM operation."[64] Had the UNSCOM weapons inspectors restricted their activities solely to its nonproliferation agenda, which had widespread support in the world, they could have preserved the high esteem in which most member states held them. Instead, news leaks and speculation from one of the inspectors (Scott Ritter, a former U.S. Marine intelligence officer) raised suspicions that UNSCOM had gone beyond just trying to find Saddam's weapons. According to these reports, the CIA had used UNSCOM in 1996 as an umbrella for its own intelligence collection operations as well as for covert actions designed to topple Saddam Hussein.[65] The Clinton administration conceded that the CIA had been assisting UNSCOM "through intelligence, logistical support, expertise, and personnel" but denied using the team to plot a coup against the Iraqi leader.[66] Wherever the truth lay, UNSCOM was fatally wounded by these charges, and the independence of the United Nations was severely compromised, in perception if not in reality. In order to advance its plans to destroy Saddam Hussein, the UN liaison operations of the U.S. intelligence community (presumably acting under White House orders) had instead destroyed an international effort to halt the proliferation of dangerous strategic weapons.

To avoid the problem of national bias that comes with relying on individual nations' intelligence services for its information, the UN must create its own intelligence capabilities—professional intelligence officers committed to making the UN work (with all the necessary safeguards against misusing shared information). The UN is already taking some steps in this direction. It has set up a situation center, which is creating a computer infrastructure for collecting, storing, and retrieving open-source information on world affairs. Its resources, though, are modest.

The United Nations has also recently gained the authority to construct a satellite surveillance system that would allow its International Drug Control Program to monitor the cultivation of illegal drug crops in the major source countries. By this means, the UN can establish an internationally accepted benchmark for verifying countries' promises to reduce their production of drugs. "For the first time the international community will have a very reliable instrument to measure the extent of illegal crops," according to the program's executive director.[67] The European Space Agency is contributing the necessary satellites and technical expertise to support the operation.

These experiments in international intelligence remain alive despite the UNSCOM setback. Nonetheless, it has been difficult to overcome the old view of the UN as either a target or a cover for intelligence operations, rather than a customer for information and analysis provided by the secret agencies of member nations for the benefit of the whole world. This change in attitude is "ill thought out and haphazard," in the words of a former British ambassador to the United Nations.[68]

The relationship between international organizations and intelligence raises a paradox: how can these organizations be effective if they are so poorly informed about the outlaw nations they are expected to tame? The UN is supposed to resolve conflicts, keep the peace, enforce economic sanctions, control the spread of large-scale weapons, combat organized crime, fight drug trafficking, and bring to justice war criminals and human rights violators. All of these tasks require intelligence, yet the UN has little at its disposal. International organizations cannot afford to develop their own full-service intelligence agencies. Besides, member nations are unlikely to tolerate the risk that the UN might end up peering into their own backyards. Member states could provide more intelligence assistance themselves, but they fear leaks of sensitive sources and methods. Moreover, the UN must worry about biased intelligence from member states.

Despite these dilemmas, both nations and NGOs could give to the UN and other international organizations extra or "secondhand" satellites and other surveillance equipment for monitoring global environmental conditions, refugee flows, arms trade, and suspicious military mobilizations. Satellites can even track mosquito populations around the globe, by focusing on vegetation patterns and breeding grounds that attract the disease-bearing insects.[69] The UN could establish an assessment board made up of retired senior intelligence analysts from member states: men and women with extensive analytic experience who could evaluate the quality and objectivity of member-state intelligence reports solicited by the UN secretary-general. As a specialist on the United Nations observes, "The UN must be given the means, including information-gathering and analysis, to make manifest its goal, as stated in the opening words of the UN Charter, of 'saving succeeding generations from the scourge of war.'"[70] So far members of the UN have fallen far short of satisfactory intelligence cooperation, although some individual nations (like Great Britain) have been responsive to requests from UN officials for intelligence assistance. Increased intelligence burden sharing within the framework of the United Nations would enable a global dissemination of information to all member nations, carefully reviewed by an assessment board to filter out national biases. This would be a valuable contribution toward the search for solutions to the challenges that confront all the world's people.

# PART III

# Smart Intelligence—
# and Accountable

# EIGHT

# More Intelligent Intelligence

America's fundamental aspiration is the preservation of peace. To this end we seek to develop policies and arrangements to make the peace both permanent and just. This can be done only on the basis of comprehensive and appropriate information.

—President Dwight David Eisenhower, dedication of the new CIA headquarters building in Langley, Virginia, 1959

American intelligence after the cold war has been a balance of old approaches that still seem useful (such as the satellite surveillance of distant battlefields), along with new approaches necessitated by changing conditions (covert actions that attack international terrorists' computer networks and bank holdings).

## Continuities and Changes in Intelligence

Counterintelligence, covert action, collection, and analysis—the mainstays of the espionage business during the cold war—continue into the twenty-first century as the principal methods used by the secret agencies to carry out their missions overseas. Within each of these categories, however, have been some significant innovations.

### Counterintelligence

The purpose of counterintelligence (CI) is the protection of America's government and its secrets against hostile forces. Today counterintelligence depends on the same methods always used by the counterintelligence corps, from barbwire fences and guard stations to coded messages and stringent security clearances. New is the current emphasis on safeguards against "information operations" (once known as "information warfare") or "cyberterrorism," especially the protection of government computers against foreign access (or American teenagers, for that matter). Currently, one of the intelligence community's main recruitment efforts at home is hiring computer specialists who can use their knowledge to help the secret agencies protect their databases, although the best computer experts are difficult to entice, since the private sector is able to pay so much more for their services. Appeals to patriotism and the lure of working for interesting clandestine agencies are the best hopes.

Beginning with the Ames spy scandal, in which Aldrich Ames of the CIA's Operations Directorate was uncovered in 1994 as a long-time Soviet mole, Congress has appropriated additional funds for counterintelligence. Internal security has been tightened at Langley since this embarrassment, which tipped off the Kremlin to more than two hundred CIA spy operations in the former Soviet republics and led to the execution of at least nine key Agency assets. Ironically, U.S. officials have paid more attention to counterintelligence since the end of the cold war than they did during some of the most confrontational years with the Soviets under Presidents Carter, Ford, Reagan, and Bush. Guided by James J. Angleton, the CIA's chief of counterintelligence (a man of enormous skill and resolve, however paranoid he may have been), CI enjoyed its highest profile from 1953 to 1974, until a seam of discord split open between William Colby and Angleton over how to handle the Agency's relations with Israeli intelligence and Colby fired Angleton.

With Angleton's departure, responsibilities for counterintelligence were dispersed throughout the CIA and given a lower profile by intelligence managers. A series of foreign spy revelations in 1985 (most notably the Walker family's espionage against U.S. naval intelligence) renewed the attention of intelligence managers in CI, and the Ames spy scandal a decade later provided an additional jolt. The Los Alamos spy case in 1999 set off the most recent counterintelligence alarm in the Energy Department and the nation's science laboratories. Based on these experiences, the current DCI is strengthening counterintelligence throughout the community, as well as in the labs and another vulnerable site, the security connections between the secret agencies and the private industries contracted to build surveillance platforms and other intelligence hardware.

Counterintelligence covers a number of subspecialties beyond catching foreign spies trying to steal America's secrets. Beneath its umbrella resides counterterrorism. The Counterterrorist Center (CTC), the oldest center (founded in 1986 by DCI William J. Casey), has received the most funding since the end of the cold war and is now also the largest, even "bloated," according to a former CIA officer.[1] Some insiders view the CTC as the most integrated from a personnel perspective (others point to the Crime and Narcotics Center). Most of the CTC's experts are on loan from CIA's Operations Directorate, which has command-and-control authority over the center, even though the CIA's three other directorates also participate in its activities.[2] Despite the strong CIA staffing component, the center has twenty-four officers (known as "detailees") from a dozen other agencies, including the FBI and the Department of State (the two most important links), the Department of Defense, the Secret Service, the Department of Energy, the Bureau of Alcohol, Tobacco and Firearms, the Naval Investigative Service, the Federal Aviation Agency (another vital participant in this mission), the NSA, and the Immigration and Naturalization Service. A State Department official heads the Interagency Intelligence Committee on Terrorism for purposes of government-wide coordination.

By all accounts, the CTC demonstrates that a high level of cooperation can be achieved through the community-wide sharing of personnel, information, and insights:

> The whole concept behind the CTC was to bring elements from all four [CIA] Directorates together and put them under one single chain-of-command, so that we'd have all the necessary resources together to tackle the problem. In addition, we brought in these detailees from outside, so that we'd have a very close relationship with the intelligence community. These people can pick up a secure [telephone] line and cut through the bureaucratic thickets that we normally face.[3]

Especially innovative and productive has been the center's placement of CIA analysts and clandestine DO officers in the same location, working side by side for the first time ever in the Agency's history (and encouraging further experiments in "co-location" elsewhere at Langley, though with uneven results). Turf battles still are fought in the CIA and throughout the community; but according to CTC participants, having in place a center for counterterrorism means that the battles are now less brutal and more easily stopped than used to be the case. In addition, the center has excelled in providing intelligence for tracking and capturing fugitive terrorists. Some fifty have been apprehended in the past five years—although Fugitive No. 1, Osama bin Laden, continues to elude the intelligence dragnet.[4] He is thought to be hiding somewhere in Afghanistan under the protection of the Taliban regime, a fundamentalist government that controls about 85 percent of the nation. But even when U.S. intelligence knows precisely where he is, getting to him is another matter.

The bombing of the World Trade Center in New York City (1993)—what one terrorism authority refers to as "the first battle of the twenty-first century"[5]—and a federal building in Oklahoma City (1994), as well as the U.S. embassies in Kenya and Tanzania (1998), has encouraged Congress to allocate more money to those agencies combating terrorism, including the CTC (even though it does not deal with U.S. domestic terrorism). Congress has yet to appropriate the funds requested by the State Department to enhance security at ("harden") its embassies, in yet another instance of a long-standing tendency among legislators to support the supposedly hard-nosed warriors of the secret agencies over the "pinstriped" negotiators in the diplomatic corps.

The CTC and its counterpart units in allied nations appear to have made some progress in the war against terrorists, as the number of terrorist incidents against the United States and worldwide has decreased in the last few years.[6] When terrorism does strike, though, America is a favorite target. This nation suffered more than 35 percent of the total number of international terrorist attacks in 1998, up from 30 percent in 1997 and 25 percent in 1996.[7] Worrisome, too, is the fact that the terrorists' weapons have become increasingly more lethal. Moreover, as government experts have stated, the objective of terrorists allied with bin Laden "is not to influence, but to kill, and in large numbers—hence their declared interest in acquiring chemical and even nuclear weapons."[8]

Some forms of terrorism are nearly impossible to stop, especially a suicide attack carried out by one person or a group, as happened to Egyptian President Anwar Sadat in 1979, the U.S. Marine base in Lebanon in

1982, and the Israel embassy in Buenos Aires in 1992. Among the most troubling scenarios pondered by intelligence officials is the launching of a nuclear-tipped ballistic or cruise missile against an American target from an offshore surface vessel, disguised perhaps as a freighter.[9] "No matter how well protected you are, or how well trained a president's security detail," acknowledged a CTC expert, "if you've got someone in a truck—or whatever—loaded to the gills with bombs (and probably loaded to the gills with hashish, too), the chances of him getting through are pretty strong."[10]

To combat terrorism, the CTC works closely with the Nonproliferation Center (NPC), since both have a mandate to curb the use of dangerous weapons against mass populations. Both centers have concluded that a terrorist organization is more likely to use biological or chemical weapons than a nuclear weapon against the United States. "They can really only get a nuclear weapon from a state sponsor," points out a CTC official, "and state sponsors would be reluctant to give that sort of weapon to a terrorist group, because the retaliation against the state by the United States would be like a sledgehammer."[11] The NPC concentrates on the supply side of the weapons problem, trying to stem their flow at the origins of production and distribution, whereas the CTC focuses on the demand side, preventing terrorist groups from acquiring the weapons in the first place. If these efforts fail, the CTC cooperates closely with the FBI to catch the perpetrators following the terrorist attack.

The most important defense against terrorism is information about its likely occurrence, so that law enforcement officials can intercede before the attack takes place. To this end, the perfection of HUMINT and other collection methods stands at the top of the CTC's priorities, especially the infiltration of terrorist organizations or the wooing of a defector from the enemy camp. These are difficult tasks, since modern terrorist organizations are sophisticated and acutely aware of the CTC's intentions. Even when the CTC is successful, its achievements usually remain hidden (at the center's own insistence), for fear that valuable tradecraft will become known to future terrorists.

Based on the CTC's HUMINT and TECHINT intelligence sources, the United States retaliated in 1998 against suspected terrorist facilities and encampments in Sudan and Afghanistan. In Sudan, the target was the Al Shifa Pharmaceuticals plant in Khartoum, suspected by CTC officials of producing chemical weapons; in Afghanistan, it was a cluster of tent encampments outside the town of Khost in Paktia Province, where terrorists, including Osama bin Laden, had gathered for meetings. As mentioned earlier in this book, the Sudanese air attack became controversial when the government of Sudan claimed the factory was making only aspirin and other harmless medicines, not, as claimed by the CTC, a precursor chemical (known as Empta) necessary for producing the deadly nerve agent VX. As for the bombing near Khost, it was subsequently learned that the terrorist gathering had disbanded only two hours before the U.S. Tomahawk missiles struck. Bin Laden and his associates were lucky. Yet once more in the eyes of the media, the CIA had suffered another humiliating failure. In self-defense, CTC officials point out that no one has a crystal ball, not even the media. No human being is able to predict with confidence when a tent encampment of terrorists in a remote Afghan desert might decide to steal away in the night.

The CTC concedes that most of the time the United States will not have the luxury of a clear, advance warning about an impeding terrorist attack. As a result, it has been given presidential authority to resort to more disruptive and preemptive counterterrorist activities, namely, covert action.

## Covert Action

Just as during the cold war, covert action (CA) is still an important tool for the intelligence community or, more accurately, for the CIA and its Operations Directorate and some of the DCI centers, which are responsible for conducting aggressive secret operations against foreign nations and groups that intend to harm the United States. The main difference in the use of CA now and during the cold war is that today it is focused more on the so-called transnational issues (proliferation, narcotics, international crime) and less on specific regimes.[12]

Collection and analysis are an important foundation for effective covert action against terrorists, since before the CTC can take direct action, it must first know through what channels weapons are flowing to terrorists, where the terrorists are located, and how they intend to carry out their activities. Based on this information and in cooperation with the Pentagon and paramilitary elements within the CIA (the Special Operations Group of the Operations Directorate), the CTC's job is to make life difficult for terrorists in most every way possible, from intercepting their weapons and sowing doubt, confusion, and dissention within their ranks to fouling their computers and tying up their financial resources.

In this new age, the CIA continues to use old forms of covert action against hostile foreign nations, too, including propaganda, political and economic disruption, and even secret warfare. The most recent examples of the last are the funding of Iraqi opposition groups in 1998/99 (largely routed by Saddam Hussein's armies but still supported by U.S. officials, especially in Congress) and support for the anti-Serbian Kosovo Liberation Army in Kosovo and other anti-Milosevic factions within Serbia (with results so far not much better than in Iraq).[13]

The newest forms of CA carried out by the CIA are designed to complement the counterintelligence corps in blocking information operations directed against the United States. These covert actions seek especially to disrupt the communications of adversaries—from terrorists to rogue nations—by degrading their telecommunications and computer facilities.[14] Another tactic is to manipulate international financial transactions through computer hacking, say, emptying out bin Laden's accounts in the Dubai Islamic Bank in Dubai of the United Arab Emirates and in the National Commercial Bank in Saudi Arabia, as well as other locations around the world where he reportedly has hidden his copious assets.[15]

Whatever form the covert action may take, it remains subject to a series of extensive internal clearances before being implemented, a review process put into effect in 1974 with the Hughes-Ryan amendment to the National Security Act of 1947 and refined over the intervening years through more amendments. In-house CIA panels initially scrub each covert action proposal, both before and after an NSC interagency group looks at it. Then the proposal must pass muster in the DCI's office, the NSC Deputies Committee, and the NSC itself. Within the NSC, the proposal must obtain the president's written authority in a document called a "finding," the chief executive's finding that the proposal merits adoption. Finally, the covert action must be reported to the two congressional oversight committees in which legislators may occasionally object to the proposed operation and ask that it be modified or shelved altogether (although Congress has no formal authority to stop a covert action, in extreme cases—as with Nicaragua in the 1980s—it can vote down the money to support it).

## The Assassination Option

From time to time, the argument is raised that out of a misplaced sense of morality, the U.S. government has tied its hands in dealing with terrorists and violent dictators by removing a useful instrument of foreign policy: the assassination plot, an extreme form of paramilitary covert action. It is true that for a brief time during the cold war (the late Eisenhower and early Kennedy administrations), the United States did engage in assassination attempts.[16] The best-known plots were aimed at Fidel Castro of Cuba and Patrice Lumumba of the Congo. Neither plot succeeded (Lumumba died at the hands of African rivals not connected to the CIA), nor has any other known CIA assassination attempt against a foreign leader.

Despite this record of failure, some advocate a revival of this approach to resolving America's foreign policy headaches.[17] After all, diplomacy is slow and often ineffectual, and air strikes or sending in the marines are noisy, bloody alternatives that might trigger a major war. In between lies the prospect of neatly removing someone like Iraq's Saddam Hussein or Serbia's Slobodan Milosevic with a silent dart gun or a vial of poison. No endless diplomatic haggling, no great expense (cruise missiles cost $1 million each if surface-launched, $2 million if by air), no still greater tribute in blood and treasure that would accompany a major invasion. Just a single bullet in the head of an annoying dictator or a few drops of Blackleaf-40 in his morning orange juice.

Is the assassination option a valid answer to this nation's international woes? With a couple of important exceptions, the answer should be a resounding no. The case against assassination has strong legal, practical, and moral dimensions. President Gerald R. Ford signed an executive order in 1976 prohibiting assassination plots, a policy that has never been rescinded by his successors. The language of the order, signed again by President Ronald Reagan in 1981, reads, "No person, employed by or acting on behalf of the United States Government, shall engage in, or conspire to engage in assassination."[18]

True, President Reagan had Mu'ammar Gadhafi's house bombed as part of an air raid against Libya, and George Bush ordered the bombing of Baghdad (including Saddam's palaces) during the Persian Gulf War and would not have been unhappy if the Iraqi president had been one of the victims; indeed, the Bush White House "lit a candle every night hoping Saddam Hussein would be killed in a bunker" during the Baghdad bombing.[19] Nevertheless, these were acts of overt warfare. In contrast, successive presidents have felt an obligation to honor the executive order with respect to the CIA's more clandestine operations. The Bush administration even prevented the CIA from supporting a Panamanian group intent on overthrowing President Manuel Noriega in 1989, for fear that the coup might lead to his murder.[20] Indeed, President Ford did not arrive at the assassination prohibition lightly, declaring unequivocally that he was opposed to political assassination.

Should a president decide to waive the executive order and adopt the assassination option, a still more daunting consideration has to do with the practicalities. The United States has never been adept at assassinating foreign leaders. Castro lives on after many attempts against his life concocted during the Kennedy administration. Even locating targets like warlord Mohamed Farah Aidid of Somalia or Saddam Hussein proved impossible during the 1990s. Dictators are paranoid, well guarded, and elusive; they live in closed societies where it is easy for them to hide.

The consequences of a murder plot raise another practical consideration. Would the elimination of Castro have led to freedom in Cuba, or merely the rise to power of his like-minded brother, Raul? How many more Saddam Husseins wait in line to replace the current Iraqi dictator? How many individuals must be assassinated before a regime changes its colors? Should it be U.S. policy to assassinate a long queue of potential tyrants, just to be on the safe side? The venal leader plus all his close relatives, too? And at what point do foreign leaders decide that if the United States is going to target them, perhaps they ought to retaliate against America's president—who lives in an open society and is easily targeted? Finally, to what extent is murder compatible with American values? Does the United States seek a world in which countries kill one another's heads of state? For America, the world's leading democracy, the role of global godfather is contradictory and inappropriate. Means matter, not just ends.[21]

Now the exceptions. First, if the president is engaged in a war authorized by Congress (not simply by NATO or even the UN), the enemy's leaders are just as subject to combat operations as is the lowliest soldier in a trench. Formal warfare overrides the executive order against assassination. Second, if America's president has reliable intelligence that a dictator or a terrorist is on the verge of using lethal force against the United States or its vital interests (not merely manufacturing weapons, as every nation does), it would be absurd to stand by and do nothing. The CIA has established an informal agreement with its congressional oversight committees (SSCI and HPSCI) that if a terrorist were known to be driving a truck loaded with explosives toward a U.S. building, the CIA would be expected to shoot the driver if there were no other way of preventing the bombing.[22] This is a far cry from a preemptive plot to kill a dictator. Short of these exceptions, though, the United States is well advised to keep President Ford's executive order intact and, however tempting at times, to resist the odious role of International Godfather.

## Intelligence Collection

Most of the intelligence budget is spent on collection hardware, especially satellites, eavesdropping antennae, and a variety of reconnaissance aircraft (piloted and pilotless). But in recent years, intelligence officials have become more aware of the limits of these surveillance platforms. Satellites and aircraft cannot see through roofs or into underground caverns.[23] Moreover, the construction and positioning of large satellites—more than $1 billion for the launch alone—is a great drain on the intelligence budget.

In light of these shortcomings, intelligence managers have begun the long, slow task of building up America's HUMINT capabilities, doubly important since the intelligence community is presently witnessing the mass retirement of a generation of case officers responsible for recruiting and managing spies during the cold war. Training the new recruits and sending them overseas to find new foreign assets will take time, and so in the first years of the twenty-first century the United States' HUMINT intelligence abroad will be less effective until the new case officers begin to establish their own spy networks.

The targets of HUMINT operations have changed, too. While

Russian politicians, diplomats, generals, and spies will continue to be the preferred targets (and the careers of those CIA case officers who successfully turn anyone from this group will benefit), high-ranking officials inside rogue nations are valuable as well. North Korea is a prime example. The recruitment of a leading official from this isolated nation is probably the most difficult assignment in the world today. It is almost impossible to recruit anyone inside North Korea because American travel there is so restricted. The only real chance is to approach and try to "pitch" (recruit with promises of money or perhaps resettlement in the West) a North Korean diplomat when he attends meetings abroad. Even this scenario is unlikely, since North Korean officials and their security guards travel in clusters, a precaution intended to ward off approaches from foreign intelligence officers. Foreign scientists are valuable targets for recruitment, too; China is not the only nation approaching experts in other countries in hopes of gaining access to weapons secrets and other technological advances.

A key theme of this book is that the United States has been too fascinated with "gold-plated" technical intelligence at the expense of human collection. Without losing this nation's comparative advantage in TECHINT, the intelligence community is capable of developing a world-class HUMINT service if it is supported by the president and Congress. To do so will require a more extensive recruitment and training of case officers familiar with the language and culture of targets not of great interest to the United States during the cold war (for example, Serbia). The goal should be smaller spy satellites and better foreign agents.

The intelligence community must recognize that much of what policymakers need to know can be found in the open literature. Even in the days of DCI Allen Dulles (1953–62), about 80 percent of the information in classified intelligence reports was based on open information. The DCI did not sit down and identify exactly what an "information item" was and then compute the percentage of those items (weighted according to importance) that came from each source. Rather, this presumably was a "guesstimate" based on a rough comparison of what Dulles saw in the newspapers and what he learned from his network of spies and spy machines. Today the figure is thought to be more like 90 percent and growing as the secret agencies become more proficient at picking through the world's open sources and then stirring into the reports for policymakers their own secret findings.[24] The use of these percentages, however imprecise, is more than a just a rhetorical device; they are the pretty good hunches of those who read a lot of intelligence reports and much of the open literature.

## Analysis

In the lexicon of U.S. intelligence professionals, "analysis" refers to the interpretation by experts of unevaluated ("raw") information collected by the CIA and the other agencies in the intelligence community. The information may come from open sources, such as Iraqi television broadcasts, or from covert sources, say, SIGINT collected from Serbia by way of a reconnaissance satellite. The analyst's responsibility is to assemble all these data, from a variety of sources, both open and clandestine, a process known as "all-source analytic fusion."

Even though a large percentage of this information may be in the public domain, these sources can be difficult for most people to reach, such as the hundreds of magazines and newspapers now published in Russia or obscure scientific papers presented at distant international conferences (a form of "gray literature"). Logically, we would think that the intelligence analysts would begin with open sources of information and then turn to covert sources to look for the missing parts of the puzzle he or she has been assigned to solve. In practice, they often do just the opposite. Analysts frequently say they are too busy reading secret information from foreign agents to spend much time on open sources. The covert or secret information ("intelligence," in the narrow sense of that term) is derived from across the "ints": signals intelligence, imagery intelligence, measurement-and-signatures intelligence (MASINT, technically derived data other than imagery and SIGINT, including such telltale signs as energy emitted from a nuclear warhead), and espionage or human intelligence. After it is captured by a global web of mechanical platforms and human assets, this information moves into the hands of analytic experts in the intelligence community (the producers of intelligence reports) and then on to the officials whom the entire complex sequence is meant to serve: the president and other leading policymakers (the consumers).

At its best, intelligence analysis can offer policymakers just the right data and assessments they need to make wise decisions, presented with accuracy, timeliness, and clarity. When the United States entered into war against Iraq in the Persian Gulf in 1991, President George Bush and his military commanders had a better understanding of the battlefield situation than any other leaders have in the history of armed conflict, in large part a result of the multiple U.S. intelligence platforms above and around the war zone.

At its worst, intelligence analysis can be wrong, late, or muddled and sometimes all three at once. Just before war broke out between North and South Korea in 1950, a national intelligence estimate (NIE, the most elaborate of the intelligence-reporting formats) forecast peace on the peninsula. In 1956, analysts failed to anticipate the Soviet invasion of Hungary and again, in 1968, the Soviet invasion of Czechoslovakia. A former national security adviser in the Nixon administration recalls that the President's Daily Brief arrived early one morning in 1973 announcing that the Egyptians would not attack Israel, even though at that very moment the attack was under way![25]

## The Perils of Analysis

The information gathered by America's secret agencies travels a perilous course from its acquisition by sensors and assets in the field (collection) through its evaluation by experts (analysis) and finally—often the most difficult stage of the journey—to its delivery at the offices of policymakers in Washington and U.S. military commanders overseas (dissemination). In this so-called intelligence cycle, many things can go wrong.

### Determining Policy Needs

At the very beginning, the policymaker may not know exactly what kinds of information and analysis he or she requires, and so the intelligence agencies are left to guess what collection targets might be most helpful. Or the policymaker may be too busy to determine what information he or she needs, or sometimes the policymaker does not know whom in the intelligence community to contact. The result is a cueless collector and clueless policymaker.

### *Pre-Analysis Collection Barriers*

Assume that the policymaker enjoys a close working relationship with the intelligence community and requests specific information from abroad. Even then, another formidable obstacle quickly arises: the secret agencies must be able to gain access to the information. Sometimes this is simple. Whether the beaches along Kuwait's coast are firm enough to support amphibious landing craft, and the circle of likely heirs to the Russian presidency in its next cycle of change (if not the exact individual, any more than one can predict with full assurance House or even presidential elections in the United States), can be readily determined. But consider these questions: Does North Korea have nuclear weapons? Is Russia violating the Chemical-Biological Warfare Convention of 1992? Has Pakistan purchased M-11 missiles from China? Such information is closely guarded and harder to acquire.

Intelligence officers distinguish between secrets and mysteries. Secrets are information that a foreign nation is trying to keep concealed, for instance, the blueprint for Russian stealth technology or Iraqi order-of-battle data, but with skill and luck, the United States may find them. A mystery is something that may defy the most cunning espionage and the most advanced technical surveillance; even the target country itself may be unable to answer the question. How long will Castro last as Cuba's leader? Or during the cold war, would the Iranian army support the shah in 1979 or tilt toward the Islamic revolution? Would the Soviets decide to invade Czechoslovakia in 1968 or just rattle their sabers? The answers to questions like these are not to be found in documents but, rather, are imponderables about which one can only speculate (unless there is an agent deep within the enemy camp).

Even using open sources, acquiring just the right information can be daunting, given today's deluge of television reports, newspapers, magazines, books, Internet data, and gray literature from around the world. Modern intelligence agencies must be as proficient in open-information management and retrieval as they are in classic espionage and spying with satellites and other machines.

Time is a constraint. In 1991, the United States had the advantage of anticipating war in the Persian Gulf. The president ordered troops and supplies sent to the region. The DCI, in cooperation with the Pentagon, encircled the expected battleground with an armada of listening and watching posts. But moving satellites into the correct geosynchronous position takes time, as does "surging" other assets, including spies on the ground. During the early stages of the war planning, America's secret agencies disagreed over the Iraqi order-of-battle numbers, and for several weeks, collectors and analysts pored over their data to determine which agency had the more reliable figures. Seldom, however, does a nation have this luxury of time to prepare the battlefield.

### Processing

Deciphering the information that has been collected takes time, as adversaries often encode their communications. Moreover, some countries (including Russia) use such complicated mathematical codes that the messages are essentially undecipherable. Even communications in exotic foreign languages require skill and patience to unravel.

The keys to good analysis, then, are not just sharpening the skills of the analysts themselves, nor can analysts sit and wait for the information to land on their desks. From the beginning, they must help policymakers understand how the secret agencies can help them and work with the collectors to determine the best targets and modus operandi. The new "partnership" between co-located case officers from the CIA's Operations Directorate and analysts from the Intelligence Directorate is one of several reforms adopted since the end of the cold war to make HUMINT targeting more effective.[26]

### Searching for Insights

Next is the actual analysis of the information, efforts to interpret the espionage findings in light of open-source knowledge and to give policymakers valuable insights into world affairs—what the British call "assessment." Sometimes the open sources will be sufficient to answer the policymaker's question. On other topics, though, covert information may be needed. Imagery (IMINT) can be a good source of data on the location of foreign troops; SIGINT and HUMINT on the plans of adversaries; MASINT (measurement and signature intelligence) on the specifications of the enemy's weapons. Ideally, the skillful analyst is able to weave together each of these sources, revealing the hidden figure in the carpet. More likely, the analyst confronts the existential dilemma of ambiguity and uncertainty in human affairs. As skillful a weaver of all-source evidence as he or she may be, some of the necessary strands of information will probably be missing. The carpet, richly textured in some places, may be frayed or even have gaping holes in others.

Even when the analyst has all the facts, they rarely speak for themselves, so their meaning must be extracted from among a number of often conflicting ("noisy") possibilities. Was the Soviet Backfire bomber a tactical or a strategic weapons system? During the cold war, analysts had an enormous amount of data on the capabilities of the Backfire, but they disagreed about how the Soviet military might use the aircraft. Probably the airplane was meant for tactical purposes. But if the Kremlin ordered pilots to fly a one-way, kamikaze mission to the United States, the Backfire did have just enough fuel capacity to serve this mission (however unlikely). That is, the answer rested on the *intentions* of Kremlin leaders, a dimension of their behavior much harder to fathom than the straightforward counting of their weapons through IMINT photography. Irrefutable evidence is a luxury seldom provided to the analyst; more common is a shadowy landscape studded like a surrealist painting with question marks and darkened doorways.

### Better Information, Better Analysis

In the 1950s—the "dark ages of intelligence," in the phrase of a CIA historian[27]—the secret agencies had no overhead reconnaissance capabilities and knew little about weapons production and other important events behind the Iron Curtain. Finally, critical technological breakthroughs in surveillance capabilities—first the U-2 spy plane and then the CORONA satellites and the SR-71 surveillance aircraft (1963)—provided analysts with the hard data they needed to prepare reliable reports on Soviet military developments, supplemented by an occasional and valuable HUMINT asset (Oleg Penkovsky being the most famous). Besides these remarkable IMINT breakthroughs, the intelligence community made major advances in SIGINT and MASINT capabilities.[28]

From 1950 to 1970, America's intelligence analysts went from a state of near blindness with respect to the USSR to something approaching 20/20 vision on at least selected aspects of Soviet society, especially weapons capabilities and numbers. During the next two decades, the progress continued. Imagery cameras gained sharper resolution and flexibility, incorporating color film and stereoscopic lenses and radar and infrared capabilities; SIGINT "ears" grew ever larger, more sensitive, and ubiquitous; MASINT sensors were refined; and America's stable of HUMINT assets expanded (although most proved ineffectual). The Kremlin's military intentions, political machinations, and economic strategies remained murkier than its weaponry, although even these mysteries became less opaque as analysts gained experience.

Many of this nation's intelligence accomplishments must remain classified to protect methods that may be useful again. One success story disclosed by the Aspin-Brown commission in 1996 was the discovery that North Korea was planning to construct a nuclear weapons capability. U.S. intelligence also tracked the clandestine efforts of several countries to acquire weapons of mass destruction and delivery systems. In some cases, this information provided the basis for diplomatic actions by the United States and the United Nations to counter this proliferation. American intelligence also has helped other countries identify and arrest several notorious terrorists, including Carlos the Jackal in Sudan, the alleged ringleader of the World Trade Center bombing in the Philippines, the head of the "Shining Path" terrorist group in Peru, and those involved in the bombing of Pan Am 103.[29]

Intelligence analysts have alerted this nation's leaders to a vast number of events abroad of importance to the interests of the United States. Armed with these early warnings, policymakers have been able to make decisions with the greater degree of confidence that comes with knowing all the facts of a situation. From time to time these decisions have been flawed, of course, like the human beings who made them. But often the errors have occurred not so much from failures of intelligence collection or analysis as from the policymakers' unwillingness to accept the facts and judgments of the intelligence experts. It is during the final stage of the intelligence cycle, known as dissemination, that the analyst faces his or her greatest obstacle.

### Dissemination and the Paradox of Rejection

American intelligence holds a central paradox: the nation spends some $26 billion to $30 billion a year to gather and analyze information deemed useful to policymakers, only to find that often it is never used.

How can policymakers spend so much money to acquire all this information and then ignore it?

The reasons vary and begin at the starting point of the intelligence cycle, when policymakers have the chance to tell the DCI and other intelligence managers exactly what kinds of information they need. If they do not and the secret agencies are forced to guess what the policymakers want, the information that they receive may not be what they expected. Sometimes policymakers simply refuse to hear the truth—the well-known problem of speaking truth to power.[30] President Lyndon B. Johnson rejected the CIA's reports on Vietnam when they failed to match his hopes for a quick victory. More recently, a well-regarded former director of the DCI Nonproliferation Center, Gordon Oehler, claimed that the Clinton administration disliked inconvenient intelligence on nuclear weapons, choosing to disregard facts that failed to fit "a pre-conceived view of what the world ought to look like."[31]

### The Limits of Time and Understanding

The importance of a close relationship between intelligence producers and consumers seems so patently obvious that one must wonder why the policymakers are AWOL at the crucial starting point. Time constraints and a lack of awareness are central explanations. Many in high office find themselves too harried to block out time for meetings with intelligence officials. Others lack an understanding about how the secret agencies can help them with their specific information needs. Moreover, sometimes policymakers convince themselves that they can find all the intelligence they need in the nation's major newspapers, along with their own informal contacts in Washington and abroad.

### Ideology

Ideology frequently is the reason for disregarding intelligence. The Aspin-Brown commission heard this comment from a former NIO, echoed by many other intelligence officers: "Intelligence is of use to decision makers primarily when it accords with their own views."[32] Accordingly, analytic reports from the intelligence agencies that question the policymaker's basic convictions or previous public pronouncements may be dismissed out of hand. This form of self-delusion has been widely reported by historians. During World War II, Joseph Stalin embraced

Nazi Germany in a nonaggression pact and subsequently rejected the counsel of his advisers who warned that Russia was about to be attacked by its erstwhile ally. During the Vietnam War, President Johnson escalated his rhetoric in favor of defending South Vietnam and thereafter dismissed all judgments of the CIA that the United States was engaged in an unwinnable war of attrition. More recently, CIA officers charged Vice President Al Gore with casting aside in 1995 conclusive intelligence on the personal corruption of his counterpart and professional friend in Russia, Prime Minister Viktor S. Chernomyrdin. According to several intelligence officials, the vice president reportedly sent the analysis back to Langley with a barnyard epithet scrawled across its cover.[33] "Policymakers are like surgeons," a member of the Aspin-Brown commission pointed out. "They don't last long if they ignore what they see when they cut an issue open."[34]

### Relevance

Sometimes policymakers discount intelligence information because they have been disappointed in it in the past, or perhaps the analyst delivered a report too late for it to matter any longer. "Relevance" is the word one hears most often in speaking with policymakers about their intelligence needs. "We publish too much intelligence of questionable relevance to policymakers," longtime CIA analyst Robert Gates admitted during his DCI confirmation hearings. It thus is essential that the secret agencies provide useful information—what the professionals call "value added"—beyond what the policymaker can find in the daily media and weekly news periodicals. The evidence is strong that the secret agencies have passed this test on numerous occasions, particularly on technical matters (such as Soviet weapons development), transnational issues (terrorism and arms trade), and a range of diplomatic initiatives.[35] Public sources are often better, though, on political reporting. Moreover, newspapers and magazines have the advantage of a more readable style and better "atmospherics" (more vivid details of some events).

### Format

The form of intelligence reporting is important. "If the intelligence product is not two pages or less," an assistant secretary of defense told the Aspin-Brown commission, "it is unlikely to be read. I have only about five minutes that I can devote [each day] to reading intelligence."[36] He obviously preferred what is known in intelligence circles as "current intelligence," brief memoranda on key issues of importance to his daily agenda.

But some senior officials prefer to read a longer analysis. This is true even of busy cabinet secretaries. Les Aspin and Harold Brown of the Defense Department serve as examples.[37] Even though most senior officials prefer two-page intelligence reports, their aides may appreciate the more thorough analysis offered in deeper "research intelligence." Commented a cabinet aide: "No one reads an encyclopedia from A to Z, but it is still helpful to have encyclopedias."[38]

The secret agencies have therefore crafted a range of written products, from fax and interactive e-mail intelligence over secure lines to "in brief" spot intelligence reports of paragraph length and—the analyst's research showcase—the omnibus NIEs. The challenge is to find which format works best for each official, which is more difficult than it seems, because the policymaker may not take the time to sample these menu offerings or express a preference to intelligence managers.

At times the answer may be none of the above. As one intelligence scholar noted, "Some policymakers don't read, some won't read, and some can't read."[39] They thus may seek oral briefings rather than written reports. Accordingly, the intelligence community has trained a cadre of oral briefers, from those who travel to the Oval Office at the request of the president to those who meet with a cabinet member or an aide the first thing each morning, sometimes in the limo on the way to work.

### Marketing

The intelligence cycle ends with the job of marketing. Ideally, the policymaker retrieves the desired intelligence product from a secure computer terminal linked to the analyst's workstation. More commonly, the intelligence agencies use attractive visual presentations of information in hopes of catching the policymaker's attention: fascinating IMINT photographs, detailed maps in four colors, catchy sidebars, time lines, succinct profiles of foreign personalities, boxed quotations from foreign leaders, and many other techniques normally associated with glossy magazine publishing. The agencies even produce intelligence videotapes and CD-ROMs, for those (like President Reagan) who prefer watching movies to reading reports. Once again, the idea is to meet the needs of the consumer as far as possible without destroying the credibility of the substance.

## Improving the Quality of Analysis

How can analysis be improved in this new world since the end of the cold war? First, the intelligence cycle must keep the needs of the individual policymakers foremost in mind; that is, intelligence must be consumer driven. Only if the collector and the analyst know exactly what information a decision maker needs will the secret agencies be able to provide assistance that is both timely and relevant. The wise intelligence officer is responsive both to what the policymaker *thinks* he or she needs to know and what the intelligence officer believes the policymaker *really* needs to know. Second, the intelligence community must present evidence to policymakers that is as objective as possible.

## Tasking for Collection

Determining where to focus America's collection capabilities must be based on a close working relationship with policy officials in whatever venue these decision makers find most effective and convenient, to improve both the quality of tasking instructions and the dissemination of the final analytic product.

There is no one way to solve this communications problem. Rather, intelligence managers must regularly consult with policymakers to determine their preferences for a liaison relationship with intelligence analysts. Some departments and agencies may want analysts or oral briefers (perhaps both) to be assigned directly to their offices, just down the hallway from policymakers and available for consultation at a moment's notice. This "forward observer" model of consultation has been successful in some locations. The Department of Commerce, for example, has a dozen intelligence officers on loan from the intelligence community to service 120 top policymakers in the department.[40] Other policymakers may prefer an early morning briefing on the way to work or the first thing at the office, or perhaps exchanges throughout the day using secure fax or e-mail facilities. Still others may want a briefing on demand or an opportunity to gather with a group of analysts from time to time. One innovative official in the Bush administration established an ad hoc study group that became known as the "East Asian Informals," various collectors, analysts, and policymakers discussing that region of the world. Whatever the desired format for tasking intelligence officers or receiving their product, it must be decided by the consumer. And some consumers may want no help at all from the intelligence community.

### The Dependence of Analysis on Reliable Data

The intelligence community must use its expertise to decide which "int" is most promising for a particular assignment. The starting point should be a greater emphasis on using open sources before turning to clandestine sources of information.

At the beginning of the 1990s, intelligence managers set up a Community Open Source Program Office (COSPO) inside the CIA's Directorate for Science and Technology. Its purpose was to coordinate the community's collection, processing, and dissemination of open-source information. In turn, COSPO created the Open Source Information System (OSIS), a computer network that uses the Internet to give analysts and policymakers access to worldwide public information. Nonetheless, the intelligence community has slipped behind the sharply rising curve of modern information management, and one expert on open-source intelligence has concluded that even COSPO is "dead in the water," has become a victim of inattention.[41]

Enriching the computer hardware and software inside the secret agencies is only one way of improving the access of analysts to open materials. In addition, the intelligence community must offer more open conferences on international topics, with both "inside" and "outside" experts on world affairs. The National Intelligence Council should have each of its NIEs vetted by an outside panel of scholars known for their expertise and objectivity. Then if the two groups come to different conclusions, the presidential and congressional oversight panels should take a close look at the reasons for the disagreement.

One of America's most important resources is its knowledge base, an asset that needs to be more effectively used in the government's foreign policy deliberations. The intelligence community should draw up a list of respected experts willing to contribute their education and experience to an interpretation of international events. The idea of an external review for intelligence products raises the broader question of whether intelligence assessments might well be conducted completely outside the intelligence community, perhaps in a National Intelligence Council–like entity affiliated with the National Security Council or perhaps by an independent think tank. At a minimum, the current National Intelligence Council should be located away from the CIA, where it is now. A good location would be near the White House where it once stood (on E Street near the Old Executive Office Building), situated closer to the policymakers it serves and away from possible domination by analysts at the CIA.

But not everyone likes the idea of moving the National Intelligence Council out of the CIA.[42] Some analysts believe that then it would be too close to the policymakers, and the alternative of lodging the National Intelligence Council in a think tank would take it too far from the often useful clandestine resources of the intelligence community. Others have more practical, and perhaps more compelling (if prosaic), arguments: the CIA has more parking places at Langley, and, besides, purchasing an old building in D.C. would be expensive—and they are riddled with asbestos. So much for lofty rationales for deciding how best to conduct the affairs of state!

The idea of placing the NIC downtown (though still within the intelligence community's organizational framework) continues to have appeal, however, and was endorsed by the Aspin-Brown commission. This would make the NIC—or, in the commission's Anglophile terminology, a new National Assessment Center (NAC)—more independent from the secret agencies and, therefore, possibly more attractive to outstanding academic scholars concerned about the potential stigma associated with working inside the walls of the CIA. A relocated NIC would continue to have constant access to the extensive analytic resources of the CIA's Directorate of Intelligence, by means of secure electronic linkages and frequent conferencing (at the CIA, where there is a place to park).

In sum, the most important requirement for effective intelligence in this new world is niche analysis. The analyst must design the intelligence product to suit the informational—though certainly not the political—needs of the consumer.[43] Without this quality, personnel in the secret agencies can retire and spend their time fishing; they are no longer needed. How can this laudable goal be achieved? "Understanding what the policymaker wants—that's the key to the intelligence business," a seasoned intelligence manager asserts.[44] In turn, that means having an intelligence officer close to the policymaker. "The key," advises a former ambassador, "still is getting close enough to the individual policymaker to find out what he needs."[45] The greatest successes seem to be associated with having an analyst or a liaison officer in the next room, or at least not too far down the corridor, or traveling with the policymaker abroad, sitting in on staff meetings, or providing a daily briefing. If the intelligence product offers a crisp response to the main issues on a policymaker's desk at that moment, it will not only be read; it will be devoured.

# NINE

# Balancing Liberty
# and Security

We know that many Americans are uneasy about CIA and
U.S. intelligence activities. They understand the need for information, and even, on occasion, for covert action. But they
are uncomfortable with secrecy. And therein lies the value of
congressional oversight: the reassurance to Americans that the
laws are being obeyed and that there is accountability.
> —DCI Robert M. Gates, *Hearings*, U.S. Senate
> Committee on Intelligence, 1991

## The Sharing of Governmental Power

By constitutional design, the executive branch of government in the
United States is required to share its powers with the legislative and
judicial branches. While this can lead to frustrations and inefficiencies,
its virtue lies in the accountability that sharing provides. This legislative monitoring or review is usually referred to by the awkward term
"oversight."

The concept of power sharing has roots that run deep in American
tradition. "If angels were to govern men, neither external nor internal
controls on government would be necessary," James Madison observed in 1788. Perhaps unable to recollect any angels he had met in
public life, he advised the adoption of more secular safeguards against
government abuse. "A dependence on the people" would be paramount, especially a cycle of elections. Though necessary, voting in itself would not be sufficient, however. "Experience has taught mankind
the necessity of auxiliary precautions," Madison added. Between elections, the three branches of government would have to keep a close

watch on one another. In his most famous dictum, "Ambition must be made to counteract ambition."[1]

This concern about the dangers of concentrated power was widespread in the new republic. Jefferson scoffed at the notion that loyal citizens should exhibit an obsequious confidence in their leaders; instead, he recommended vigilance over those serving in high office. "Confidence is everywhere the parent of despotism," he warned. "In questions of power, then, let no more be heard of confidence in man, but bind him down from mischief by the chains of the Constitution."[2] The preeminent link in these chains was the Constitution's first article, which enumerated the powers of Congress and made it clear that legislators would have a major role to play in the exercise of the war, treaty, and spending powers, along with an opportunity to impeach an executive or judicial official who violated the public trust. Contemporary political scientists have refashioned this idea as "separated institutions *sharing* powers" as a more accurate portrayal of the day-to-day reality of how the Constitution operates in practice.[3]

This idea of power sharing was endorsed in modern times by Supreme Court Justice Louis Brandeis, who reminded a new century of Americans that the founders had sought "not to promote efficiency but to preclude the exercise of arbitrary power. The purpose was not to avoid friction, but, by means of the inevitable friction incident to the distribution of the governmental powers among three departments, to save the people from autocracy."[4]

The governing arrangements envisioned by the founders have never worked perfectly. Institutional struggles over the war and the treaty powers have been particularly heated. Sometimes the powers of the president have expanded to alarming proportions, as when Abraham Lincoln assumed the status of an autocrat during the early phases of the Civil War, when Andrew Johnson acted capriciously during Reconstruction, when Lyndon B. Johnson escalated the war in Vietnam without a meaningful congressional debate, and when Richard M. Nixon helped cover up a White House espionage operation against the opposition party (the Watergate scandal).

On other occasions, the powers of Congress have grown too large, as when Joseph R. McCarthy (R, Wisconsin) grossly misused the Senate's investigative powers to harass the Truman and Eisenhower administrations and scores of private citizens. Sometimes the judiciary has over-reached, as in 1936 when Justice George Sutherland issued sweeping dicta in favor of expanded presidential powers in foreign affairs.[5]

For the most part, though, the government has abided by the founding principle of power sharing, though its precise form has always been dependent on the personalities and conditions of the times. Some personalities have been expansive in the interpretation of their office's inherent constitutional powers (compare Franklin D. Roosevelt with the more passive William Howard Taft). Some events have compelled a greater concentration of power in the hands of the executive, in times of emergency and for the sake of secrecy and swift action. The Depression, World War II, and the cold war have been the major centralizing forces of the modern era that encouraged an aggrandizement of power by the executive branch.

Yet almost always (the Civil War excepted), dialogue and accommodation have mollified disputes among the departments of government. Presidents Andrew Johnson and Bill Clinton barely escaped removal from office through the impeachment procedure, and President Richard Nixon resigned rather than face almost certain removal. Usually, though, those in high office have been willing to display (however begrudgingly) a spirit of comity on which power sharing depends. Always at the heart of these governing arrangements is the principle of checks against power imbalances, that is, accountability, except for one domain of government that has always stood out as a conspicuous exception to the rule. Throughout most of their history, the nation's intelligence agencies have enjoyed immunity from close oversight by outside supervisors.

## The Exceptional Case of Intelligence

During America's early history, intelligence operations eluded serious supervision by Congress and the courts.[6] But even in the modern era with all the congressional oversight capabilities (budgets, staff, frequent hearings, strengthened subpoena, and other investigative authorities), the CIA and its companion agencies have sidestepped the government's usual checks and balances. Members of Congress have deferred to the expertise of intelligence officers and preferred anyway to avoid responsibility for controversial secret operations like the Bay of Pigs fiasco (1961).[7]

A former director of Central Intelligence, James R. Schlesinger, re-membered a meeting he had in 1973 with John Stennis (D, Mississippi), chair of the subcommittee dealing with intelligence on behalf of the Sen-ate Armed Services Committee. "I went up to the Hill and said, 'Mr. Chairman, I want to tell you about some of our programs.' To which the Senator quickly replied: 'No, no, my boy, don't tell me. Just go ahead and do it—but I don't want to know!'"[8] With little scrutiny, the leaders of the Armed Services Committees in both chambers quietly allocated funds for the secret agencies into the Defense Department's annual ap-propriations bill.

Nor did the Executive Office of the President offer reliable account-ability for the intelligence establishment. Key members of the National Security Council rarely—in some cases, never—even laid eyes on the in-telligence budget. "I never saw a budget of the CIA, although I was a statutory member of the National Security Council," Dean Rusk once said, looking back over his long tenure as secretary of state during the Kennedy and Johnson administrations.

> The CIA's budget apparently went to two or three specially cleared peo-ple in the Bureau of the Budget, then run briefly by the president, turned over to Senator [Richard] Russell [D, Georgia], and that was the end of it. He would lose the CIA budget in the Defense budget and he wouldn't let anybody question it. There were no public hearings on it. So again his judgment, his word on that, was the last word.[9]

Many of the CIA's activities (including aggressive covert action, col-lection, and counterintelligence operations) never received a thorough examination—or, in some cases, even approval—by the National Secu-rity Council.[10] When the council did endorse a covert action proposal, the decision process became slippery, according to Clark Clifford, an ad-viser to several presidents from Truman onward.

> I believe on a number of occasions a plan for covert action has been pre-sented to the NSC and authority is requested for the CIA to proceed from point A to point B. The authority will be given and the action will be launched. When point B is reached, the persons in charge feel it is neces-sary to go point C, and they assume that the original authorization gives them such a right. From point C, they go to D and possibly E, and even further. This has led to some bizarre results, and when an investigation is

started the excuse is blandly presented that authority was obtained from the NSC before the project was launched.[11]

Mindful of the need for closer supervision of the intelligence community, a few members of Congress attempted from time to time to devise new controls (particularly in the wake of intelligence flaps such as the Bay of Pigs and the CIA's infiltration of the National Student Association). But these initiatives were always defeated, as a majority of legislators remained content to abide by the rule of exception for intelligence activities, persuaded by the argument that the nation's secret operations were too delicate for oversight and wary of consenting to operations that might prove embarrassing.

Nonetheless, some of the oversight proposals were modest efforts to strengthen the review of intelligence programs, and had they been adopted, they might have helped avoid later scandals. Other proposals were more extreme, including one—the Abourezk amendment—designed to abolish all covert actions, regardless of type or circumstance.[12] Whatever the merits of the various oversight initiatives, Congress proved unwilling to extend the doctrine of power sharing to the darker recesses of American government.

In December 1974, however, this attitude changed abruptly. In a series of articles, reporter Seymour M. Hersh of the *New York Times* disclosed that the CIA had spied on American citizens during the Vietnam War and had also attempted to topple the constitutionally elected president of Chile (Salvador Allende). Although Congress might have ignored the revelations about covert action in Chile as just another necessary chapter in the cold war against Soviet interference in the developing world, spying on American citizens—their constituents—was an allegation they found difficult to dismiss. Both the executive and legislative branches immediately launched investigations, in what became known as the "Year of Intelligence" (or the "Intelligence Wars," in the embittered view of some CIA officials).[13]

During these inquiries in 1975, a parade of horrors emerged, everything from murder plots against foreign leaders to widespread espionage operations against American citizens whose only crime had been to protest the war in Vietnam or join the civil rights movement. The Ford administration revived the President's Foreign Intelligence Advisory

Board and created the Intelligence Oversight Board, both part of the Executive Office of the Presidency and now expected to monitor the secret agencies on behalf of the chief executive. By executive order, President Gerald R. Ford banned assassination plots and tightened CIA and National Security Council approval procedures for the use of covert action. His successor, Jimmy Carter, further codified and strengthened the council's accountability for intelligence activities by means of another executive order and supporting directives.

The zeal for reform was most evident on Capitol Hill. Indeed, President Ford's initiatives were widely considered more an attempt to preempt congressional action than bold steps to rein in the secret agencies. On the last day of the legislative session in 1974, Congress enacted the first-ever statute to place controls on the use of covert action. The landmark Hughes-Ryan amendment made two far-reaching changes: first, before a covert action could be carried out, the president would have to authorize the operation through a special approval called a "finding," and second, the finding would have to be reported to the appropriate committees of Congress "in a timely fashion," thereby alerting legislative overseers that a covert action had been authorized by the White House.[14] With the enactment of this law, a few legislators were allowed into the small group of people told about covert actions, the "witting circle," in spytalk. Legislators stopped short of granting themselves authority to approve or disapprove covert actions, but at least they would have an opportunity to know about them and (by implication) to voice their objections or, at the extreme, even shut off funding for a proposal if they strongly opposed it.

By the spring of 1976, senators had established a permanent committee on intelligence oversight, named the Senate Select Committee on Intelligence (SSCI, pronounced "sissy" by everyone except its members and staff, which they would sometimes prove to be) and given a mandate to provide a close accounting of intelligence budgets and day-to-day operations. The next year the House followed suit, establishing the House Permanent Select Committee on Intelligence (HPSCI, pronounced "hipsee") with largely comparable duties and expectations.

Since then, this congressional experiment in power sharing has evolved in fits and starts. Sometimes legislators have tightened the reins, most notably with passage of the Intelligence Oversight Act of 1980, the

Boland amendments to curtail covert action in Nicaragua during the Reagan administration, the Intelligence Oversight Act of 1991, and, in the same year (both responses to the Iran-contra scandal), the creation of a CIA inspector general confirmed by and accountable to Congress. At other times, legislators have loosened the reins when they proved to be too restrictive, as in 1985 with the repeal of the legislation prohibiting covert action in Angola and the buckling under of legislators to President George Bush's insistence on greater presidential discretion over reporting to the Congress on covert actions. On still other occasions, Congress has helped the intelligence agencies shelter their legitimate activities, as with the passage of an Intelligence Identities Protection Act in 1982 to prohibit the exposure of undercover intelligence officials through the publication of their names. While the pulling and tugging continued, one conclusion was without dispute: at last the secret agencies had become a part of America's system of shared powers.

## On the Merits of Accountability

Has the new system of accountability been successful? Opinion remains divided on this question, as reflected in two recent studies of intelligence.[15] For one author, Kathryn Olmsted, the movement to introduce accountability into this secret world has largely failed, however well intended and proper the attempt. Despite the year-long investigations by three separate panels—one in the Senate led by Senator Frank Church (D, Idaho), another in the House led by Representative Otis Pike (D, New York), and a third in the White House led by Vice President Nelson Rockefeller (R, New York), the end result was little reform. The Congress was, she writes, "ultimately unwilling to shoulder its responsibilities for overseeing the intelligence community."

In her effort to determine why this was the case, Olmsted begins with an observation from Richard Helms, a former DCI pilloried by Senate investigators in 1975. Helms commented sarcastically: "Where is the legislation, the great piece of legislation, that was going to come out of the Church committee hearings? I haven't seen it."[16] Though for quite different reasons, Olmsted, too, is unimpressed by the will of legislators to supervise the intelligence community. The preference of Capitol Hill overseers is "to maintain their basic deference" to the secret agencies, she maintains, rather than hold them to high standards of accountability. In regard to accountability from outside the government, she finds the nation's media equally feckless. While much of Olmsted's criticism of legislative oversight is compelling, she too easily discounts the improvements that have come about as a result of the investigations in 1975. She (and Helms) is wrong: it is not the number of laws or their level of detail that matters so much but, rather, the day-to-day monitoring of the secret agencies by legislators and their staff. By this measure, the creation of the two intelligence oversight committees has led to a much closer check on America's secret government than existed earlier.

Moreover, the oversight laws that have been passed should not be so easily discounted, especially their reporting requirements. The Intelligence Oversight Act of 1980 considerably enhanced accountability. It included a provision for *advanced* notice to Congress of *every* important covert operation (not just covert actions). Significant, too, are the Foreign Intelligence Surveillance Act (FISA) of 1978, which brought the judiciary into the ambit of intelligence oversight by requiring a special court review of requests for national security wiretaps; and the Intelligence Oversight Act of 1991, which insists on a prior, written presidential finding for important covert actions, not *ex post facto* oral approval, as once given by President Reagan.[17] These initiatives are not shadows on the wall but, like the new inspector general statute, tough laws that have given genuine meaning to intelligence accountability. This is particularly evident when compared with the statutory void that existed before passage of the Hughes-Ryan Act.

The media also deserve more credit than Olmsted gives them. Clearly, a number of American reporters erred in the past when they accepted secret stipends from the CIA for intelligence work, blurring the line between independent journalism and espionage.[18] Moreover, reporting on intelligence matters has often been superficial (Olmsted's central point). Yet the reason for the thin coverage warrants some empathy. The secret agencies are enclosed by both real and figurative walls, just as daunting for journalists as for scholars and other outsiders. Expectations that the media will be able to break down these walls with any frequency is unrealistic, nor would most American citizens want the nation's secrets so easily breached.

Furthermore, the media have occasionally behaved in a manner that has been not so much deferential as irresponsible. Columnist Jack Anderson had his moments of commendable reporting in the public interest, but his disclosure of Operation Guppy (U.S. wiretapping of Soviet limousines in Moscow) and the *Glomar Explorer* story (when the CIA attempted to salvage a sunken Soviet submarine) undermined two potentially valuable intelligence-collection operations.[19] Several members of the media with access to these stories prudently decided against printing them, on grounds that the best interests of the United States might be harmed. There are times—however few—when the media should restrain itself in the national interest.

In Olmsted's view, the "secret agencies clearly emerged the winners of their long battle with the investigators [in 1975]," for the inquiries resulted "only in restoring the CIA's credibility." Yet consider the whole new set of arrangements for closer intelligence supervision on Capitol Hill, including the establishment of SSCI and HPSCI by lopsided votes (the White House and the intelligence community lobbied vigorously against them). The two committees enjoy line-by-line budget authorization, competent staffs, subpoena powers, and a mandate to prevent further abuses. Consider, too, the exposés of assassination plots, domestic spying, covert action in Chile, and drug experimentation. The intelligence agencies were hardly winners in 1975. True, the CIA was not dismantled, as some feared (including then DCI William Colby). The end result, though, was nonetheless a significant tightening of legislative supervision over the secret agencies.

As for restoring the CIA's credibility (which Olmsted seems to view as a dubious outcome), it was never the intention of the Church committee to undermine the intelligence agencies' ability to perform their legitimate work. Rather, Senator Frank Church hoped to improve U.S. intelligence by rooting out its rotten branches. Church's only major speech during the inquiry praised the CIA for its analytic skills and solid reporting to policymakers over the years.[20] His purpose was to extol the virtues of intelligence (he himself had served as an intelligence officer during World War II), renewing its legitimacy even as he criticized its excesses.

Olmsted ends her study with an important question about the evolution of intelligence oversight in the United States: Have the legislative committees caved in to the very agencies they were created to supervise? Once more she discerns a pattern of deference toward the secret agencies by their overseers, citing as an illustration a journalist's observation that within a decade after 1975, the House Intelligence Committee "was staffed largely by former CIA officers."

From time to time, the two oversight committees have disappointed outside advocates of strong accountability, but at other times they have also demonstrated firm resolve, depending on the mix of members and how seriously they have taken their oversight responsibilities. Representative Edward P. Boland (D, Massachusetts) stood up to the covert action chicanery in Nicaragua directed by the National Security Council staff during the Reagan years, as did Iran-contra congressional investigators in 1987. And throughout 1995–96, both intelligence committees engaged in a wide-ranging, constructive review of intelligence reform proposals.

"For a brief moment," Olmsted concludes, "[congressional investigators] forced the nation to debate the perils of secrecy in a democracy." On the contrary, this has been an energetic and ongoing debate, continuing through the Carter years and heating up during the Reagan and Bush administrations with the Iran-contra affair. It was revived again during the Clinton years with the report of the Aspin-Brown commission in 1996, along with concomitant efforts by Congress and scholars in the private sector to ponder intelligence reform. How much intelligence is enough? What is the proper balance between liberty and security? When should legislators and the media be supportive or openly critical of sensitive intelligence operations? These are questions without definitive answers.

Whereas Olmsted is dismayed by the lack of robust intelligence oversight, the second study takes quite the opposite view. Steven F. Knott is aghast that the overabundance of oversight has supposedly stifled America's secret agencies. He reminds us that Washington, Jefferson, and Lincoln periodically resorted to unsavory covert practices. He derives from this history lesson a dubious conclusion, however, namely, that a reliance on executive discretion over intelligence activities served the nation well in the past and would in the future as well if only the Congress would step out of the way. According to Knott, intelligence operations frequently are delicate and perishable and rely on secrecy, flexibility, timeliness, and efficiency, all of which are lost when Congress enters the picture.

Knott is impressed by precedents set in the nation's early history and understandably so, for the founders' accomplishments are indeed impressive. His enthusiasm, though, goes too far. During the Watergate scandal, defenders of the Nixon administration insisted that the president had done nothing more than what earlier presidents had done. "I do not share this view," properly responded a legislator during the impeachment proceedings against the president, "or the view of those who hold that all presidents have lied, have broken the law, have compromised the Constitution. And if George Washington accepted bribes, it would not make bribery a virtue, nor would it be grounds for overlooking such acts by his successors."[21] Similarly, the fact that earlier presidents engaged in intelligence operations without serious accountability should not condone the practice today.

Knott is a fervent critic of the post-Watergate rebellion against the imperial presidency. He laments the "myth of innocence" that enveloped Frank Church and his band of reformers in Congress. Instead, he reminds Americans of how their most venerated early leaders were willing to engage in operations that today would send pantywaist legislators running into the press room crying foul. "The most important reform that should be made to the current system," Knott writes, "would be the elimination of the intelligence committees and the restoration of the system that existed from 1947 to 1974." In place of the congressional oversight committees, he would prefer a system of unfettered executive dominance. President Ford's "ludicrous" executive order prohibiting the assassination of foreign leaders should, for instance, be immediately repealed.

What disturbed legislators in 1975 was the extent to which many of the modern intelligence agencies had violated the law and their charters. Most legislators were shocked by the discovery of assassination plots; the creation of more than a million intelligence files on U.S. citizens; illegal mail openings, wiretaps, and cable interceptions; drug experiments against unsuspecting citizens; unlawful sequestering of chemical-biological materials; a White House spy plan against American citizens; an intelligence scheme to blackmail Dr. Martin Luther King Jr. and encourage his suicide; the CIA's infiltration of this country's media, universities, and church groups; the FBI's incitement of violence among African

Americans; covert harassment of Vietnam War dissenters and civil rights activists; and covert actions directed against not just autocracies but duly elected governments in democratic regimes.

Throughout most of the republic's history, secret operations remained small and peripheral. Now, however, our intelligence establishment has grown beyond the capacity of the president alone to monitor. The Congress must help. In Knott's opinion, however, this legislative supervision ("micromanagement," in the preferred slight) has only stymied the secret agencies. Yet most of the intelligence directors since 1975 take a different view. They have welcomed the opportunity to share the burden of their heavy responsibilities with members of Congress. Moreover, no administration has sought to repeal the core set of laws and oversight procedures that currently guide intelligence activities. Legislators understand that this nation must continue to have, when needed, a viable covert action capability and one that can move swiftly. According to Knott, the new oversight has caused the CIA to shy away from this option, but in fact, covert action was most extensively used during the Reagan and Bush years, well after the reforms were in place.[22]

Knott does Congress a further disservice by blaming it for the unauthorized disclosure of classified information. Studies on the subject of leaks consistently trace most back to the executive branch.[23] Knott also maintains that the oversight exercised by Congress from 1947 to 1974 was sufficiently vigorous. Every other credible study disagrees.[24] He then shifts from the improbable to the impossible: a defense of the relations between DCI William J. Casey of the Reagan administration and Congress. The fact is that Casey's standing on Capitol Hill reached rock bottom. He had nothing but disdain for the legislative branch and even managed to alienate the CIA's archdefenders in Congress (including the SSCI chair, Barry Goldwater, R, Arizona).

The choice is not between executive or legislative sovereignty over intelligence. The challenge is to use the best attributes of both branches in the service of the nation's security. Members of Congress have a strong sense of what the American people will support, plus a large amount of foreign policy expertise in their own right. Congress provides a second opinion, carefully tendered in the executive (closed) sessions of the oversight committees by a small group of legislators in each chamber. On sensitive matters that can involve great cost and danger for the United States, a second opinion can be vital.

During the Iran-contra investigation, Vice Admiral John M. Poindexter (President Reagan's national security adviser) conceded that he had bypassed the intelligence committees in order to avoid "outside interference"[25]—as if Congress were an outsider. Granted, in the intelligence domain, debate must often take place behind closed doors. The new system of oversight, though, provides an opportunity for at least some degree of independent review by elected representatives of the American people, beyond just the president and vice president. The alternative is covert operations by executive fiat. The unfortunate consequences of that approach, well documented by investigators in 1975 and again in the wake of the Iran-contra scandal, remain fresh in the memory of the attentive public.

## Adapting to the New Era of Accountability

Regardless of whether or not one likes the idea of greater intelligence accountability, the fact remains that 1975 was a critical turning point in the history of American intelligence. Since then, the quality of oversight has depended on the degree of commitment displayed by individual legislators toward their supervisory responsibilities and how often (and persuasively) the media have reported incidents of intelligence impropriety. Generally, the level of oversight has remained relatively high compared with its near absence before 1975. With the passage of a series of amendments sponsored by HPSCI chair Edward Boland, legislative overseers responded quickly to block untoward covert actions in Nicaragua during the first half of the Reagan administration. Congress failed to sniff out the Iran-contra shenanigans at first, but disclosure of the operations (never reported to Congress, as required by law, but by a Middle Eastern newspaper) jolted the overseers back to their senses.

### A New Partnership

Despite these fluctuations, the overall trend during the latter stages of the cold war was unmistakable: Congress and the executive branch had entered into a new era of partnership in the conduct of intelligence activities. As a recent DCI put it, the CIA found itself equidistant between the two branches: "responsible and accountable to both, unwilling to act at presidential request without clearance from Congress."[26] Between 1986 and 1990, the number of CIA briefings to the congressional oversight committees, individual members, and staffers rose from a few hundred a year to 1,040 in 1986, 1,064 in 1987, 1,044 in 1988, 947 in 1989, 1,012 in 1990, and 1,000 in 1991.[27] The number of written reports sent to Congress, most of them classified, has also sharply increased since 1986. In 1991 alone, 7,000 intelligence reports went to Capitol Hill.[28]

The frequency of contact between the CIA and Congress has accelerated since the cold war. In 1993, 1,512 meetings took place between members of Congress and the CIA's legislative liaison staff, along with 154 one-on-one or small-group meetings between legislators and the DCI; 26 congressional hearings with the DCI as a witness; 128 hearings with other CIA witnesses; 317 other contacts with legislators; and 887 meetings and contacts with legislative staff, a 29 percent increase over 1992. In 1993, the Agency provided 4,976 classified documents to legislators, along with 4,668 unclassified documents and 233 responses to constituency inquiries.[29] In 1998, CIA officials briefed members or staffers on Capitol Hill on 1,350 occasions (about five times each working day).[30]

Another sign of a more serious effort to monitor the CIA and keep American citizens informed of at least some of its activities was the series of hearings in Congress, held from 1991 to 1994, in which witnesses from the intelligence community testified in public, a rarity during the cold war. President Clinton's first DCI, R. James Woolsey, appeared in eight open hearings in 1993, whereas in previous years— even after the congressional investigations of 1975 and calls for greater openness—DCIs often never appeared in public hearings during an entire session of Congress or, if testifying, never more than once or twice a year.

The result is that the Agency now has two masters: the president as well as Congress, and sometimes a third, as the courts increasingly adjudicate intelligence-related litigation and regularly examine requests for electronic-surveillance warrants against national-security targets.

## Backsliding

The degree of CIA openness should not be overstated, however. That Congress was still kept in the dark on key aspects of intelligence policy was underscored in 1994. Although the HPSCI had been briefed, SSCI members learned only through a chance audit that the National Reconnaissance Office (NRO) had engaged in cost overruns amounting to $159 million for its new headquarters in the Virginia countryside. Subsequent reports in 1995–96 revealed further that the NRO had accumulated a $4 billion slush fund of appropriations, without keeping Congress informed of its magnitude.[31] R. James Woolsey produced a raft of documents purportedly showing that when he had been DCI, Congress had been briefed on the NRO budget nine different times. A CIA/Department of Defense inquiry subsequently indicated, however, that the NRO had presented this matter to legislators in piecemeal fashion that (to quote the report) "left unclear the total project cost."[32] However inadvertent the inadequacy of briefings may have been, the fact remained that the NRO had failed to keep Congress fully informed of its activities, as the spirit and the letter of the oversight laws intend. The "fully informed" standard means that intelligence officials must patiently reiterate their testimony to busy committee members and staff again and again, if necessary, with respect to any departure from normal practices (including cost overruns). Overseers have every right to this information.[33]

It was revealed in 1995 that another secret agency, this time the CIA, had also failed to report to Congress about dubious activities. The issue concerned the Agency's ties to a controversial military colonel in Guatemala, Julio Roberto Alpirez, who had been providing intelligence to the United States from time to time. The media suspected the officer of being involved in the murder of an American citizen in Guatemala and also in the death of a local guerrilla insurgent married to an American woman. Under the oversight rules, the CIA should have reviewed with the congressional oversight panels the propriety of an ongoing relationship with the colonel. "Guatemala's most important lesson," concluded the *New York Times*, "is that the C.I.A. cannot be trusted to police itself."[34]

Another, more recent case of an intelligence official who failed to understand the concept of accountability is the chief of counterintelligence in the Energy Department. In 1999, he criticized the SSCI and HPSCI chairs for their vigorous inquiry into the spy scandal at the Los Alamos National Laboratory, complaining that he had "to testify about this before fourteen different committees for two months."[35] The Los Alamos spy incident, however, revealed a serious counterintelligence breach. If legislative overseers wish to hear from the CI chief in charge of the nation's labs one or one hundred times, that is an important part of his job. As an experienced former intelligence officer explained, "Dealing with the public is as much a function of intelligence these days as the recruiting of agents or the forecasting of future events."[36]

At least the Energy Department's CI chief avoided the even worse stance adopted by the Iran-contra bureaucrats. They either failed to inform Congress at all, or, the ultimate offense against accountability, they lied to legislators. Other officials in the Energy Department, though, did exhibit some of this regrettable behavior, despite the still-fresh memory of Iran-contra. In 1998, the department failed to file an annual report on the status of security at the nation's labs, as required by Congress.[37] Moreover, two of the department's senior officials, including its acting head of intelligence, withheld information on the Los Alamos scandal from the House Armed Services Subcommittee on Military Procurement, even under oath and in executive session.[38]

For some people, the lessons of Iran-contra seem easily forgotten (if they were ever learned). "To my mind, to disclose as little as necessary to Congress, if they can get away with it, is not a bad thing," a former intelligence officer reportedly observed in 1991, referring to colleagues caught up in the Iran-contra affair. "I have trouble myself blaming any of those guys."[39] Similarly, the new NRO director concedes that the old ethic at his organization—which he vows he is determined to change— was at best a grudging acceptance of congressional accountability. "Legislators were considered pimples on the face of progress," he recalls. "The attitude was: 'We're not going to tell you and you can't make us.'"[40] Yet as a former SSCI staff member observed, the only hope for oversight to work depends ultimately on the "honesty and completeness in what the members of the intelligence community tell their congressional overseers."[41]

During the Congress's Los Alamos inquiries in 1999, even DCI George Tenet—formerly the SSCI staff director and well versed in the ethos of oversight—refused to provide information about the spy case to his former committee (evidently so ordered by the Department of Justice). The SSCI chairman, Senator Richard Shelby, was correct in asserting his committee's right to "have access to all information in unredacted form that pertains to our oversight responsibility."[42] Without full access to information about all intelligence activities, the oversight committees would be unable to provide the institutional balance envisioned by the nation's founders as a safeguard against the abuse of power.

The evolution of reliable accountability for intelligence was dealt yet another blow at the beginning of the new century when it came to light in February 2000 that the CIA had never reported to the congressional oversight committees or the Justice Department evidence that implicated former DCI John Deutch in the improper handling of classified materials (while director, he took large amounts home to work on, thereby violating security procedures). There was "no excuse" for failing to report the impropriety, conceded Deutch's successor, George Tenet. "It should have been done promptly, certainly by the spring of 1997."[43] The intelligence community's degree of openness and cooperation with legislative overseers, then, has been uneven since the institution of greater accountability in 1975. How well have other overseers, inside and outside the government, fared in their efforts to keep the secret agencies accountable?

## Oversight by the White House

During the Reagan years, the intelligence community benefited from a close relationship with the White House, mainly because DCI Casey was a personal friend of the president and had served as his national campaign manager. Casey became the first DCI accorded the largely honorific "cabinet rank." Furthermore, Reagan was supportive of Casey's enthusiasm for covertly countering the worldwide influence of the Soviet Union. But this free rein given to the intelligence community and the NSC staff led to the Iran-contra excesses. When former DCI George Bush became president, the CIA had the luxury of a chief executive who understood and appreciated intelligence as well as anyone who has served in the nation's highest office. Accordingly, President Bush was sympathetic to most of the funding requests from the secret agencies, though he did reduce the CIA's involvement in covert actions.[44]

The Clinton administration has been almost a polar opposite, with its relative inattentiveness to foreign policy (at least in the early years). Then, during the administration's first significant foreign policy crisis in Somalia, intelligence deficiencies—among them, a failure to understand the intentions, or even the whereabouts, of tribal leader General Mohamed Farah Aideed—raised doubts among White House officials about the effectiveness of the secret agencies.

In 1994, President Clinton turned to a proposal advanced by his former secretary of defense, Les Aspin, Vice President Al Gore, and his national security adviser, Anthony Lake, to establish a presidential reform commission on intelligence, the president's first expression of interest in the direction that intelligence should take during his tenure. This was prompted not just by the events in Somalia; the CIA's failure to have forecast the fall of the Soviet Union, also produced widespread criticism in Washington. Some critics further excoriated the intelligence agencies for underestimating the nuclear weapons programs in Iraq and North Korea. Others simply argued that with the end of the cold war, America no longer needed a large intelligence establishment. In addition, its annual budget was an inviting target for budget cutters concerned about the spending deficit.[45] The final straw was the discovery in 1994 of a highly placed Russian mole inside the CIA, Aldrich H. Ames.

Although President Clinton understood that something had to be done, Senator John Warner (R, Virginia) had in mind something quite different. As chapter 6 discussed, he envisioned a legislative probe whose main objective would be to reassure the American people that the CIA was an effective organization and should be preserved, not abolished or even substantially downsized. The SSCI, of which Warner was a senior member, accepted his view and pushed for a congressional panel of inquiry, rather than what might have been a more probing executive branch inquiry with Aspin at the helm.

The eventual compromise between the branches was a law passed in 1994 that created a joint presidential-congressional commission on the roles and capabilities of the U.S. intelligence community. It authorized the president to select nine members, which he drew from the President's Foreign Intelligence Advisory Board (including its chair and subsequently the commission's chair, Les Aspin). Congressional leaders from both parties picked the remaining eight members, Senator Warner among them. The commission began its work in March 1995. When Aspin tragically died three months later, he was replaced by another former secretary of defense, Harold Brown (of the Carter administration).

The report issued by the commission in March 1996 largely met Warner's objective. Instead of recommending major reforms, the blue-ribbon panel—the first significant official inquiry into intelligence policy in twenty years—extolled the good work of the secret agencies, kept their budgets intact, offered a few modest suggestions for improvement, and disappeared as a footnote to history.

The commission's boldest initiative was its attempt to help President Clinton's second intelligence chief, John M. Deutch, expand his powers (see chapter 5). The panel recommended that the DCI have joint approval—along with the relevant department secretaries—over all intelligence agency directors. The commission further advocated greater DCI authority over communitywide budget decisions. The individual intelligence agencies (and especially the military ones) immediately laid siege to these proposals, however, drawing on the assistance of the armed services committees and other powerful allies in the Congress. The reform proposals largely collapsed.

## Interest Groups

In 1975, a senior intelligence officer resigned from the CIA to establish the Association of Retired Intelligence Officers (ARIO).[46] Its purpose was to lobby legislators and the American people on behalf of the secret agencies. Other pressure groups came into existence soon thereafter, some for and some against the intelligence community. For example, as the Pentagon's budget began to shrink after the collapse of the Soviet Union, industrial manufacturers cast an eye toward the government's ongoing requirements for espionage hardware—especially expensive satellites—to supplement dwindling contracts for tanks, ships, and aircrafts. Members of Congress in districts with weapons plants—and jobs at risk—were solicited by the manufacturers for assistance in procuring intelligence-hardware deals, in the manner they once were used to obtain Department of Defense acquisitions and to forestall base closures. By the cold war's end, interest-group politics had entered the once relatively insulated domain of intelligence policy.[47]

With respect to the intelligence community's own lobbying efforts on Capitol Hill, known in Washington euphemistically as "legislative liaison," in the wake of the investigations of 1975, intelligence managers began to understand a lesson already well learned by the FBI and the Pentagon, namely, the importance of defending (read selling) one's programs on Capitol Hill and beyond. The Agency's Office of Congressional Affairs expanded from two staffers in 1974 to more than a dozen in 1994. The CIA's Office of General Counsel soared from two in 1974 to sixty-five in 1994 (although most of these individuals were employed to administer the new accountability rules, and only a few were given lobbying tasks). Forced somewhat out into the open in 1974 by the *New York Times* allegations of improprieties, the CIA and the other secret agencies began to devote additional resources to their public defense, in the manner of most other government bureaucracies.

## Scholarly Inquiries

The same forces that led to the creation of an intelligence commission in 1994 stirred various nongovernment groups to study intelligence reform, including panels at Georgetown University, the Council on Foreign Relations (CFR), and the Twentieth Century Fund. Perhaps the most controversial views expressed by the members of these outside panels came from the project director for the CFR report, who tried to turn back the clock on twenty years of bipartisan intelligence reform.[48] He recommended the restoration of assassination plots; use of the Peace Corps as a cover for CIA officers abroad (which has never been done); permission for intelligence officers to pretend they are American journalists, academics, or clergy traveling overseas; and more aggressive participation in coups d'état against regimes deemed unfriendly to the United States, all of which had been rejected by every major government panel of inquiry from Church, Pike, and Rockefeller through Aspin-Brown.

## The Debate Continues

Since the end of the cold war, intelligence officials have been more forthcoming in their public release of selected documents from the organization's early history, including analytic reports on the USSR in the 1950s, documents on the Cuban missile crisis, and some 4 million pages of secret records on the Agency's probe of possible foreign ties to the assassination of President John F. Kennedy.[49] Moreover, the current DCI, George Tenet, stated in 1998 that "we plan to release well over one million pages of documents this year and more than two million next year. The C.I.A. has done more in recent years to release information than ever before, and certainly far more than any other intelligence service in the world."[50]

However heartening these statistics may appear as an expression of greater openness, they do not mean that the information released by the intelligence community has been of high quality or that the quality is likely to improve in the future. More telling than the DCI's reassurances is the CIA's request in 1999 that the Justice Department rescind the authority of the Interagency Security Classification Appeals Panel (ISCAP) to declassify Agency documents, a panel that has overruled denials of declassification by the secret agencies in over 50 percent of the cases.[51] A researcher with the National Security Archives concluded that the Clinton administration's release of documents on the CIA's involvement with the Pinochet government in Chile during the 1970s indicates that the Agency "has much to offer here, and much to hide. They clearly are continuing to hide this history."[52]

The secret agencies remain a loose association of individual fortresses that seldom give up information about their clandestine activities. This continues to be true, even though every credible study on secrecy in America has concluded that most documents that are classified need not be if the criterion for release is whether the national interests of the United States would be injured. Of course, the government must keep concealed the names of its agents overseas, its nuclear weapons secrets, and its sensitive methods of intelligence collection; but if we wish to remain a democracy, the government must also keep the people better informed about the many activities of its intelligence agencies that can be made public, especially events that took place decades ago.

With its subpoena powers, budget review, control of the intelligence purse strings, and a capacity to focus public attention by way of open hearings, the Congress remains the strongest *potential* overseer for intelligence. This potential rests, though, on the question of whether its members have the will to perform these duties, a mixed record so far. For the most part, intelligence accountability has rested on the shoulders of a few dedicated legislators and their staff aides. This limited scrutiny has led to gaps in legislative coverage of intelligence activities and sometimes an insufficient "critical mass" among legislators to focus the full committee's attention on problems that could benefit from more serious oversight. In 1996—three years before the scandal over the alleged Chinese spying at Los Alamos—the two congressional intelligence committees were told about the possible theft of nuclear secrets from the lab but reportedly did nothing to strengthen counterintelligence at the site or at the other national laboratories.[53]

Even if the SSCI and HPSCI members spent more time on their oversight duties, they could never hope to monitor, or even understand, all the complexities of U.S. intelligence. Furthermore, the secret agencies will sometimes ignore the oversight guidance provided by Congress, no matter how good the counsel may be. In 1988, for instance, the General Accounting Office (GAO, an investigative arm of Congress) found lax counterintelligence procedures at the nation's weapons laboratories that allowed foreign visitors too easy access to data on America's nuclear weapons. The GAO recommended appropriate corrective measures. Nine years later its investigators conducted a follow-up study, only to discover these security problems had grown much worse.[54]

Though certainly imperfect, accountability from Congress and other legitimate entities (like the Intelligence Oversight Board) remains important, if only for the selective examination of programs it provides; for the questioning of intelligence officers on enough things to keep people more honest; for its latent capacity to punish those who do violate their oath of office, if only by embarrassing them in the public light of investigative hearings; and for the guidance that overseers can give to bureaucrats about what the public expects from its intelligence agencies. As former DCI Robert Gates has observed, "Some awfully crazy schemes might well have been approved had everyone present [in the White House] not known and expected hard questions, debate, and criticism from the Hill. And when, on a few occasions, Congress was kept in the dark, and such schemes did proceed, it was nearly always to the lasting regret of the Presidents involved."[55] The current DCI concurs. "I dare say the CIA receives more oversight from the Congress than any other agency in the federal government," George Tenet stated. "This is not a complaint. In fact, this oversight is our most vital and direct link to the American people—a source of strength that separates us from all other countries of the world."[56]

The success of democracy will continue to depend on these checks, along with an equally indispensable ingredient, the attitudes of people in high office. One of the most thoughtful DCIs, the late William Colby, expressed a sense of optimism about the new era of intelligence accountability that came to pass on his watch.

> With today's supervision, and with the command structure trying to keep things straight, the people in CIA know what they should do and what they should not do—as distinct from the fifties, in which there were no particular rules. If CIA people today are told to violate their limits, or if they are tempted to violate those limits, one of the junior officers will surely raise that question and tell the command structure, and, if not satisfied there, he will tell the Congress, and, if not satisfied there, he will tell the press, and that is the way you control it.[57]

The Iran-contra scandal erupted not long after these words were recorded, reminding the nation how important a personal commitment to law and integrity is to those who govern.

A cause for celebration in America's experiment with intelligence accountability is the fact that the overwhelming majority of those who serve in the intelligence agencies are men and women of enormous talent and integrity, among the best anywhere in public service or in the private sector. Jefferson's eternal vigilance will remain necessary, though, because inevitably in any organization, a few will lack honor. They will dismiss the rule of law, the philosophy of power sharing, and the principle of accountability.

Scholars and practitioners are likely to carry on the debate about the proper degree of supervision over the hidden side of America's government. Proponents of meaningful accountability will cite Madison, Jefferson, and Brandeis; opponents, Jefferson again (this time his unchecked use of covert action in simpler days), the *Curtiss-Wright* case, and the Machiavellian perspectives of Admiral John Poindexter's testimony during the Iran-contra hearings. Proponents will warn of Big Brother intrusion at home and against tampering with democratic regimes abroad; opponents will point to the paralysis that accompanies legislative micromanagement, and the foolishness of turning the CIA into a nunnery.

The champions of oversight want reliable safeguards to preserve liberty; its critics seek more effective secret operations to shield the United States from enemies at home and abroad. The rub comes from this obvious conclusion: the nation wants and deserves both civil liberties and a shield against foreign dangers. So the search continues to find the right formula for power sharing in this most difficult of government domains—knowing full well that no formula exists, only the hope that in a spirit of comity, the Congress, the executive, and the courts will carry on the quest for a modus vivendi that takes into account liberty and security.

# America's Intelligence Leadership, 1941–2000

## Coordinator of Information and Director of Strategic Services

1941–45    William J. Donovan

## Directors of Central Intelligence

1946    Sidney W. Souers
1946–47    Lieutenant General Hoyt S. Vanderberg
1947–50    Rear Admiral Roscoe H. Hillenkoetter
1950–53    General Walter Bedell Smith
1953–61    Allen W. Dulles
1961–65    John A. McCone
1965–66    Vice Admiral William F. Raborn Jr.
1966–73    Richard Helms
1973    James R. Schlesinger
1973–76    William E. Colby
1976–77    George H. W. Bush
1977–81    Admiral Stansfield Turner
1981–87    William J. Casey
1987–91    William H. Webster
1991–93    Robert M. Gates
1993–95    R. James Woolsey
1995–97    John M. Deutch
1997–    George J. Tenet

## Chairs, U.S. Senate Select Committee on Intelligence

| | |
|---|---|
| 1976–77 | Daniel K. Inouye, Democrat, Hawaii |
| 1977–81 | Birch Bayh, Democrat, Indiana |
| 1981–85 | Barry Goldwater, Republican, Arizona |
| 1985–87 | David Durenberger, Republican, Minnesota |
| 1987–93 | David L. Boren, Democrat, Oklahoma |
| 1993–95 | Dennis DeConcini, Democrat, Arizona |
| 1995–97 | Arlan Specter, Republican, Pennsylvania |
| 1997– | Richard C. Shelby, Republican, Alabama |

## Chairs, House Permanent Select Committee on Intelligence

| | |
|---|---|
| 1977–85 | Edward P. Boland, Democrat, Massachusetts |
| 1985–87 | Lee H. Hamilton, Democrat, Indiana |
| 1987–89 | Louis Stokes, Democrat, Ohio |
| 1989–91 | Anthony C. Beilenson, Democrat, California |
| 1991–93 | Dave McCurdy, Democrat, Oklahoma |
| 1993–95 | Dan Glickman, Democrat, Kansas |
| 1995–97 | Larry Combest, Republican, Texas |
| 1997– | Porter Goss, Republican, Florida |

# NOTES

## Notes to the Introduction

1. My notes on President Bill Clinton's remarks to the CIA, Langley, VA, July 14, 1995.

2. Remark at the National Intelligence and Technology Symposium, CIA, Langley, VA, November 6, 1998.

3. Remark to me, Washington, DC, November 7, 1998.

4. This list is from presentations by senior intelligence officers at the National Intelligence and Technology Symposium.

5. John Millis, staff director, U.S. House Permanent Select Committee on Intelligence, speech to the Central Intelligence Retirees Association (CIRA), October 5, 1998.

6. William E. Burrows and Robert Windrem, *Critical Mass: The Dangerous Race for Superweapons in a Fragmenting World* (New York: Simon & Schuster, 1994), 26.

7. Millis, speech.

8. Interview, Washington, DC, November 7, 1998. All interviews were conducted by me unless otherwise noted.

9. Phyllis Oakley, director, Intelligence and Research, Department of State, remarks at the National Intelligence and Technology Symposium, italics in original.

10. The 35 percent increase in the DI's travel funds authorized by the CIA in 1999 so that more analysts could visit "their country" more frequently is a step in the right direction. But this budget needs to be doubled in order to ensure that analysts throughout the Agency have up-to-date language skills and knowledge of events overseas.

## Notes to Chapter 1

1. Robert M. Gates, remarks at the Conference on U.S. Intelligence, Langley, VA, June 11, 1984, and, while serving as director of Central Intelligence, remarks to the Economic Club of Detroit, April 13, 1992.

2. Robert M. Gates, "In War, Mistakes Happen," *New York Times*, May 12, 1999, A27.

3. Loch K. Johnson, "Reinventing the CIA: Strategic Intelligence and the End of the Cold War," in Randall B. Ripley and James M. Lindsay, eds., *U.S. Foreign Policy after the Cold War* (Pittsburgh: University of Pittsburgh Press, 1997), 152.

4. See Abraham H. Maslow, *Motivation and Personality* (New York: Harper & Row, 1987).

5. Anthony Lake, *Managing Complexity in U.S. Foreign Policy* (Washington, DC: U.S. Department of State, Bureau of Public Affairs, March 14, 1978), 1.

6. U.S. Department of State, Bureau of Public Affairs, *Fundamentals of U.S. Foreign Policy* (Washington, DC: U.S. Department of State, Bureau of Public Affairs, March 1988), 1.

7. Joseph S. Nye Jr., "Redefining National Security," *Foreign Affairs* 78 (July/August 1999): 35.

8. See Michael Mastanduno, "Economics and Security in Statecraft and Scholarship," *International Organization* 4 (Autumn 1998): 825–54.

9. Samuel P. Huntington, "The Erosion of American National Interests," *Foreign Affairs* 76 (September/October 1997): 28–49.

10. Mickey Kantor, quoted in "Cool Winds from the White House," *Economist*, March 27, 1993, 58.

11. R. James Woolsey, "World Threat Assessment Brief," Statement for the record, *Hearings*, U.S. Senate Select Committee on Intelligence, 104th Cong., 1st sess., January 10, 1995, 8.

12. Daniel Williams and John M. Goshko, "Reduced U.S. World Role Outlined but Soon Altered," *Washington Post*, May 26, 1993, A1.

13. Louis Freeh, "Economic Espionage," testimony, *Hearings*, U.S. Senate Select Committee on Intelligence, 104th Cong., 2d sess., February 28, 1996.

14. Pietro S. Nivola, "American Trade Policy after the Cold War," in Ripley and Lindsay, *U.S. Foreign Policy after the Cold War*, 249.

15. Ibid., 254.

16. See, for example, Jeffrey E. Garten, *A Cold Peace: America, Japan, Germany, and the Struggle for Supremacy* (New York: Times Books, 1992); and Edward N. Luttwak, *The Endangered American Dream* (New York: Simon & Schuster, 1993).

17. Thomas L. Friedman, "A Manifesto for the Fast World," *New York Times Magazine*, March 28, 1999, 43.

18. The usual precedence of military over economic matters can also be seen in America's reaction to the theft by foreigners of U.S. military and economic se-

crets. Discovery of the former stirs an outrage, as when Jonathan Pollard of the Office of Naval Intelligence passed highly classified military documents to Israeli intelligence in the 1980s and when a Chinese American scientist at the Los Alamos labs was thought to have provided the Chinese government with U.S. nuclear-weapons designs in the 1990s. Yet when French intelligence infiltrated American aerospace firms, when Israeli intelligence penetrated Recon/Optical (an Illinois company that manufactures satellite cameras), and when South Korean intelligence targeted the acquisition of microwave technology used in the F-16 fighter, the American response was in each case little more than a slap on the wrist. See Duncan L. Clarke and Robert Johnston, "Economic Espionage and Interallied Strategic Cooperation," *Thunderbird International Business Review* 40 (July/August 1998): 413–31. The authors point out that nations involved in economic espionage against one another also seek mutual assistance with respect to such transnational threats as terrorism, nuclear proliferation, and organized crime; therefore, they are prepared to accept some level of economic spying directed against them, even by allies, in return for cooperation on these greater dangers of strategic security.

19. See the polling data in John E. Rielly, ed., *American Public Opinion and U.S. Foreign Policy 1991* (Chicago: Chicago Council on Foreign Relations, 1991), 15; and John E. Rielly, "Americans and the World: A Survey at Century's End," *Foreign Policy* 114 (Spring 1999): 101.

20. Mary E. Wilson, "Infectious Diseases: An Ecological Perspective," *British Medical Journal*, December 23, 1995, 1681–84.

21. C. R. Neu, national intelligence officer for economics, "Comments on Economic Intelligence," Institute for International Economics, April 25, 1995, 5.

22. Nye, "Redefining National Security," 24. Scholars of international relations also use the dichotomy of "high" and "low" politics in reference to hard and soft power, respectively.

23. Anthony Lewis, "When We Could Believe," *New York Times*, June 12, 1987, A31.

24. Michael Wines, "Two Views of Inhumanity Split the World, Even in Victory," *New York Times*, June 13, 1999, sec. 4, p. 1.

25. See Craig R. Whitney, "Fewer Bombs Fall on a Cloudy Day in Balkan Battle," *New York Times*, April 12, 1999, A10; David E. Rosenbaum, "U.S. Official Calls Tallies of Kosovo Slain Too Low," *New York Times*, April 19, 1999, A10; and David Stout, "U.S. Photos Show Ground Work at Suspected Site of Mass Grave," *New York Times*, June 10, 1999, A18.

26. On the use of Jstars, see Edmund L. Andrews, "Aboard Advanced Radar Flight, U.S. Watches Combat Zone," *New York Times*, June 14, 1999, A12.

27. Interview with an Apache pilot in Kosovo, National Public Radio, July 7, 1999.

28. George J. Tenet, quoted by Tim Weiner, "U.S. Spy Agencies Find Scant Peril on Horizon," *New York Times,* January 29, 1998, A3.

29. Michael Wines, "Straining to See the Real Russia," *New York Times*, May 2, 1999, sec. 4, p. 1.

30. George J. Tenet, statement, *Hearings*, U.S. Senate Armed Services Committee, 106th Cong., 1st sess., February 2, 1999, 2.

31. Indeed, ironically U.S. officials explicitly informed the Indian government about the timing of U.S. satellite coverage for South Asia in hopes of impressing on them the futility of trying to conceal test activity. But even without this unintended assistance, the Indians could no doubt have figured out the cycles for themselves. On the ease with which even amateurs can follow the orbits of U.S. spy satellites, see Vernon Loeb, "Hobbyists Track Down Spies in Sky," *Washington Post*, February 20, 1999, A1.

32. Interviews with senior intelligence officials in the DCI Nonproliferation Center and the DCI Crime and Narcotics Center, Central Intelligence Agency, Langley, VA, June 14 and 15, 1999. According to the DCI's special assistant for nonproliferation, eight to ten nations are "key proliferators," and another sixty to seventy warrant close watch for suspected activities in this area. On the North Korean missile threat, see James Risen, "C.I.A. Sees a North Korean Missile Threat," *New York Times*, February 3, 1999, A6; and on attempts by the Russian mafia and former KGB agents to sell guided missiles, plutonium for bombs, Semtex explosives, and other armaments, see *Observer*, September 11, 1994, 6. For an example of North Korean weapons sales abroad (including the 500-kilometer-range Scud-C missiles to Iran and Syria and the 1,000-kilometer-range Nodong 1 missile to Libya), see "U.S., Russian Intelligence Agencies Offer Proliferation Assessments," *Arms Control Today* 23 (March 1993): 21.

33. Rielly, "Americans and the World," 101.

34. *The Chemical and Biological Warfare Threat*, undated and without attribution (although with all the earmarks of a CIA publication and probably printed in 1995, the year it was distributed to various agencies and congressional committees in Washington, DC).

35. R. James Woolsey, testimony, *Hearings*, U.S. Senate Select Committee on Intelligence, 103d Cong., 2d sess., March 6, 1993.

36. Mary Anne Weaver, "The Real bin Laden," *New Yorker*, January 24, 2000, 36. Weaver reports that the missiles hit facilities in the area belonging to Inter-Services Intelligence or ISI, the Pakistani intelligence agency, killing five officers and twenty trainees and enraging the Pakistani government.

37. A still more embarrassing mistake as the twentieth century wound down was not in the proliferation field but the flawed targeting instructions supplied by the U.S. intelligence community that led to the NATO bombing of the Chinese embassy in Belgrade. This appalling error led comedian Jay Leno to suggest a new meaning for the acronym CIA: "Can't Identify Anything." The accidental killing of ISI intelligence personnel in Pakistan (see the preceding note) was an equally serious error, though less visible to the general public.

38. The CIA continues to maintain it has solid evidence that Empta was in fact being made and that the plant in question had ties to the terrorist Osama bin Laden. The Agency refuses to provide proof to the public, however, on grounds that its modus operandi would be compromised for future operations (interviews with senior intelligence officers, Langley, VA, February 18 and June 15, 1999). Other government "officials" suggested to a reporter, however, that the plant "was probably making nothing more dangerous than pharmaceuticals," Daniel Schorr, "Washington Notebook," *New Leader*, May 17–31, 1999, 5.

39. John Lauder, director, DCI Nonproliferation Center, comment at Oxford University, Oxford, September 26, 1999.

40. George J. Tenet, remarks at annual dinner, Nashua (NH) Chamber of Commerce, June 28, 1999, 5.

41. This statistic is derived from my interviews with senior intelligence officials, Central Intelligence Agency, June 14 and 15, 1999, and comments by the director of the DCI Nonproliferation Center.

42. Interview with Gates, Washington, DC, March 28, 1994.

43. See William E. Burrows and Robert Windrem, *Critical Mass: The Dangerous Race for Superweapons in a Fragmentary World* (New York: Simon & Schuster, 1994).

44. Judith Miller with William J. Broad, "Iranians, Bioweapons in Mind, Lure Needy Ex-Soviet Scientists," *New York Times*, December 8, 1998, A1.

45. Special assistant to the DCI for nonproliferation, "Worldwide WMD Threat," *Statement for the Record*, Commission to Assess the Organization of the Federal Government to Combat the Proliferation of Weapons of Mass Destruction, April 29, 1999, 2, 3.

46. According to a high-ranking former CIA official, comment at Oxford University, Oxford, September 25, 1999.

47. Special assistant to the DCI for nonproliferation, Statement on the World Wide Biological Warfare Threat, *Hearings*, U.S. House Permanent Select Committee on Intelligence, 106th Cong., 1st sess., March 3, 1999, 4.

48. The Deutch commission on proliferation, quoted by Walter Pincus, "U.S. Preparedness Faulted," *Washington Post*, July 9, 1999, A2.

49. David Johnston, "Finding Spies Is the Easy Part," *New York Times*, May 23, 1999, E4.

50. Tim Weiner, "Opponents Find That Ousting Hussein Is Easier Said Than Done," *New York Times*, November 16, 1998, A10; and Jane Perlez, "Albright Says Hussein's Foes Are Building Unified Front," *New York Times*, May 25, 1999, A4.

51. Interview with UN officials, New York City, May 26, 1999.

52. Interview at Central Intelligence Agency, Langley, VA June 15, 1999.

53. Comment at Oxford University, Oxford, September 25, 1999.

54. Interview with R. James Woolsey, Central Intelligence Agency, Langley, VA September 29, 1993.

55. Interview with the NPC director, Central Intelligence Agency, Langley, VA, July 8, 1993.

## Notes to Chapter 2

1. Samuel D. Porteous, "Looking out for Economic Interests: An Increased Role for Intelligence," *Washington Quarterly* 19 (1996): 192.

2. A survey of key policy agencies conducted by the Bush administration, to clarify the government's projected intelligence needs between 1991 and 2005, foreshadowed the rising interest in economic intelligence; National Security Council, *National Security Review Directive no. 29* (Washington, DC: National Security Council, November 1991).

3. David M. Kennedy, "Sunshine and Shadow: The CIA and the Soviet Economy," Case Program no. C16-91-1096.0, John F. Kennedy School of Government (Cambridge, MA: Harvard University, 1991), 2.

4. Kristen Lundberg, "CIA and the Fall of the Soviet Empire: The Politics of 'Getting It Right,'" Case Program no. C16-94-1251.0, John F. Kennedy School of Government (Cambridge, MA: Harvard University, 1991).

5. See Commission on the Roles and Capabilities of the U.S. Intelligence Community, "Preparing for the 21st Century: An Appraisal of U.S. Intelligence," *Report* (Washington, DC: U.S. Government Printing Office, March 1, 1996), 88 (hereafter cited as the Aspin-Brown commission). Intelligence community information derived from open sources and provided to private firms (usually through intermediaries like the Department of Commerce) is commonly referred to as "business intelligence."

6. Harold Brown, comment at a public meeting of the Aspin-Brown commission, Washington, DC, January 19, 1996.

7. Statement provided to me by the DCI's Office of Congressional Affairs, Langley, VA, February 7, 1995. Robert M. Gates's and R. James Woolsey's reaf-

firmations may be found, respectively, in Gates, remarks to the Economic Club of Detroit, April 13, 1992, 9; Woolsey, "The Future of Intelligence on the Global Frontier," address to the Executive Club of Chicago, November 19, 1993; Woolsey, testimony, U.S. Senate Select Committee on Intelligence, February 2, 1993.

8. Quoted by Gates in remark to the Economic Club of Detroit, 6. Hale said to the British, who were about to hang him for espionage in 1776, "I only regret that I have but one life to lose for my country."

9. On the involvement of other nations in industrial espionage, see Mike Frost and Michel Gratton, *Spyworld: Inside the Canadian and American Establishments* (Toronto: Doubleday, 1994), 224–27; American Institute for Business Research, *Protecting Corporate America's Secrets in the Global Economy* (Washington, DC: American Institute for Business Research, 1992), 41, 45; Craig Whitney, "German Finds That Spies Are Still Doing Business," *New York Times*, September 9, 1993, 1; and Randall M. Fort, "Economic Espionage: Problems and Prospects," *Consortium for the Study of Intelligence* (Washington, DC: Georgetown University, 1993), 3.

10. See Stansfield Turner, "Intelligence for a New World Order," *Foreign Affairs* 70 (Fall 1991): 151–52. Then-chairman of the Senate Select Committee on Intelligence, David L. Boren (D, Oklahoma) endorsed this view as well; see his "The Intelligence Community: How Crucial?" *Foreign Affairs* 71 (Summer 1992): 58. In the early 1970s, the President's Foreign Intelligence Advisory Board (PFIAB) also advocated U.S. industrial espionage. See Maurice C. Ernst, "Economic Intelligence in CIA," *Studies in Intelligence* 28 (Winter 1984): 1–22, reprinted in H. Bradford Westerfield, ed., *Inside CIA's Private World* (New Haven, CT: Yale University Press, 1995).

11. Interviews with senior officials in the Departments of State and Commerce, June 24, 1999; see also John Maggs, "From Swords to Plowshares," *Journal of Commerce*, August 18, 1995, 1.

12. Robert M. Gates, testimony, U.S. House Judiciary Committee, Subcommittee on Economic and Commercial Law, 102d Cong., 2d sess., April 29, 1992.

13. See the statistics in S.1556, 104th Cong., 2d sess., January 2, 1996, reported by Edwin Fraumann (an FBI official), "Economic Espionage: Security Missions Redefined," *Public Administration Review* 57 (July/August 1997): 303.

14. The survey was published by the American Society for Industrial Security in 1996 and reported in John J. Fialka, "Stealing the Spark: Why Economic Espionage Works in America," *Washington Quarterly* 19 (1996): 180.

15. U.S. House Select Committee on U.S. National Security and Military/Commercial Concerns with the People's Republic of China, *Report*, 106th

Cong., 1st sess. (Washington, DC: U.S. Government Printing Office, May 1999).

16. Duncan L. Clarke and Robert Johnston, "Economic Espionage and Interallied Strategic Cooperation," *Thunderbird International Business Review* 40 (July/August 1998): 415.

17. Fraumann, "Economic Espionage: Security Missions Redefined," 308.

18. Quoted in "Votre Secrets, Monsieur?" *Security Management,* October 1992, and cited by Merrill E. Whitney and James D. Gaisford, "Economic Espionage as Strategic Trade Policy," *Canadian Journal of Economics* 29 (April 1996): 627.

19. Fort, "Economic Espionage: Problems and Prospects"; Fraumann, "Economic Espionage: Security Missions Redefined," 308. The Overseas Security Advising Agency at the Department of State also helps U.S. businesses with their security needs abroad.

20. Fraumann, "Economic Espionage: Security Missions Redefined," 306.

21. 18 U.S.C., secs. 1831–39.

22. Jeff Gerth and David E. Sanger, "Citing Security, U.S. Spurns China on a Satellite Deal," *New York Times,* February 23, 1999, A1. The Clinton administration subsequently allowed the sale.

23. Gregory F. Treverton, "Intelligence since Cold War's End," in Report of the Twentieth Century Fund Task Force on the Future of U.S. Intelligence, *In from the Cold* (New York: Twentieth Century Fund Press, 1996), 115.

24. Woolsey, "World Threat Assessment Brief," Statement for the record, *Hearings,* U.S. Senate Select Committee on Intelligence, 104th Cong., 1st sess., January 10, 1995, 9.

25. C. R. Neu, national intelligence officer for economics, "Comments on Economic Intelligence" (Washington, DC: Institute for International Economics, April 25, 1995), 2.

26. On this hostility, see Michael Wines, "Straining to See the Real Russia," *New York Times,* May 2, 1999, 1, sec. 4.

27. Nicholas D. Kristof and Sheryl WuDunn, "Of World Markets, None an Island," *New York Times,* February 17, 1999, A9.

28. The poll was conducted by the Russian newspaper *Izvestiya* (January 23, 1998) and provided to me during an interview with the director of the DCI Crime and Narcotics Center, Central Intelligence Agency, Langley, VA, June 21, 1999.

29. "The struggle of the last half century was to defeat Communism," Representative James A. Leach (R, Iowa) observed in an op-ed piece on international criminal activity emanating from Russia, "the challenge in the years ahead will be

to constrain corruption"; "The New Russian Menace," *New York Times*, September 10, 1999, A27.

30. For a catalog of the staggering range of international criminal activity directed toward the United States and its allies, see the White House report entitled *International Crime Control Strategy*, May 1998.

31. Interview with CNC director, CIA Headquarters, Langley, VA, June 14, 1999. Not everyone is so sanguine about CIA-FBI relations. "It's like that book on male-female relations," suggests a former high-level CIA official. "One agency is from Venus, the other from Mars. They just don't get along." Comment at Oxford University, September 25, 1999.

32. Ambassador Robert D. Blackwill, former NSC staffer for European and Soviet affairs, interviewed by Jack Davis, "A Policymaker's Perspective on Intelligence Analysis," *Studies in Intelligence* (Summer 1994): 3.

33. Remarks at the conference Does America Need the CIA? Gerald R. Ford Library, Ann Arbor, MI, November 19, 1997, 3–4.

34. Porteous, "Looking out for Economic Interests," 199. For ample documentation of this institutional jealousy during recent international financial crises, see Philip Zelikow, "American Intelligence and the World Economy," in *In from the Cold*, 137–262; and Ernest R. May, "Intelligence: Backing into the Future," *Foreign Affairs* 48 (Summer 1994): 63–72.

35. Porteous, "Looking out for Economic Interests," 199.

36. Neu, 2–3.

37. According to Neu; see ibid., 3.

38. R. James Woolsey, during a question-and-answer period following his address, "The Future Direction of Intelligence" (Washington, DC: Center for Strategic and International Studies, July 18, 1994).

39. Aspin-Brown commission, 23. Intelligence officials claim to have uncovered bribes affecting $30 billion in foreign contracts between 1992 and 1995. See James Risen, "Clinton Reportedly Orders CIA to Focus on Trade Espionage," *Los Angeles Times*, July 23, 1995, A14.

40. Treverton, "Intelligence since Cold War's End," 115.

41. Quoted by David E. Sanger and Tim Weiner, "Emerging Role for the C.I.A.: Economic Spy," *New York Times*, October 15, 1995, A1.

42. Interview with an official in the Office of U.S. Trade Representative, Washington, DC, August 22, 1997.

43. See Maggs, "From Swords to Plowshares"; Sanger and Weiner, "Emerging Role for the C.I.A."

44. Sanger and Weiner, "Emerging Role for the C.I.A.," A1. On the importance of NSA signals intelligence in reportedly gaining a $6 billion contract from

Saudi Arabia against European competitors, see Ian Traynor, "Bridge of Spies," *Guardian*, March 26, 1997, 2–3.

45. Sanger and Weiner, "Emerging Role for the C.I.A."

46. Jane Perlez, "Clinton Pushes for Treaty to Ban the Worst Child Labor Practices," *New York Times*, June 17, 1999, A17.

47. Woolsey, "World Threat Assessment Brief," 10.

48. Interview with the CNC director, June 14, 1999.

49. Ibid.

50. On Haiti's growing prominence in the cocaine trade, see Larry Rohter, "Haiti Paralysis Brings a Boom in Drug Trade," *New York Times*, October 27, 1998, A1.

51. Interview with CNC director, June 14, 1999.

52. Loch K. Johnson, "Smart Intelligence," *Foreign Policy* 89 (Winter 1992/93): 53–70.

53. This profile of drug users is based on remarks made by a government drug enforcement expert (at the time, the top aide to drug czar William Bennett), Senior Conference, U.S. Military Academy, June 9, 1990, West Point, NY. More recently, the current director of the Office of National Drug Control Policy, General Barry R. McCaffrey, noted that the "typical drug user is not poor and unemployed" and that in 1997, young adults, men, whites, and those with less than a high school education were more likely to use drugs than other workers. AP report, *New York Times*, September 9, 1999, 19.

54. Christopher S. Wren, "A Purer, More Potent Heroin Lures New Users to a Long, Hard Fall," *New York Times*, May 9, 1999, 27.

55. David Broder, "To Win the War on Drugs," *Washington Post*, May 2, 1999, B7.

56. Interview, Langley, VA June 21–24, 1999.

57. Ibid.

58. Ibid.

59. Interview with Bo Cutter, Washington, DC June 26, 1995.

60. Ibid.

61. Interviews with senior intelligence officers, Langley, VA, February 18, 1999.

62. Testimony, *Hearings*, U.S. Senate Foreign Relations Committee, 103d Cong., 1st sess., November 4, 1993.

63. Quoted by John M. Broder, "President's Sober Response Assures Public of Counterespionage Measures," *New York Times*, May 26, 1999, A15.

64. Highly placed policymakers are frequently unaware of the intelligence origins of information they receive in staff briefings and government reports. As a result, they may blithely dismiss the secret agencies as largely unhelpful, whereas

the deputy assistant secretaries who actually read the intelligence reports often have a more charitable view.

65. May, "Intelligence: Backing into the Future," 65.

## Notes to Chapter 3

1. See Thomas Homer-Dixon, "On the Threshold: Environmental Changes as Acute Causes of Conflict," *International Security* 16 (Fall 1991): 76–116; and his "Environmental Scarcities and Conflicts: Evidence from Cases," *International Security* 19 (Summer 1994): 5–40; Marc Levy, "Is the Environment a National Security Issue," *International Security* 20 (Fall 1995): 35–62; Thomas Homer-Dixon and Marc Levy, "Correspondence: Environment and Security," *International Security* 20 (Winter 1995/96): 189–98. See also the excellent study by David D. Dabelko and Geoffrey D. Dabelko, "The International Environment and the U.S. Intelligence Community," *International Journal of Intelligence and Counterintelligence* 6 (Spring 1993): 21–42.

2. Interview with DS&T scientist, CIA, Langley, VA, January 24, 1996.

3. Quoted in Loch K. Johnson, "Smart Intelligence," *Foreign Policy* 89 (Winter 1992/93): 59.

4. Matthew Paterson and Michael Grubb, "The International Politics of Climate Change," *International Affairs* 68 (1992): 296.

5. Mostafa K. Tolba with Iwona Rummel-Bulska, *Global Environmental Diplomacy: Negotiating Environmental Agreements for the World, 1973–1992* (Cambridge, MA: MIT Press, 1998), 13–14.

6. This quotation is from the report of a research group consisting of members of the U.S National Academy of Sciences and its counterpart institutions from Israel, Jordan, and the Palestinian Authority, cited in William A. Orme Jr., "International Study on Water in Mideast Leads to a Warning," *New York Times,* March 3, 1999, A9.

7. Tolba and Rummel-Bulska, *Global Environmental Diplomacy*, 15.

8. These observations on Haiti's ecological conditions are based on an interview with a former CIA analyst who covered the Caribbean, Washington, DC, June 5, 1997.

9. Stephen Kinzer, "Where Kurds Seek a Land, Turks Want the Water," *New York Times*, February 28, 1999, E3.

10. Interview with NSA official, Washington, DC, September 26, 1996.

11. Tolba and Rummel-Bulska, *Global Environmental Diplomacy*, 100.

12. Dr. Sherwood Rowland, public lecture, University of Georgia, Athens, March 19, 1999.

13. This summary draws on interviews with intelligence officials, Washington, DC, September 26–28, 1996.

14. Interview with senior intelligence analyst, CIA, Langley, VA, February 18, 1999.

15. For details on the key agreements, see Tolba and Rummel-Bulska, *Global Environmental Diplomacy;* Stephen Hopgood, *American Foreign Environmental Policy and the Power of the State* (New York: Oxford University Press, 1998); and Jessica T. Matthews, "Preserving the Global Environment," in Eugene R. Wittkopf, ed., *The Future of American Foreign Policy,* 2d ed. (New York: St. Martin's Press, 1994), 108–16.

16. This list draws on interviews with intelligence officials, September 26–28, 1996; the 900 figure is from an unclassified intelligence report entitled "Global Trends 2010" National Intelligence Council, Langley, VA November 1997.

17. Interview with senior EPA official, Washington, DC, September 27, 1997.

18. Interview, Washington, DC, September 27, 1997.

19. Interview with senior DS&T manager, Langley, VA, February 20, 1999.

20. See William J. Broad, "U.S. Will Deploy Its Spy Satellites on Nature Mission," *New York Times,* November 27, 1995, A1; and Tim Beardsley, "Environmental Secrets: MEDEA Brings Intelligence in from the Cold," *Scientific American* 273 (July 1995): 28–30.

21. Interviews with DS&T personnel, September 26–28, 1996; and Beardsley, "Environmental Secrets."

22. The United States has no national fire detection capability, despite spending $600,000 a year to control fires on federal lands.

23. These advantages are highlighted in an unclassified document given to me by the Directorate of Science and Technology, entitled "ETF Fiscal Year 1993 Experiments Summary" (unpaginated and undated but probably 1994).

24. Ibid.

25. Robert Wright, "Private Eyes," *New York Times Magazine,* September 5, 1999, 52, 54.

26. Interview, CIA, Langley, VA, February 18, 1999.

27. National Intelligence Council, "The Environmental Outlook in Russia," *Intelligence Community Assessment,* ICA 98-08 (January 1999): 33–35.

28. Edward O. Wilson, *The Diversity of Life* (New York: Penguin Books, 1994).

29. Tolba and Rummel-Bulska, *Global Environmental Diplomacy,* 182.

30. Remarks at National Intelligence and Technology Symposium, CIA, Langley, VA, November 6, 1998.

31. See the Rockefeller commission's report (Washington, DC: U.S. Gov-

ernment Printing Office, 1975), 230–31. This commission noted that intelligence imagery of U.S. locations has been used "for such diverse civilian projects as mapping, assessing natural disasters such as hurricane and tornado damage and the Santa Barbara, California, oil spill, conducting route surveys for the Alaska pipeline, conducting national forest inventories, determining the extent of snow cover in the Sierras to facilitate the forecast of runoff and detecting crop blight in the Plains States." The commission found no impropriety in permitting the civilian use of aerial photography systems, though it balked at using intelligence imagery to detect areas of high concentrations of industrial pollutants in the air and water. The concern was that these data might then be used in a criminal action against polluters—a law enforcement activity beyond the intelligence community's mandate. (Based on this same reasoning, the CIA turned down a request from the Treasury Department to help locate moonshine stills in North Carolina using the infrared photography of spy satellites, another domain of law enforcement.)

32. Interview, Washington, DC, July 14, 1994.

33. Two that have been declassified and placed into the public domain are the National Intelligence Council's "Environmental Outlook in Russia," 1–35; and "The Environmental Outlook in Central and Eastern Europe," *Intelligence Community Assessment*, ICA 96-08D (December 1997): 1–33. These reports are good illustrations of the intelligence community's often well-crafted products, whose four-color graphs, sophisticated charts, and maps (even occasional centerfolds featuring, say, a photograph of earthquake damage in an urban locale), along with readable, magazinelike prose, have attracted widespread praise in the upper reaches of the government—even if the analysis itself is incorrect from time to time. The reports also provide an unclassified demonstration of the ways in which sophisticated imagery can be helpful in the public domain without jeopardizing sources and methods, through the technique of converting the photographs into simplified but still useful artist's depictions of the more detailed photographic data captured by the camera's lens.

34. NIC, "Environmental Outlook in Russia," 1.

35. Interviews with policymakers in the EPA, NSC, and State Department, Washington, DC, July and August 1995.

36. Interview, Washington, DC, July 15, 1994.

37. Interview, Washington, DC, July 16, 1994.

38. Interview, Washington, DC, July 15, 1994.

39. See Kim A. McDonald, "NASA Satellites May 'Revolutionize' Earth Sciences," *Chronicle of Higher Education*, July 9, 1999, A20, A22.

40. Interview, Washington, DC, July 15, 1994.

## Notes to Chapter 4

1. Intelligence Authorization Act for Fiscal Year 1995, PL 103-359, sec. 903(b)(2), signed by the president on October 14, 1994.

2. For arguments to this effect, see Laurie Garrett, *The Coming Plague: Newly Emerging Diseases in a World out of Balance* (New York: Farrar, Straus & Giroux, 1994); Frank Ryan, *Virus X: Tracking the New Killer Plagues* (Boston: Little, Brown, 1997); Thomas Homer-Dixon, "Environmental Scarcity, Mass Violence, and the Limits to Ingenuity," *Current History* 95 (November 1996): 359–65; Thomas Homer-Dixon and Valerie Percival, *Environmental Security and Violent Conflict* (Toronto: University of Toronto Press, 1996); Dennis Pirages, "Microsecurity: Disease Organisms and Human Well-Being," *Washington Quarterly* 18 (Fall 1995): 5–12; C. F. Ronnfeldt, "Three Generations of Environment and Security Research," *Journal of Peace Research* 34 (November 1997): 473–82; and Jessica T. Matthews, "Power Shift," *Foreign Affairs* 76 (January/February 1997): 50–66.

3. Pirages, "Microsecurity," 11. Another expert reminds us that "because diseases have been the biggest killers of people, they have also been decisive shapers of history"; Jared Diamond, *Guns, Germs, and Steel: The Fate of Human Societies* (New York: Norton, 1997): 197. On the military front, Colonel Gerard Schumeyer, director of the Armed Forces Medical Intelligence Center, writes that "the medical threat may be the most serious threat to future [U.S. military] operational deployments"; "Medical Intelligence: Making a Difference," *American Intelligence Journal* 17 (1996): 11.

4. Quoted by Walter Pincus, "Military Espionage Cuts Eyed," *Washington Post*, March 17, 1995, A6.

5. National Science and Technology Council, Office of Science and Technology Policy, Executive Office of the President, *The National Security Science and Technology Strategy* (Washington, DC: U.S. Government Printing Office, 1996), 55.

6. Ibid., foreword by President Bill Clinton, unpaginated.

7. Diane C. Snyder, interview with a senior officer in the CIA's Directorate of Science and Technology, shared with me, Washington, DC, November 1994.

8. On the threat of global disease, see Garrett, *The Coming Plague*; Robin Marantz Henig, *A Dancing Matrix: Voyages along the Viral Frontier* (New York: Knopf, 1993); and Schumeyer, "Medical Intelligence," 11–15. A useful web site on this subject is Program for Monitoring Emerging Diseases (ProMED), Federation of American Scientists, at http://www.fas.org/pub/genfas/promed.

9. C. A. Hart and S. Kariuki, "Antimicrobial Resistance in Developing Countries," *British Medical Journal* 317 (1998): 647.

10. For a recent study on one of these dangers, see Susan E. Robertson, Barbara P. Hull, Oyewale Tornori, Okwo Bele, James W. LeDuc, and Karin Esteves, "Yellow Fever: A Decade of Reemergence," *Journal of the American Medical Association*, October 9, 1996, 1157–62.

11. Sheryl Gay Stolberg, "DDT, Target of Global Ban, Finds Defenders in Experts on Malaria," *New York Times*, August 29, 1999, A1, A6.

12. Associated Press, "Fatal Virus in Malaysia Confounds U.S. Scientists," *Atlanta Journal and Constitution*, April 9, 1999, A4.

13. World Health Organization, "Emerging and Other Communicable Diseases (EMC)," http://www.who.ch/programmes/emc/news.htm, October 2, 1996; see also Sharon Begley, "Commandos of Viral Combat," *Newsweek*, May 22, 1995, 48–54.

14. This estimate is from travel to the United States in 1993, calculated by Work Activity Data System, Plant Protection and Quarantine, APHIS-USDA, Hyattsville, MD, cited in Corrie C. Brown and Barrett D. Slenning, "Impact and Risk of Foreign Animal Diseases," *Journal of the American Veterinary Medical Association* 208 (1996): 1039.

15. Ryan, *Virus X*, 9, 359.

16. *The National Security Science and Technology Strategy*, 43.

17. Commission on the Roles and Capabilities of the United States Intelligence Community, *Preparing for the 21st Century: An Appraisal of U.S. Intelligence* (Washington, DC, U.S. Government Printing Office, March 1, 1996), 26.

18. For a nonfictional account of this possibility, see Office of Technological Assessment, "Proliferation of Weapons of Mass Destruction: Assessing the Risks," report OTA-ISC-559 (Washington, DC: U.S. Government Printing Office, August 1993), 53. Two authorities recently concluded that the likelihood of terrorists using biological agents as weapons is "probably increasing, as biological weapons proliferate and the stability of the cold war balance of power passes"; Robert H. Kupperman and David M. Smith, "Coping with Biological Terrorism," in Brad Roberts, ed., *Biological Weapons: Weapons of the Future?* vol. 15 (Washington, DC: Center for Strategic and International Studies, 1993), 45. An analyst in the Canadian Security Intelligence Service concluded similarly that "the likelihood of future terrorist use of CB [chemical-biological] agents is both real and growing"; Ron Purver, "Understanding Past Non-Use of C.B.W. by Terrorists," presentation to the conference on ChemBio Terrorism: Wave of the Future? sponsored by the Chemical and Biological Arms Control Institute, Washington, DC, April 29, 1996. See also Richard Betts, "Weapons of Mass Destruction," *Foreign Affairs* 77 (January/February 1998): 26–41, who calls for "standby programs for mass vaccinations and emergency treatment with antibiotics" to increase the protection or recovery from biological terrorist attacks

(37); Jonathan B. Tucker, "Chemical/ Biological Terrorism: Coping with a New Threat," *Politics and the Life Sciences* 15 (September 1996): 167–85, along with accompanying commentaries by a host of experts; and Glenn E. Schweitzer with Carole C. Dorsch, *Super-Terrorism: Assassins, Mobsters, and Weapons of Mass Destruction* (New York: Plenum Trade, 1998), chap. 4. On May 22, 1998, President Clinton announced a series of measures to improve U.S. defenses against bioterrorism, including the stockpiling of antibiotics and vaccines; William J. Broad, "How Japan Germ Terror Alerted World," *New York Times*, May 26, 1998, A1.

19. For an example of an intelligence assessment that examines the tie between warfare and a public health issue, see Central Intelligence Agency, "CIA Report on Intelligence Related to Gulf War Illnesses" (Langley, VA: Central Intelligence Agency, September 24, 1996), 1–9.

20. On the U.S. intelligence community's psychological profiling of foreign leaders (a narrow-gauge intelligence focus on the mental health of individuals, in contrast to the broad-gauge global health issues that are the primary concern of this chapter), see Tom Omestad, "Psychology and the CIA: Leaders on the Couch," *Foreign Policy* 95 (Summer 1994): 105–22. These individual health profiles are important to U.S. officials as a form of political-risk analysis. Periodically the President's Daily Brief carries reports on the well-being of prominent foreign leaders, particularly in recent years the chronic poor health of Russian President Boris N. Yeltsin (interview with former Secretary of Defense Les Aspin, Washington, DC, January 27, 1995). On the uncertainties of Yeltsin's health and how this matter became an "inescapable issue for Washington" in the waning years of the twentieth century (he resigned as president on December 31, 1999), see Jane Perlez, "Uncertainty Is Persisting Word on U.S.-Moscow Relationship," *New York Times*, June 20, 1999, A12. During the war in Kosovo (1999), the intelligence community displayed sharp divisions over the likely behavior of Yugoslavian leader Slobodan Milosevic. According to a reliable newspaper report, one classified intelligence assessment predicted that he would remain resolute despite NATO bombing, while another said his confidence would soon break; Elaine Sciolino and Ethan Bronner, "How a President, Distracted by Scandal, Entered Balkan War," *New York Times*, April 18, 1999, A13. The intelligence community goes to great lengths to determine the health of important world leaders. During the cold war, CIA assets in the Middle East managed to infiltrate the plumbing infrastructure beneath the palace of a reigning head of state. When the exalted personage flushed the royal toilet, the assets were ready, test tubes in place, far below in the labyrinth of pipes beneath the palace. The urine samples were rushed back to DS&T labs for detailed medical

analysis to assay the leader's current state of wellness (interview with retired CIA Middle East case officer, Washington, DC, May 12, 1980).

21. Richard Preston, "The Demon in the Freezer," *New Yorker*, July 12, 1999, 44, 47.

22. This scenario is based on remarks by physicist Richard L. Garwin in William J. Broad, "After Many Misses, Pentagon Still Pursues Missile Defense," *New York Times*, May 24, 1999, 23.

23. See the account by Richard Preston, *The Hot Zone* (New York: Random House, 1994).

24. See "Another Sort of Asian Contagion," *Economist*, December 20, 1997/January 2, 1998, 125.

25. Garrett, *Microbes,* 40.

26. William J. Broad and Judith Miller, "Government Report Says 3 Nations Hide Stocks of Smallpox," *New York Times*, June 13, 1999, A1; and their "The Threat of Germ Weapons Is Rising," *New York Times*, December 27, 1999, E1.

27. Ken Alibek with Stephen Handelman, *Biohazard* (New York: Random House, 1999).

28. Both cited by Broad and Miller, "The Threat of Germ Weapons Is Rising," E1, E5.

29. Judith Miller and William J. Broad, "Clinton Describes Terrorism Threat for 21st Century," *New York Times*, January 22, 1999, A1.

30. Broad and Miller, "3 Nations Hide Stocks of Smallpox," D4.

31. Judith Miller and William J. Broad, "Clinton to Announce That U.S. Will Keep Sample of Lethal Smallpox Virus," *New York Times*, April 22, 1999, A12.

32. Ken Alibek and Stephen Handelman, "Smallpox Could Still Be a Danger," *New York Times*, May 24, 1999, A31.

33. Special assistant to the DCI for nonproliferation, Statement, "Worldwide Biological Warfare Threat," U.S. House Select Committee on Intelligence, 106th Cong., 1st sess., March 3, 1999, 3. On bioweapons generally, see Richard Danzig, secretary of the navy, "The Next Superweapon: Panic," *New York Times*, November 15, 1998, A12; Richard Falkenrath, Robert Newman, and Bradley Thayer, *Nuclear, Biological and Chemical Terrorism and Covert Attack* (Cambridge, MA: MIT Press, 1999); Joshua Lederberg, *Biological Weapons: Limiting the Threat* (Cambridge, MA: MIT Press, 1999); Peter Pringle, "Bioterrorism," *Nation*, November 9, 1998, 11–17; and John D. Steinbruner, "Biological Weapons: A Plague upon All Houses," *Foreign Policy* (Winter 1997/98): 85–96.

34. Patrick E. Tyler, "China Concedes That AIDS Virus Infected Common Blood Product," *New York Times*, October 25, 1996, A1. Garrett writes that many nations have deliberately tried to cover up their epidemics "for political and economic reasons"; *Microbes*, 19.

35. See, for example, Michael Specter, "Deep in the Russian Soul, Lethal Darkness," *New York Times*, June 6, 1997, E1.

36. This statistic is from an interview with hospital officials in Janeiro conducted by former President Jimmy Carter and reported in his "State of Human Rights Address," Carter Center, Atlanta, 1991, 5.

37. The Zimbabwe statistic is from Donald G. McNeil Jr., "AIDS Is the Silent Killer in Africa's Economies," *New York Times*, November 15, 1998, A1; the TB death rates, from Alimuddin Zumla and John Grange, "Tuberculosis," *British Medical Journal* 316 (1998): 1962.

38. Interviews with CIA analysts, Langley, VA, September 26–27, 1996.

39. Maurice Strong, secretary-general of the United Nations Conference on Environment and Development (held in Brazil in 1992), statement, "40 Chernobyls Waiting to Happen," *New York Times*, March 22, 1992, E15.

40. Bradley Graham, "Military Chiefs Back Anthrax Inoculations," *Washington Post*, October 2, 1996, A1.

41. Interviews with CIA managers, Langley, VA, September 26–27, 1996.

42. Reuters, "Zaire Fighting Endangers Refugees, U.N. Says," *New York Times*, October 25, 1996, A7; and George A. Gellert, "International Migration and Control of Communicable Diseases," *Social Science and Medicine*, December 15, 1993, 1489–99.

43. Schumeyer, "Medical Intelligence."

44. For the USAMRMC's role in combating the West Nile virus that surfaced on the East Coast of the United States in 1999 (via mosquito bites), see Jennifer Steinhauer and Judith Miller, "In New York Outbreak, Glimpse of Gaps in Biological Defenses," *New York Times*, October 11, 1999, A1.

45. Ibid. Steinhauer and Miller note the failure of the myriad federal, state, and local health agencies to communicate well with one another during the response to the West Nile virus scare (A19).

46. Interview with NIC director, Langley VA, January 31, 1995.

47. Ryan, *Virus X*, 351.

48. Interviews with CIA analysts, Langley, VA, September 26–27, 1996.

49. R. Jeffrey Smith and Thomas W. Lippman, "FBI Plans to Expand Overseas," *Washington Post*, August 20, 1996, A1.

50. As Schumeyer observes, open-source medical indicators can also provide early warning with respect to an adversary's military intentions, say, by way of the enemy's "unusual acquisition or movement of medical resources, scheduled blood drives, and implementation of vaccination programs"; "Medical Intelligence," 14.

51. Barbara Hatch Rosenberg, e-mail to Diane C. Snyder, shared with me, October 16, 1996.

52. According to my periodic interviews with intelligence analysts (1998/99), Washington, DC, and Langley, VA.

53. *The National Security Science and Technology Strategy*, 54.

54. Tucker, "Chemical/Biological Terrorism," 177. For a plea to improve the coordination of the broader U.S. public health infrastructure in the fight against global infectious diseases, see Stephen S. Morse, "Controlling Infectious Diseases," *Technology Review* 98 (October 1995): 54–61.

55. Cited by Thomas W. Lippman, "Success Stories, Symbolism Draw Christopher to Africa," *Washington Post*, October 8, 1996, A12.

## Notes to Chapter 5

1. See especially Report of the Commission on the Roles and Capabilities of the U.S. Intelligence Community, *Preparing for the 21st Century: An Appraisal of U.S. Intelligence* (Washington, DC: U.S. Government Printing Office, March 1, 1996) (hereafter cited as the Aspin-Brown commission); Task Force, Council on Foreign Relations, *Making Intelligence Smarter* (New York: Council on Foreign Relations, 1996); Allan E. Goodman, Gregory F. Treverton, and Philip Zelikow, *In from the Cold* (New York: Twentieth Century Fund, 1996); John H. Hedley, "The Intelligence Community: Is It Broken? How to Fix It," *Studies in Intelligence* 39 (1996): 11–19; National Institute for Public Policy, *Modernizing Intelligence* (Fairfax, VA: National Institute for Public Policy, 1997); and U.S. House Permanent Select Committee on Intelligence, *IC21: The Intelligence Community in the 21st Century*, 104th Cong., 1st sess. (Washington, DC: U.S. Government Printing Office, 1996).

2. On reform and abolition, respectively, see Daniel P. Moynihan, "Do We Still Need the C.I.A.? The State Dept. Can Do the Job," *New York Times*, May 19, 1991, E17; and Seymour M. Hersh, "Spy vs. Spy," *New Yorker*, August 8, 1994, 4. On a plea in favor of wider discretion for the intelligence agencies, see Stephen F. Knott, *Secret and Sanctioned* (New York: Oxford University Press, 1996).

3. Stansfield Turner, *Secrecy and Democracy* (Boston: Houghton Mifflin, 1985), 185.

4. Robert M. Gates, *From the Shadows* (New York: Simon & Schuster, 1996), 43.

5. Bert A. Rockman, "America's *Departments* of State," *American Political Science Review*, December 1981, 912. Between Schlesinger and Turner came Robert M. Gates, an insider, and George Bush, another outsider—but one who avoided tampering with the CIA's staffing and operations.

6. Gates, *From the Shadows*, 140.

7. Colin Campbell, "Political Executives and Their Officials," in Ada W. Finifter, ed., *Political Science: The State of the Discipline* (Washington, DC: American Political Science Association, 1993), 383–406.

8. Interviews with intelligence officials (1993–99), Washington, DC. For published newspaper accounts on the size of the U.S. intelligence budget, see chapter 6.

9. James Q. Wilson, *Thinking about Reorganization* (Washington, DC: Consortium for the Study of Intelligence, 1993), 1.

10. Edward G. Shirley, "Can't Anybody Here Play This Game?" *Atlantic Monthly*, February 1998, 45–61.

11. Quoted by Walter Pincus, "Tenet Seeks Coordination of Intelligence Gathering," *Washington Post*, February 12, 1999, A33. The ICS is now known as the Community Management Staff (CMS).

12. R. James Woolsey, remark to me, Oxford, England September 24, 1999.

13. Interviews with James J. Angleton, Washington, DC, September–December 1975.

14. For a damaging critique of the polygraph's value, written by a scientist, see Robert L. Park, "Liars Never Break a Sweat," *New York Times*, July 12, 1999, A19.

15. Turner, *Secrecy and Democracy*, 186.

16. Ibid., 57.

17. Interviews with senior intelligence officials, Washington, DC, June 8–10, 1997.

18. Quoted in Loch K. Johnson, *Secret Agencies: U.S. Intelligence in a Hostile World* (New Haven, CT: Yale University Press, 1996), 51.

19. Rockman, "America's *Departments* of State," 916.

20. Wilson, *Thinking about Reorganization*, 5.

21. Quoted in Victor L. Marchetti and John D. Marks, *The CIA and the Cult of Intelligence* (New York: Knopf, 1974), 96.

22. Aspin-Brown commission, 131.

23. Remark by Frederick L. Wettering, panelist at the annual meeting of the International Studies Association, Washington, DC, February 17, 1999.

24. Richard E. Neustadt, *Presidential Power* (New York: Wiley, 1960).

25. John Millis, speech to Central Intelligence Retirees Association (CIRA), October 5, 1998. Not everyone at the CIA is trying to resist the SMO trend in favor of more national intelligence; some have recommended jumping on the tactical military bandwagon. As a former senior CIA officer noted, the Agency "is trying hard to get in on SMO, because that's where the money is." See Wettering, remark.

26. Charles G. Cogan, "The New American Intelligence: An Epiphany," *Working Paper no. 3*, Project on the Changing Security Environment and American National Interests, John M. Olin Institute for Strategic Studies (Cambridge, MA: Harvard University, January 1993), 29.

27. Panelist's remarks at the CIA's "The Brown Commission and the Future of Intelligence," a roundtable discussion, *Studies in Intelligence* 39 (1996): 9.

28. Comment at the National Intelligence and Technology Symposium, CIA, Langley, VA, November 6, 1998.

29. In 1992, Senator David Boren (D, Oklahoma) and Representative Dave McCurdy (D, Oklahoma) joined forces (via S. 2198 and H.R. 4165) in an earlier attempt to strength the Office of the DCI. They envisioned a new director of National Intelligence, or DNI, who would have significantly greater authority over budgets, personnel, and operations than does the current DCI. A few minor elements of their reform package made it into the Intelligence Organization Act of 1992. See Report 102-963, U.S. House of Representatives, 102d Cong., 2d sess. (Washington, DC: U.S. Government Printing Office, 1992). The more sweeping reforms of the Boren-McCurdy Act died, however, strangled by allies of the secretary of defense waiting in ambush inside the Hill's two Armed Services Committees.

30. See U.S. House, "Intelligence Authorization Act for Fiscal Year 1997," *H.R. 3259*, 104 Cong., 2d sess. (Washington, DC: U.S. Government Printing Office, 1996).

31. Among others, see the report of the Aspin-Brown commission and the U.S. House *IC21* inquiry. This is not to say that other important points of view do not exist. In fact, some reformers advocate further disaggregation, especially placing the CIA's analytic staff into the various policy departments where they would have closer immediate interaction with the consumers they serve (for example, National Institute for Public Policy, *Modernizing Intelligence*). The drawbacks of this approach are discussed in chapter 8 of this book.

32. Panelist's remark at the CIA, "The Brown Commission," 6.

33. Charles G. Cogan, formerly of the CIA, concluded, "How do you overcome the problem of a weak DCI vis-à-vis a strong secretary of defense? You can't." Comment to panel at the annual meeting of the International Studies Association, Washington, DC, February 17, 1999. For his reform suggestions within the framework of a weak DCI, see Cogan, "The New American Intelligence."

34. Quoted in Hedley, "The Intelligence Community," 17.

35. Representative Porter Goss, remarks at National Intelligence and Technology Symposium.

36. Millis, speech to Central Intelligence Retirees Association (CIRA), October 5, 1998.

37. Quoted by Pincus, "Tenet Seeks Coordination of Intelligence Gathering."

38. For a view that the DCI's main concern for national (civilian) intelligence does not really require much access to SIGINT and IMINT anyway, see Ernest R. May, "Intelligence: Backing into the Future" *Foreign Affairs* 71 (Summer 1992): 63–72.

39. The Intelligence Organization Act of 1992 recommended this rotation reform for implementation by the DCI; yet it has been honored more in the breach than in the commission, in part because many CIA officers believe they will be harmed in their internal promotion opportunities if they are away from their home offices.

40. Seymour M. Hersh, "The Traitor," *New Yorker*, January 18, 1999, 27.

41. Interview with the external affairs coordinator, Counterterrorist Center, Langley, VA, September 30, 1993.

42. Rockman, "America's *Departments* of State," 925.

43. Bruce D. Berkowitz, "The CIA Needs to Get Smart," *Wall Street Journal*, March 1, 1999, A22.

## Notes to Chapter 6

1. Harold Lasswell, *Who Gets What, When, and How* (Chicago: University of Chicago Press, 1936).

2. The $26 million to $30 billion figure has been reported in many newspaper accounts. See, for example, Tim Weiner, "C.I.A. Chief Defends Secrecy, in Spending and Spying, to Senate," *New York Times*, February 23, 1996, A5. Examples of spending on intelligence activities occasionally surface in the media, giving the public some sense of how the monies are dispensed. According to a newspaper account drawing on newly released U.S. intelligence documents, "for much of the 1960s, the CIA provided the Tibetan exile movement with $1.7 million a year for operations against China, including an annual subsidy of $180,000 for the Dalai Lama." See Jim Mann, "CIA Papers Detail 1960s Payments to Dalai Lama," *Los Angeles Times*, September 16, 1998, 4. A news magazine reported that federal agents paid $3.5 million to informants to help catch Mir Aimal Kansi, arrested in Pakistan four years after shootings outside CIA headquarters left two dead and three wounded. See *Newsweek*, June 30, 1997, 6. In 1998, $97 million went to Iraqi opposition groups, including the Iraqi National Congress. See James Risen, "C.I.A. Proposal for Iraq Action Reportedly Turned Down," *New York Times*, May 11, 1998, 16. And the CIA's support to anti-Soviet mujahideen ("soldiers of god") fighters in Afghanistan during the

1980s reportedly totaled more than $3 billion, including $500,000 in 1987 alone. See Mary Anne Weaver, "The Real bin Laden," *New Yorker*, January 24, 2000, 34–35. For comparison, Great Britain reportedly spends the equivalent of about $1.6 billion on intelligence. See Michael Herman, *British Intelligence towards the Millennium: Issues and Opportunities*, London Defence Studies no. 38 (London: Centre for Defence Studies, 1997), 7–9.

3. On the French case, see William Drozdiak, "France Accuses Americans of Spying, Seeks Recall," *Washington Post*, February 23, 1995, A1. On the German case, see wire services, "Germany Expels U.S. Diplomat Reportedly Accused of Espionage," *Los Angeles Times*, March 9, 1997, A4; and Alan Cowell, "Bonn Said to Expel U.S. Envoy Accused of Economic Spying," *New York Times*, March 10, 1997, A6.

4. See Ernest R. May, "Intelligence: Backing into the Future," *Foreign Affairs* 71 (Summer 1992): 66, citing former DCI Richard Helms. For a Brookings Institution deduction based on open sources that the CIA's budget in recent years has been $3 billion (secretly folded into a nondescript air force budget line called "Selected Activities"), see *Business Week* 27 (July 1998): 45.

5. On the more general question of NRO budget legerdemain, see Tim Weiner, "After Errant $2 Billion, Spy Satellite Agency Heads Are Ousted," *New York Times*, February 27, 1996, A9; and David Wise, "The Spies Who Lost $4 Billion," *George*, October 1998, 82–86. According to the former staff director of the House Intelligence Committee, his panel knew of this funding, but the counterpart committee in the Senate was apparently unaware of it (correspondence with me, December 5, 1999).

6. Director of Central Intelligence William J. Casey spent so much money on intelligence hardware, covert action, and new personnel that according to a subsequent DCI, Robert M. Gates, the Agency was "stacking people like cordwood in the corridors." Quoted by Tim Weiner, "Big Cash Infusion Aims to Rebuild Anemic C.I.A.," *New York Times*, October 22, 1998, A3.

7. Charles E. Lindblom, *The Policy-Making Process* (Englewood Cliffs, NJ: Prentice-Hall, 1968), 26–27; and, generally, Aaron Wildavsky, *The Politics of the Budgetary Process* (Boston: Little, Brown, 1964).

8. See Commission on the Roles and Capabilities of the U.S. Intelligence Community, "Preparing for the 21st Century: An Appraisal of U.S. Intelligence," *Report* (Washington, DC: U.S. Government Printing Office, March 1, 1996), 131–32 (hereafter cited as the Aspin-Brown commission).

9. *New York Times*, October 16, 1997, A17.

10. Quoted by Steven Aftergood, "Spending Increase Impedes 1999 Intel Budget Disclosure," *Secrecy & Government Bulletin*, Federation of American Scientists 76 (January 1999): 2.

11. Cited in "Cloak over the CIA Budget," *Washington Post*, November 29, 1999, A22.

12. The HPSCI staff director reports making "about three or four hundred changes" in the intelligence budget submitted by the community in 1998: John Millis, speech to Central Intelligence Retirees Association, October 5, 1998.

13. While serving as the special assistant to Chairman Les Aspin of the Aspin-Brown commission in 1995, I was assigned to compare top-secret CIA reports on an outbreak of ethnic violence in Burundi with information in the public domain (such as from Oxford Analytica, Lexis-Nexis, and *Jane's Weekly*) over a period of days at the height of the crisis. The open sources did a remarkably good job in providing thorough coverage of the events in Burundi, but the CIA did in fact add considerable value to the open reporting, especially its detailed maps of where the fighting was going on and a deeper understanding of the main points of contention.

14. Interviews with intelligence managers, Washington, DC, November 7, 1998.

15. This phrase is from President George Bush in his remarks to the CIA, Langley, VA, November 12, 1991.

16. See John D. Steinbruner, "Nuclear Decapitation," *Foreign Policy* 40 (Winter 1981/82): 16–28.

17. R. W. Apple Jr., "Vietnam's Student," *New York Times Magazine*, December 31, 1995, 32.

18. "Indiana Jim and the Temple of Spooks," *Economist*, March 20, 1993, 34.

19. See Mark Thompson, "Why the Pentagon Gets a Free Ride," *Time*, June 5, 1995, 26–27.

20. With Speaker Newt Gingrich (R, Georgia) and Senator Sam Nunn (D, Georgia) no longer in the Congress, Lockheed-Martin (an Atlanta-based weapons manufacturer) ran into trouble with the production of the F-22, in one of the few times that the House—led by pro-defense Republicans, no less—voted against funding further production of the fighter plane on grounds of its exorbitant costs.

21. Loch K. Johnson, *Secret Agencies: U.S. Intelligence in a Hostile World* (New Haven, CT: Yale University Press, 1996), chap. 4. The current HPSCI chairman, Porter Goss, is a former CIA officer and the first to gain a committee chair in the Congress.

22. See, for example, John Mintz, "Lockheed Martin Lawsuit Delayed by Pentagon, CIA," *Washington Post*, February 28, 1996, A13; and Robert Kohler, *The Intelligence Industrial Base: Doomed to Extinction?* monograph, Working

Group on Intelligence Reform (Washington, DC: Consortium for the Study of Intelligence, 1994), 1–22.

23. Remarks at the National Intelligence and Technology Symposium, CIA, Langley, VA, November 6, 1998.

24. Quoted by Jim Abrams (AP), "CIA Error Led to Embassy Bombing," *Athens* (GA) *Daily News*, May 10, 1999, A4. Emphasizing that "intelligence isn't just something for the cold war," Goss promised "a long-term rebuild" of U.S. intelligence capabilities; see Weiner, "Big Cash Infusion."

25. Abrams, "CIA Error."

26. Remarks by a senior intelligence official at the National Intelligence and Technology Symposium.

27. See James Risen, "C.I.A. Proposal for Iraq Action Reportedly Turned Down," *New York Times*, November 5, 1998, A16.

28. Aspin-Brown commission, 131.

29. Ibid., 131–32.

30. Remark to the National Intelligence and Technology Symposium.

31. Defense spending in 1998 was only 12 percent below the average level from 1976 to 1990; Lawrence J. Korb, "Money to Burn at the Pentagon," *New York Times*, September 25, 1998, A27.

32. Weiner, "Big Cash Infusion."

33. Ibid. "Our work force has been spread thin," stressed DCI Tenet as he argued in favor of the spending increases; Eric Schmitt, "In a Fatal Error, C.I.A. Picked a Bombing Target Only Once: The Chinese Embassy," *New York Times*, July 22, 1999, A9.

34. Millis, speech.

35. Interview with David Gries, director, Center for the Study of Intelligence, CIA, Rosslyn, VA, July 9, 1993.

36. Loch K. Johnson, *America's Secret Power: The CIA in a Democratic Society* (New York: Oxford University Press, 1989): 85; and interviews with intelligence officials, Washington, DC, June 21–22, 1996. "People get fixated on hardware," the HPSCI staff director noted; Millis, speech.

37. For remarks by Vice President Al Gore on the bloatedness of the intelligence community, see John M. Broder, "Russian Premier Warns U.S. against Role as Policeman," *New York Times*, July 28, 1999, A8.

38. Aspin-Brown commission; and interviews with former intelligence officials, , Washington, DC, June 23–24, 1997.

39. Some redundancy is important; for example, unmanned drone aircraft like the Predator and the Hunter are vulnerable to being shot down, and furthermore, they may not be deployed in time or the United States may lack

access to a convenient launching base near the battlefield site. Nevertheless, the degree of redundancy has been excessive and too costly.

40. For an analysis to this effect, see Memorandum for the Director of Central Intelligence from the Small Satellite Review Panel, undated but in May or June 1996, attached (as an unclassified synopsis of a larger classified report) to a press release issued by Representative Combest, then HPSCI chair, Washington, DC, June 28, 1996.

41. Remarks at the National Intelligence and Technology Symposium.

42. According to my interviews with people working on the Aspin-Brown commission, its staff budget experts as well as a few commission members came to this conclusion after spending a year (from March 1995 to March 1996) wading through intelligence agency budgets in search of economies, especially reductions in large and expensive surveillance satellites. The majority of commission members decided, though, not to propose this recommendation, so the commission's final report stated simply that the panel as a whole was "not in a position to make this assessment" (Aspin-Brown commission, 135). The commission's approach was to advocate savings without being specific, although its final report acknowledged that reduced intelligence funding "may be unavoidable in the long run" (134).

## Notes to Chapter 7

1. For a discussion of U.S. ties to friendly foreign intelligence services, see Jeffrey T. Richelson, *The U.S. Intelligence Community,* 4th ed. (Boulder, CO: Westview Press, 1999), chap. 13; Jeffrey T. Richelson and Desmond Ball, *The Ties That Bind: Intelligence Cooperation among the UKUSA Countries* (Boston: Allen & Unwin), 1985; H. Bradford Westerfield, "America and the World of Intelligence Liaison," *Intelligence and National Security* 11 (July 1996): 523–60; Michael Herman, *British Intelligence towards the Millennium: Issues and Opportunities,* London Defence Studies no. 38 (London: Centre for Defence Studies, 1997), chap. 12; and, for a look at the difficulties of U.S.-U.K. liaison during World War II, *British Security Coordination: The Secret History of British Intelligence in the Americas, 1940–45* (London: St Ermin's Press, 1998, reprint of a British government report prepared under the direction of Sir William Stephenson in the aftermath of World War II.

2. For evidence of how the USSR as a common threat helped sustain a close relationship between the United States and West Germany, despite periods of tension or disagreement, see Wolfgang-Uwe Friedrich, ed., *Die USA and die Deutsche Frage, 1945–1990* (Frankfurt: Campus, 1991).

3. These approximate figures are cited, respectively, in (among other sources) "The Dossier on Anthony Lake," editorial, *New York Times*, January 17, 1997, A14; and "Wir Wussten Bescheid," *Der Spiegel* 51 (1994): 27.

4. Westerfield, "America and the World of Intelligence Liaison," 523.

5. Bonn also engaged in some forms of technical intelligence collection, reportedly purchasing $700 million worth of advanced electronic listening devices from the National Security Agency between 1972 and 1977. An important condition of these sales was the expectation that the West Germans would share their information with the NSA; "Dieser Dilettanten-Verein," *Der Spiegel* 41 (1984): 38–52.

6. Christopher Simpson, *Blowback: America's Recruitment of Nazis and Its Effects on the Cold War* (New Haven, CT: Yale University Press, 1990).

7. Mary E. Reese, *General Reinhard Gehlen: The CIA Connection* (Fairfax, VA: George Mason University Press, 1990).

8. Munich also served as the base of operations for the CIA-funded Munich Institute for the Study of the USSR, which from 1950 to 1971 produced propaganda material on the Soviet system and its policies. See Charles T. O'Connell, *The Munich Institute for the Study of the USSR: Origin and Social Composition* (Pittsburgh: University of Pennsylvania, Center for Russian and East European Studies, 1990).

9. Kim Andrew Elliott, "Too Many Voices of America," *Foreign Policy* 77 (Winter 1989): 113–31. Since the end of the cold war, the stations have been moved to Prague where they continue to broadcast, with a greatly reduced budget but without the interference of Moscow's cold war jamming. See David Binder, "Protesting Changes, Leader Steps Down at Cold-War Radios," *New York Times*, January 12, 1994, A9; and "U.S. Radio Services Move Base to Prague," *New York Times*, June 6, 1995, A11.

10. From a speech recorded in the *Hansard*, March 1, 1848, and reprinted in Evan Luard, *Basic Texts in International Relations* (New York: St. Martin's Press, 1992), 166.

11. Tim Weiner, "The Case of the Spies without a Country," *New York Times*, January 17, 1999, B6.

12. Interviews with James Angleton, Washington, DC, September–December 1975.

13. See James Risen and Steven Erlanger, "C.I.A. Chief Vowed to Quit If Clinton Freed Israeli Spy," *New York Times*, November 11, 1998, A1; and James Risen, "Clinton Asks the Views of Top Aides on the Freeing of Pollard," *New York Times*, December 3, 1998, A8.

14. On the CIA's reluctance to share sensitive information with the BND

during the cold war for fear of Communist moles, see "Dieser Dilettanten-Verien."

15. James Risen, "Bonn Sniffs for Russian Moles, Worrying C.I.A.," *New York Times*, June 4, 1998, A1.

16. Ibid.

17. Robert Gerald Livingston, "The Quest for Stasi's Old Files," *Los Angeles Times*, December 27, 1998, M2.

18. See, for example, David Johnston, "Korean Spy Case Takes More Serious Turn," *New York Times*, October 3, 1996, A5, in which the U.S. ambassador in Seoul describes the CIA-Korean liaison as a "very close" working partnership with a "continued residue of suspicion." The ABC Evening News once reported strained relations between U.S. and Italian intelligence (SISDE) over a CIA/FBI counterterrorism raid in Italy that interfered with an ongoing SISDE intelligence collection operation (December 2, 1998).

19. According to the German scholar Anselm Doering-Manteuffel, "The Cold War gave the West Germans and western Europeans little room for independent action. In order to ward off the Soviet threat, they were obliged to align themselves with the United States. Thus, anticommunism became the prime and most effective impetus behind the gravitation toward the Atlantic in Germany and the political integration of western Europe"; "Turning to the Atlantic: The Federal Republic's Ideological Reorientation, 1945–70," annual lecture 1998, *Bulletin of the German Historical Institute* 25 (Fall 1999): 17.

20. Wolfram F. Hanrieder, "The German-American Connection in the 1970s and 1980s: The Maturing of a Relationship," in Carl C. Hodge and Cathal J. Nolan, eds., *Shepherd of Democracy? American and Germany in the 20th Century* (Westport, CT: Greenwood Press, 1992), 105–21.

21. On the decreasing dominance of the United States and the rising strength of West Germany during the 1970s, see Manfred Knapp et al., *Die USA und Deutschland, 1918–1975: Deutsch-Amerikanische Beziehungen zwischen Rivalitaet und Partnerschaft* (Munich: Beck, 1978).

22. Martin J. Hillenbrand, *Fragments of Our Time: Memoirs of a Diplomat* (Athens: University of Georgia Press, 1998), 280–81.

23. Wolfram F. Hanrieder, "Vom Doppelcontainment zum Umbruch in Europa," in Wolfgang-Uwe Friedrich, ed., *Die USA and die Deutsche Frage, 1945–1990* (Frankfurt: Campus, 1991).

24. See Willy Brandt, *Begegnunger und Einsichten: Die Jahre 1960–1975* (Hamburg: Hoffmann und Campe, 1976); and his *Erinnerunger* (Zurich: Propylaen, 1989).

25. Wolfram F. Hanrieder, "German-American Relations in the Postwar Decades," in Frank Trommler and Joseph McVeigh, eds., *America and the Ger-*

*mans: An Assessment of a Three-Hundred-Year History* (Philadelphia: University of Pennsylvania Press, 1985), 106, 108.

26. See Wilhelm von Sternburg, ed., *Die Deutschen Kanzler: Von Bismarck bis Kohl* (Frankfurt/Main: Fischer Taschenbuch Verlag, 1994).

27. See "Dieser Dillettanten-Verein"; and "Still in der Ackerfurche," *Der Spiegel* 51 (1994): 25–27.

28. Helmut Schmidt, *Menschen und Maechte* (Berlin: Siedler, 1987).

29. See Johannes Fischer, "Kontrolle, Konsens und Konflikt," in Oswald Hauser, ed., *Das Geteilte Deutschland in Seinen Internationalen Verflechtunger: 15 Vortaege* (Goettinger: Muster-Schmidt, 1987), 176–209; and Knapp et al., *Die USA und Deutschland, 1918–1975.*

30. On the history of the U.S.-German security relationship during these years, see Hauser, *Das Geteilte Deutschland*; Auswaertiges Amt, ed., *Aussenpolitik der Bundesrepublik Deutschland* (Cologne: Verlag Wissenschaft und Politik, 1995); Friedrich, *Die USA and die Deutsche Frage*; Knapp et al., *Die USA und Deutschland, 1918–1975*; Hans W. Gatzke, *Germany and the United States, a "Special Relationship"?* (Cambridge, MA: Harvard University Press, 1980); Steven Muller and Gerhard Schewigler, eds., *From Occupation to Cooperation* (New York: Norton, 1992); and Hodge and Nolan, *Shepherd of Democracy?*

31. Kurt Schelter, state secretary in the Federal Ministry of the Interior, address, "Symposium on International Terrorism: Are We Cooperating Enough?" New York City, October 23, 1996, 2.

32. The United States began to seek the support of German antiterrorist forces during the Carter administration. In 1986, Bonn and Washington entered into a formal agreement establishing a basis for cooperation between the U.S. Delta Force (stationed at Fort Bragg, NC) and the German GSG and British SAS counterterrorist forces. In 1987, the CIA and the German equivalent of the FBI (the BfV) reportedly ran a series of newspaper ads designed to collect information on international terrorism, an arrangement subsequently denied by both agencies; "Schnapp und Grief," *Der Spiegel* (1987): 44–48.

33. Official of the DCI Counterterrorist Center, Naples World Affairs Council, address, "International Terrorism: Challenge and Response," February 9, 1999, 8.

34. See Michael McClintock, *Instruments of Statecraft* (New York: Pantheon Books, 1992); and "NSA: Americas Grosses Ohr," *Der Spiegel* 8 (1989): 30–49. The private sale of sensitive weapons matériel by German companies to Iraq is now known to have begun in the mid-1980s; Christopher Simpson, *National Security Directives of the Reagan and Bush Administrations* (Boulder, CO: Westview Press, 1995). The BND's apparent lack of knowledge of these activities led many CIA officials to question their competence. On this point, see Imre Karacs,

"Germany Expels Three CIA Spies in Secret Deal," *Independent* (London), September 29, 1999, 16.

35. "Treffender Eindruck," *Der Spiegel* 14 (1992): 97–101. Little is known about how much U.S. officials have learned from the BND about any illegal activities of American-based exporters.

36. Interviews with BND officials, July 29, 1993, Pullach, Germany. This focus on intelligence cooperation against terrorism is broadly true with allies throughout Europe and Asia. For a European example, see the CIA tip to French intelligence in 1994 that helped the French seize the notorious international terrorist "Carlos" (Ilich Ramirez Sanchez) from a hospital room in Sudan; Craig R. Whitney, "Hunger Strike Continues for Terrorist Called Carlos," *New York Times*, November 15, 1998, A4.

37. Interview with the external affairs coordinator, CTC, Langley, VA, September 30, 1993. Personnel in the CTC are highly critical of the continuing fragmentation of the German intelligence effort against terrorism, forcing the U.S. liaison to work with three different German intelligence entities.

38. Westerfield, "America and the World of Intelligence Liaison," 530.

39. Robert D. Blackwill, "Patterns of Partnership," in Steven Muller and Gerhard Schewigler, eds., *From Occupation to Cooperation* (New York: Norton, 1992), 145.

40. See Constantine C. Menges, *The Future of Germany and the Atlantic Alliance* (Washington, DC: AEI Press, 1991); and Burkhart Koch, *Germany's New Assertiveness in International Relations: Between Reality and Misperception* (Stanford, CA: Hoover Institution, 1992).

41. The CIA acquired the bulk of the Stasi files under mysterious circumstances. The information disclosed by these documents helped seal the arrest of Aldrich Ames and has been useful in a number of CIA/FBI counterintelligence investigations. Select information from these files has led to CIA breakthroughs in Europe as well, leading to the arrest in 1993 of the NATO spy known by the code name "Topas." The CIA's unwillingness to share this information freely with the BND, however, has exacerbated relations between the two agencies. See "Files in East Germany Aided U.S. in Spy Case," *New York Times*, March 7, 1994, A13; "East German Files Aided U.S. in Spy Case," *New York Times*, March 6, 1994, 21; "CIA Blockiert Ermittlunger," *Der Spiegel* 25 (1994): 16; and "Auf den Knien zur CIA," *Der Spiegel* 32 (1993): 18–22.

42. On the capture of the no doubt red-faced CIA officer who reportedly attempted to recruit a senior official of the Economics Ministry, see Risen, "Bonn Sniffs for Russian Moles"; and Karacs, "Germany Expels Three CIA Spies," who claims that "there are estimated to be about 100 [U.S.] undercover agents in

Germany, keeping an eye on things the Germans would rather keep secret from their closest allies."

43. Karacs, "Germany Expels Three CIA Spies."

44. Karl Kaiser, "Patterns of Partnership," in in Steven Muller and Gerhard Schewigler, eds., *From Occupation to Cooperation* (New York: Norton, 1992), 173.

45. An observation made by Klaus Kinkel, German federal minister for foreign affairs, speech, Stuttgart, Germany, September 6, 1996, reprinted in German Information Center, *Statements & Speeches* 19 (1996): 8.

46. Steven Erlanger, "C.I.A.'s Role in Mideast Peace Prompts Outcry and a Call for Senate Hearings," *New York Times*, October 26, 1998, A8.

47. George J. Tenet, "What 'New' Role for the C.I.A.?" *New York Times*, October 27, 1998, A23.

48. Ibid.

49. Madeleine K. Albright, *Face the Nation*, CBS News, October 25, 1998.

50. Samuel R. Berger, *This Week*, ABC News, October 25, 1998.

51. Quoted by Eric Schmitt, *New York Times* reporter, in "CIA to Widen Role as Security Monitors," *Atlanta Constitution*, October 25, 1998, B7.

52. Ibid.

53. Harry H. Ransom, letter to the editor, *New York Times*, October 30, 1998, A34.

54. Quoted by Schmitt, "CIA to Widen Role as Security Monitors."

55. "Spies for Peace," unsigned editorial, *New York Times*, October 28, 1998, A26.

56. Commission on the Roles and Capabilities of the U.S. Intelligence Community, "Preparing for the 21st Century: An Appraisal of U.S. Intelligence," *Report* (Washington, DC: U.S. Government Printing Office, March 1, 1996), 129 (hereafter cited as the Aspin-Brown commission).

57. Ibid.; the quotation is from Seymour M. Hersh, "Saddam's Best Friend," *New Yorker*, April 5, 1999, 35.

58. Interviews with UN officials, New York City, November 29, 1995.

59. Bill Gertz, "Clinton Wants Hill off His Back," *Washington Times*, November 1, 1995, A1.

60. Tim Weiner, "The Case of the Spies without a Country," *New York Times*, January 17, 1999, E6.

61. Scott Ritter, *Endgame* (New York: Simon & Schuster, 1999); A. Walter Dorn, "The Cloak and the Blue Beret: Limitations on Intelligence in UN Peacekeeping," *International Journal of Intelligence and Counterintelligence* 12 (Winter 1999/2000): 437–38.

62. Hersh, "Saddam's Best Friend," 36.

63. Barton Gellman, "U.S. Spied on Iraqi Military via U.N.," *Washington Post*, March 2, 1999, A1.

64. Quoted in "Inspectors 'Helped Washington,'" *New Zealand Herald*, January 7, 1999, B1, citing a *Washington Post* report.

65. Ritter claims that CIA paramilitary officers were placed on the UNSCOM inspection team beginning in 1992, growing to nine members by 1996; *Endgame.*

66. "Intelligence Ties with UNSCOM Defended," *Otago* (New Zealand) *Daily Times*, January 8, 1999, 8, citing *Washington Post* and *Boston Globe* reports.

67. Quoted by Christopher S. Wren, "U.N. to Create Own Satellite Program to Find Illegal Drug Crops," *New York Times*, March 28, 1999, A10.

68. Remarks at Oxford University, September 25, 1999.

69. ABC news report, Discover News channel, October 8, 1999.

70. Dorn, "The Cloak and the Blue Beret ," 442.

## Notes to Chapter 8

1. This discussion of the CTC is based on interviews with the center's deputy director, February 18, 1999, and with senior CTC officers, September 30, 1993, CIA, Langley, VA. The former CIA officer quoted is Reule Marc Gerecht, "Alarmism Abets the Terrorists," *New York Times*, December 23, 1999, A29.

2. The Directorate of Science and Technology, for instance, plays an important role in determining the origins of weapons used by terrorists, such as explosives, detonating devices, and remote-control mechanisms. Each bomb maker has a "signature" that can reveal the identity of the terrorist, as in the case of Abra Hebrahim, a terrorist in the Middle East who crafts his explosives using a distinctive modus operandi. This identification helps the CTC trace the individual responsible for the terrorist act, an example of what CI specialists refer to as "walking back the cat."

3. Interview with the external affairs coordinator, CTC CIA, Langley, VA, September 30, 1993.

4. CTC senior official, address, Naples World Affairs Council, "International Terrorism: Challenge and Response," Italy, February 9, 1999, 8.

5. Remark at the National Intelligence and Technology Symposium, CIA, Langley, VA, November 6, 1998.

6. John Deutch, "Terrorism," *Foreign Policy* 108 (Fall 1997): 10–22; and Walter Enders and Todd Sandler, "Transnational Terrorism in the Post–Cold War Era," *International Studies Quarterly* 43 (March 1999): 145–67. For two first-rate studies on the problem of terrorism, see Jeffrey D. Simon, *The Terrorist Trap: America's Experience with Terrorism* (Bloomington: Indiana University

Press, 1994); and Stansfield Turner, *Terrorism and Democracy* (Boston: Houghton Mifflin, 1991).

7. George J. Tenet, statement, *Hearings*, U.S. Senate Armed Services Committee, February 2, 1999, 3.

8. Daniel Benjamin and Steven Simon (Clinton administration NSC experts on terrorism), "The New Face of Terrorism," *New York Times*, January 4, 2000, A23.

9. See Robert D. Walpole, NIO for Strategic and Nuclear Programs, "North Korea's Taepo Dong Launch and Some Implications on the Ballistic Missile Threat to the United States," speech, Center for Strategic and International Affairs, Washington, DC, December 8, 1998, 5.

10. Interview with senior CTC officer, CIA, Langley, VA, September 30, 1993.

11. Ibid.

12. Interview with John Millis, staff director, U.S. House Permanent Select Committee on Intelligence, Washington, DC, February 18, 1999.

13. See, for example, James Risen, "Covert Plan Said to Take Aim at Milosevic's Hold on Power," *New York Times*, June 18, 1999, A15.

14. "Information operations" by America's secret agencies can be used against this nation as well, of course, perhaps by a terrorist organization seeking to sow chaos in the financial markets of New York City through a massive computer attack aimed at Wall Street, an all-too-conceivable electronic Pearl Harbor for the United States.

15. The Dubai Islamic Bank reference is from James Risen with Benjamin Weiser, "U.S. Officials Say Aid for Terrorists Came through Two Persian Gulf Nations," *New York Times*, July 8, 1999, A8; the National Commercial Bank, from ABC Evening News, July 9, 1999.

16. See U.S. Senate Select Committee to Study Governmental Operations with Respect to Intelligence Activities (the Church Committee), "Alleged Assassination Plots Involving Foreign Leaders," *Interim Report*, S. Rept. no. 94-465 (Washington, DC: U.S. Government Printing Office, November 20, 1975).

17. Senator Orrin Hatch (R, Utah) argued that "there should be nothing that should not be on the table" when it comes to fighting terrorists; Tim Weiner, "Rethinking the Ban on Political Assassinations," *New York Times*, August 30, 1998, E3. Retired Army Lieutenant Colonel Ralph Peters declared: "Until we change the rules [to permit assassinations], we will continue to lose"; "A Revolution in Military Ethics?" *Parameters* 26 (Summer 1996): 106. Thomas L. Friedman recommended that the United States "offer a reward for removing Saddam [Hussein] from office"; "Rattling the Rattler," *New York Times*, January 19, 1999, A23. Some members of the academic community have also found

this approach worthy of closer consideration. In *The Spy Novels of John Le Carré* (New York: St. Martin's Press, 1999), Myron J. Arnoff stated, "An argument could be made that it would have been more humane (in terms of loss of life), not to mention more cost effective, to assassinate the Iraqi dictator [Saddam Hussein] than to have launched Operation Desert Storm" (193). David Newman and Bruce Bueno de Mesquita wrote, "When hundreds and even thousands of innocent people are at risk, assassination of key terrorist leaders may be an option worthy of renewed debate"; "Repeal Order 12333, Legalize 007," *New York Times*, January 26, 1989, A23. In a particularly thorough analysis, Louis Rene Beres concluded that in "rare, residual circumstances" assassination may have to be carried out by the United States; "Assassination and the Law," *Studies in Conflict and Terrorism* 18 (1995): 299–315. See also C. A. Anderson, "Assassination: Lawful Homicide and the Butcher of Baghdad," *Hamline Journal of Public Law & Policy* 13 (Summer 1992): 291–321; Louis Rene Beres, "The Permissibility of State-Sponsored Assassination during Peace and War," *Temple International & Comparative Law Journal* 5 (Fall 1991): 231–49; William Cowan, "How to Kill Saddam," *Washington Post*, February 10, 1991, C2; and Daniel Schorr, "Hypocrisy about Assassination," *Washington Post*, February 3, 1991, C7. For the CIA's latest interpretation of the assassination prohibition (a statement that generally supports the current executive order that prohibits assassinations but that points to the order's ambiguities), see Jonathan M. Fredman, CIA associate general counsel, "Covert Action, Loss of Life, and the Prohibition on Assassination," *Studies in Intelligence*, unclassified ed., 1 (1997): 15–25.

18. Executive order 12333, sec. 2.11.

19. Former Robert M. Gates, quoted by Walter Pincus, "Saddam Hussein's Death Is a Goal," *Washington Post*, February 15, 1998, A36.

20. Ibid.

21. Two recent DCIs are on record against the murder of Saddam Hussein: Robert Gates has called the idea "very counterproductive"; and James Woolsey, "extremely irresponsible." Israeli intelligence, long known to use assassination as an instrument, is reportedly under pressure to discard this approach, because most cabinet ministers and many Mossad officials have concluded that it is an "ineffective" weapon in the war against terrorism; Yossi Melman, "Israel's Darkest Secrets," *New York Times*, March 25, 1998, A23.

22. Pincus, "Saddam Hussein's Death Is a Goal."

23. When American inspectors were finally granted permission by the government of North Korea in 1999 to examine an underground cavern suspected from satellite imagery as a possible nuclear weapons lab, they found instead a

huge, empty tunnel; Philip Shenon, "Suspected North Korean Atom Site Is Empty, U.S. Finds," *New York Times*, May 28, 1999, A3.

24. On the value of OSINT, see Vernon Loeb, "Spying Intelligence Data Can Be an Open-Book Test," *Washington Post*, March 22, 1999, A17. Robert D. Steele has also written extensively and well on this topic, including "Relevant Information and All-Source Analysis: The Emerging Revolution," *American Intelligence Journal* 19 (1999): 23–30.

25. Brent Scowcroft, remarks at U.S. Intelligence and the End of the Cold War Conference, Bush School of Government and Public Service, Texas A&M University, College Station, November 20, 1999. Anwar Sadat knew that he could not win a war with Israel, and therefore the U.S. intelligence community calculated that he would not be foolish enough to start one; yet by means of an attack, he evidently hoped to prompt new negotiations.

26. Some observers fret that analysts may be contaminated by close proximity to case officers, with the latter's supposedly vested interests in backing the reports of sometimes biased DO assets in the field.

27. Comment to me, Washington, DC, September 21, 1995.

28. See the Report of the Commission on the Roles and Capabilities of the United States Intelligence Community, *Preparing for the 21st Century: An Appraisal of U.S. Intelligence* (Washington, DC: U.S. Government Printing Office, March 1, 1996). Hereafter cited as the Aspin-Brown commission.

29. Ibid.

30. See Aaron Wildavsky, *Speaking Truth to Power: The Art and Craft of Policy Analysis* (Boston: Little, Brown, 1979).

31. On President Johnson, see Thomas L. Hughes, "The Power to Speak and the Power to Listen: Reflections in Bureaucratic Politics and a Recommendation on Information Flows," in Thomas M. Franck and Edward Weisband, eds., *Secrecy and Foreign Policy* (New York: Oxford University Press, 1974): 19; and two works by Harold P. Ford: *CIA and the Vietnam Policymakers* (Rosslyn, VA: Center for the Study of Intelligence, 1997); and *CIA and the Vietnam Policymakers: Three Episodes, 1962–1968* (Washington, DC: National Technical Information Service, 1999). Gordon Oehler is quoted in Tim Weiner, "C.I.A. Inquiry Asks for an Overhaul," *New York Times*, June 3, 1998, A8.

32. Interview, Washington, DC, August 12, 1995.

33. James Risen, "Gore Rejected C.I.A. Evidence of Russian Corruption," *New York Times*, November 23, 1998, A8.

34. Jack Davis, "The Challenge of Managing 'Uncertainty': Paul Wolfowitz on Intelligence-Policy Relations," interview with Paul Wolfowitz, March 1995, 8, photocopy provided to me.

35. Robert M. Gates, *Confirmation Hearings*, U.S. Senate Select Committee on Intelligence, 102d Cong., 1st sess., September 16, 1991. In 1995, as a member of the Aspin-Brown commission staff, I had the opportunity to examine a single current copy, randomly selected, of the highly classified President's Daily Brief. The content, timeliness, readability, and attractive format of that particular issue were impressive, easily passing the "value-added" test on that day, even though the main recipient, President Bill Clinton, has expressed an overall dissatisfaction with its lack of added value. See Walter Pincus, "A Low Profile for CIA Chief," *Washington Post*, January 13, 1998, A13. The CIA would not allow me to conduct a more meaningful time-series analysis of the daily brief.

36. Joseph F. Nye, Jr., testimony, open hearing, 19 January 1995, Washington, D.C.

37. Interviews with both in Washington, DC, February and September 1996, respectively.

38. Interview, Washington, DC, August 22, 1997.

39. Allan E. Goodman, remark to Conference on U.S. Intelligence, CIA, Langley, VA, October 1, 1993.

40. Interview with a Department of Commerce official, Washington, DC, February 22, 1995.

41. Robert Steele, e-mail to me, January 5, 2000.

42. Interviews with senior intelligence officers, Washington, DC, and Langley, VA, from 1993 to 1999.

43. One of the greatest sins that an intelligence officer can commit is twisting information to suit the political needs of decision makers, a pathology called the "politicization" or "cooking" of intelligence. See Loch K. Johnson, *Secret Agencies: U.S. Intelligence in a Hostile World* (New Haven, CT: Yale University Press, 1996), 95–97.

44. Interview, Washington, DC, October 26, 1996.

45. Ambassador Robert D. Blackwill, interviewed by Jack Davis, "A Policymaker's Perspective on Intelligence Analysis," *Studies in Intelligence* (Summer 1994): 6.

## Notes to Chapter 9

1. James Madison, "Federalist Paper no. 51," February 8, 1788, reprinted in *The Federalist* (New York: Modern Library, 1937), 337.

2. Thomas Jefferson, Draft of the Kentucky Resolutions, October 1798, in *Jefferson* (New York: Library of America, 1984), 455.

3. Richard E. Neustadt, *Presidential Power and the Modern Presidents* (New York: Free Press, 1990), 29, italics in original.

4. *Myers v. United States*, 272 U.S. 52 293 (1926).

5. *United States v. Curtiss-Wright Export Corporation* 299 U.S. 304 (1936).

6. Stephen F. Knott, *Secret and Sanctioned: Covert Operations and the American Presidency* (New York: Oxford University Press, 1996).

7. Jerrold L. Walden, "The CIA: A Study in the Arrogation of Administrative Powers," *George Washington Law Review* 39 (October 1970): 66–101.

8. Interview with James R. Schlesinger, Washington, DC, June 16, 1994.

9. Richard B. Russell Library, Richard B. Russell Oral History no. 86, taped by Hughes Cates, University of Georgia, Athens, February 22, 1977.

10. U.S. Select Committee to Study Governmental Operations with Respect to Intelligence Activities, "Foreign and Military Intelligence," *Final Report*, S. Rept. 94-755, vol. 1, 94th Cong., 2d sess. (Washington, DC: U.S. Government Printing Office, May 1976), 157 (hereafter cited as the Church committee).

11. Ibid., 158; Clifford's testimony to the Church committee, December 4, 1975.

12. On the Abourezk amendment (named after its sponsor, James Abourezk, D, South Dakota), see *Congressional Record*, October 2, 1974, 33482.

13. Loch K. Johnson, *Season of Inquiry* (Lexington: University Press of Kentucky, 1986); Kathryn Olmsted, *Challenging the Secret Government: The Post-Watergate Investigations of the CIA and FBI* (Chapel Hill: University of North Carolina Press, 1996); Frank J. Smist Jr., *Congress Oversees the United States Intelligence Community, 1947–1989* (Knoxville: University of Tennessee Press, 1990).

14. Sec. 662 of the Foreign Assistance Act of 1994 (22 U.S.C. 2422).

15. Olmsted, *Challenging the Secret Government*; Knott, *Secret and Sanctioned*.

16. Olmsted, *Challenging the Secret Government*, 3.

17. See U.S. Senate Select Committee on Secret Military Assistance to Iran and the Nicaraguan Opposition and U.S. House Select Committee to Investigate Covert Arms Transactions with Iran (the Inouye-Hamilton committees), *Report on the Iran-Contra Affair*, S. Rept. 100-216 and H. Rept. 100-433 (Washington, DC: U.S. Government Printing Office, November 1987), 379.

18. Loch K. Johnson, "The CIA and the Media," *Intelligence and National Security* 1 (May 1986): 143–69.

19. Jack Anderson, "How the CIA Snooped inside Russia," *Washington* Post, December 10, 1973, B17; on the *Glomar Explorer*, see the reports in *New York Times*, March 20 and 26, 1975.

20. Frank Church, "An Imperative for the CIA: Professionalism Free of Politics and Partisanship," *Congressional* Record, November 11, 1975, 35786–88.

21. Representative Jack Brooks (D, Texas), *Impeachment Hearings*, U.S.

House Judiciary Committee, 93rd Cong., 2d sess., 1974, in "Congress: We the People," *Program 20*, WETA television, Washington, DC (1983).

22. Robert M. Gates, *From the Shadows* (New York: Simon & Schuster, 1996).

23. See, for example, the citations in Loch K. Johnson, *America's Secret Power: The CIA in a Democratic Society* (New York: Oxford University Press, 1989), 295, n. 63. At a recent conference, former DCI William Webster observed that during his tenure "more leaks came out of the White House than the [congressional] Intelligence Committees"; U.S. Intelligence and the End of the Cold War Conference, Bush School of Government and Public Service, Texas A&M University, College Station, November 20, 1999.

24. See Frederick M. Kaiser, "Congress and the Intelligence Community: Taking the Road Less Traveled," in Roger H. Davidson, ed., *The Post-reform Congress* (New York: St. Martin's Press, 1992), 279–300; Smist, *Congress Oversees the United States Intelligence Community*; and Walden, "The CIA."

25. Testimony of Vice Admiral John M. Poindexter, the Inouye-Hamilton committees, *Hearings*, vol. 8, 100th Cong., 1st sess. (Washington, DC: U.S. Government Printing Office, 1987), 159.

26. Gates, *From the Shadows*, 61.

27. Senior official, CIA, letter to me, September 21, 1991.

28. Ibid.

29. Interview with the CIA's deputy director for congressional affairs, Langley, VA, April 1, 1994.

30. Lloyd Salvetti, director, Center for the Study of Intelligence, remarks to Joint Military Intelligence College Conference, Defense Intelligence Agency, June 18, 1999.

31. Unsigned editorial, "The Keys to the Spy Kingdom," *New York Times*, May 19, 1996, E14.

32. Quoted by David Wise, "The Spies Who Lost $4 Billion," *George*, October 1998, 84. This does not excuse the all-too-frequent incidence of legislative overseers asleep at the wheel from failing to follow through on reports of illegal covert actions during the early stages of the Iran-contra affair to (more recently) a willingness to look away as the Clinton administration planned a paramilitary covert action to assassinate Saddam Hussein in violation of an executive order. The plot was subsequently called off when the operation fell apart in the field. See Walter Pincus, "Saddam Hussein's Death Is a Goal," *Washington Post*, February 15, 1998, A36.

33. President Clinton proved unwilling to back Woolsey on the NRO issue. Along with the DCI's growing frustration over seldom seeing the president, this precipitated his resignation. Woolsey no doubt understood the cardinal rule for

a DCI's success, as veteran intelligence officer Samuel Halpern defined it: "Unless the DCI is able to walk in to see the President at will, privately, except maybe for the secretary, just these persons—unless that's possible, you don't have a DCI"; interviewed by historian Ralph E. Weber, November 11, 1995, Arlington, VA, and published in Ralph E. Weber, ed., *Spymasters: Ten CIA Officers in Their Own Words* (Wilmington, DE: SR Books, 1999), 129.

34. Unsigned editorial, "Making the C.I.A. Accountable," *New York Times*, August 18, 1996, E-14.

35. Quoted by James Risen, "Energy Secretary Delays Disciplining Staff over Spy Case," *New York Times*, June 10, 1999, A6.

36. Arthur S. Hulnick, "Openness: Being Public about Secret Intelligence," *International Journal of Intelligence and Counterintelligence* 12 (Winter 1999/2000): 480. The Commission to Assess the Organization of the Federal Government to Combat the Proliferation of Weapons of Mass Destruction (the Deutch commission, led by former DCI John Deutch) had a point, though, in calling on Congress to consolidate the number of legislative committees with oversight and budgetary responsibility for nonproliferation programs, in order to reduce confusion and an unnecessary surcharge on the time and energies of executive officials in their reporting to Congress; *Report* (Washington, DC: U.S. Government Printing Office, July 1999).

37. Eric Schmitt, "Leading Senators Demand That U.S. Limit Overtures to China," *New York Times*, March 14, 1999, A6.

38. Associated Press report, "Energy Officials Admit to Ducking Spy Case Queries," *Athens* (GA) *Daily News*, April 16, 1999, 1B.

39. Quoted by Stansfield Turner in an op-ed piece, "Purge the C.I.A. of K.G.B. Types," *New York Times*, October 2, 1991, A19.

40. Remarks to National Intelligence and Technology Symposium, CIA, Langley, VA, November 6, 1998.

41. James T. Currie, "Iran-Contra and Congressional Oversight of the CIA," *International Journal of Intelligence and Counterintelligence* 11 (Summer 1998): 203.

42. Quoted by Eric Schmitt, "Senate Panel and C.I.A. Fight on China Documents," *New York Times*, June 5, 1998, A12.

43. Quoted by James Risen, "C.I.A. Admits Slow Move in Security Slip," *New York Times*, February 3, 2000, A18. Deutch's run-ins with the Operations Directorate, discussed in chapter 5, may have led him to believe its officers might be spying against him, thus causing him to seek refuge in his own home computer rather than the one on his desk at Langley (although access to a home computer would not be much of a technical challenge for DO operatives).

44. Former President George Bush, letter to me, January 23, 1994.

45. See Tim Weiner, "C.I.A. Chief Defends Secrecy, in Spending and Spying, to Senate," *New York Times*, February 23, 1996, A5.

46. This group has been renamed the Association of Former Intelligence Officers (AFIO).

47. See, for example, John Mintz, "Lockheed Martin Works to Save Its Older Spies in the Skies," *Washington Post*, November 28, 1995, D1.

48. Richard N. Haass, "Don't Hobble Intelligence Gathering," *Washington Post*, February 15, 1996, A27. For the broader, less extreme views of the council's report, see Council on Foreign Relations, "Making Intelligence Smarter: The Future of U.S. Intelligence," *Report of an Independent Task Force* (New York: Council on Foreign Relations, 1996).

49. See John M. Deutch, "C.I.A., Bunker Free, Is Declassifying Secrets," letter to the editor, *New York Times*, May 3, 1996, A10; John Hollister Hedley, "The CIA's New Openness," *International Journal of Intelligence and Counterintelligence* 7 (Summer 1994): 129–42; and Tim Weiner, "A Blast at Secrecy in Kennedy Killing," *New York Times*, September 29, 1998, A17.

50. Letter to the editor, *New York Times*, July 16, 1998, A18.

51. Steve Aftergood, "Bulletins," *Secrecy & Government Bulletin*, Federation of American Scientists 79 (June 1999): 2.

52. Quoted by Karen DeYoung and Vernon Loeb, "Documents Show U.S. Knew Pinochet Planned Crackdown in '73," *Washington Post*, July 1, 1999, A23.

53. Daniel Klaidman and Melinda Liu, "Open Secret," *Newsweek*, March 22, 1999, 31. The HPSCI staff director questions, though, whether his committee was "told directly or in such a way as to create a reaction" (personal correspondence with me, November 29, 1999), the problem again of keeping the oversight panels well and clearly informed.

54. Jeff Gerth, "Nuclear Lapses Known in '96, Aides Now Say," *New York Times*, March 17, 1999, A12.

55. Gates, *From the Shadows*, 559.

56. Remarks at Does America Need the CIA? Conference, Gerald R. Ford Library, November 19, 1997.

57. William E. Colby, "Gesprach mit William E. Colby," *Der Spiegel*, January 23, 1978, 114 (my translation).

# BIBLIOGRAPHY

Aftergood, Steven. "Bulletins." *Secrecy & Government Bulletin*, Federation of American Scientists 79 (June 1999).

———. "Spending Increase Impedes 1999 Intel Budget Disclosure." *Secrecy & Government Bulletin*, Federation of American Scientists 76 (January 1999).

Albright, Madeleine K. *Face the Nation*, CBS News, October 25, 1998.

Alibek, Ken, with Stephen Handelman. *Biohazard*. New York: Random House, 1999.

———. "Smallpox Could Still Be a Danger." *New York Times*, May 24, 1999, A31.

American Institute for Business Research. *Protecting Corporate America's Secrets in the Global Economy*. Washington, DC: American Institute for Business Research, 1992.

Anderson, C. A. "Assassination: Lawful Homicide and the Butcher of Baghdad." *Hamline Journal of Public Law & Policy* 13 (Summer 1992): 291–321.

Anderson, Jack. "How the CIA Snooped inside Russia." *Washington Post*, December 10, 1973, B17.

Andrew, Christopher. *For the President's Eyes Only*. New York: HarperCollins, 1995.

———. *Her Majesty's Secret Service: The Making of the British Intelligence Community*. New York: Viking, 1986.

———, and David Dilks, ed., *The Missing Dimension: Governments and Intelligence Communities in the Twentieth Century*. London: Macmillan, 1984.

Andrews, Edmund L. "Aboard Advanced Radar Flight." *New York Times*, June 14, 1999, A12.

Apple, R. W. Jr. "Vietnam's Student." *New York Times Magazine*, December 31, 1995, 32.

Arnoff, Myron J. *The Spy Novels of John Le Carré*. New York: St. Martin's Press, 1999.

Aspin, Les. Speech, Jewish Institute for National Security Affairs, September 21, 1992, Washington, DC.

Aspin-Brown commission. *Preparing for the 21st Century: An Appraisal of U.S. Intelligence*. Report of the Commission on the Roles and Capabilities of the

United States Intelligence Community. Washington, DC: U.S. Government Printing Office, March 1, 1996.

Bamford, James. *The Puzzle Palace.* Boston: Houghton Mifflin, 1984.

Barrett, David M. "Glimpses of a Hidden History: Sen. Richard Russell, Congress, and Oversight of the CIA." *International Journal of Intelligence and Counterintelligence* 11 (1998) 271–98.

Beardsley, Tim. "Environmental Secrets: MEDEA Brings Intelligence in from the Cold." *Scientific American* 273 (July 1995): 28–30.

Begley, Sharon. "Commandos of Viral Combat." *Newsweek,* May 22, 1995, 48–54.

Benjamin, Daniel, and Steven Simon. "The New Face of Terrorism." *New York Times,* January 1, 2000, A28.

Beres, Louis Rene. "Assassination and the Law: A Policy Memorandum." *Studies in Conflict and Terrorism* 18 (1995): 299–315.

———. "The Permissibility of State–Sponsored Assassination during Peace and War." *Temple International & Comparative Law Journal* 5 (Fall 1991): 231–49.

Berger, Samuel R. *This Week.* ABC News, October 25, 1998.

Berkowitz, Bruce D. "The CIA Needs to Get Smarter." *Wall Street Journal,* March 1, 1999, A22.

———, and Allen E. Goodman. *Strategic Intelligence for American National Security.* Princeton, NJ: Princeton University Press, 1986.

Betts, Richard K. "Analysis, War and Decision: Why Intelligence Failures Are Inevitable." *World Politics* 31 (October 1978): 61–89.

———. "Weapons of Mass Destruction." *Foreign Affairs* 77 (January/February 1998): 26–41.

Binder, David. "Protesting Changes, Leader Steps down at Cold-War Radios." *New York Times,* January 12, 1994, A9.

———. "U.S. Radio Services Move Base to Prague." *New York Times,* June 6, 1995, A11.

Bobrow, Davis B. "Prospecting the Future." *International Studies Review* 1 (Summer 1999): 1–10.

Boren, David L. "The Intelligence Community: How Crucial?" *Foreign Affairs* 71 (Summer 1992): 52–62.

Borrus, Michael, and John Zysman. "Industrial Competitiveness and National Security." In Graham Allison and Gregory F. Treverton, eds., *Rethinking America's Security: Beyond Cold War to New World Order.* New York: Norton, 1992), 136–75.

Broad, William J. "After Many Misses, Pentagon Still Pursues Missile Defense." *New York Times,* May 24, 1999, 23.

———. "How Japan Germ Terror Alerted World." *New York Times,* May 26, 1998, A1.

———. "U.S. Will Deploy Its Spy Satellites on Nature Mission." *New York Times,* November 27, 1995, A1.

———, and Judith Miller. "Government Report Says 3 Nations Hide Stocks of Smallpox." *New York Times,* June 13, 1999, A1.

Broder, David. "To Win the War on Drugs." *Washington Post,* May 2, 1999, B7.

Broder, John M. "President's Sober Response Assures Public of Counterespionage Measures." *New York Times,* May 26, 1999, A15.

———. "Russian Premier Warns U.S. against Role as Policeman." *New York Times,* July 28, 1999, A8.

Brown, Corrie C., and Barrett D. Slenning. "Impact and Risk of Foreign Animal Diseases." *Journal of the American Veterinary Medical Association* 208 (1996): 1038–40.

Burrows, William E. *Deep Black: Space Espionage and National Security.* New York: Random House, 1986.

———, and Robert Windrem. *Critical Mass: The Dangerous Race for Superweapons in a Fragmenting World.* New York: Simon & Schuster, 1994.

Bush, George H. W. Letter to Loch K. Johnson, January 23, 1994.

———. Remarks, Central Intelligence Agency, Langley, VA, November 12, 1991.

Campbell, Colin. "Political Executives and Their Officials." In Ada W. Finifter, ed., *Political Science: The State of the Discipline.* Washington, DC: American Political Science Association, 1993, 383–406.

Carr, E. H. *The Twenty Years' Crisis: An Introduction to the Study of International Relations.* New York: Harper & Row, 1939.

Carter, Jimmy. "State of Human Rights Address," Carter Center, Atlanta, 1991.

Central Intelligence Agency. "The Brown Commission and the Future of Intelligence." A Roundtable Discussion. *Studies in Intelligence* 39 (1996): 1–9.

———. "CIA Report on Intelligence Related to Gulf War Illnesses." Langley, VA: Central Intelligence Agency, September 24, 1996, 1–9.

———. Directorate of Science and Technology, "ETF Fiscal Year 1993 Experiments Summary." Langley, VA: Central Intelligence Agency, 1994.

———. National Intelligence and Technology Symposium. Central Intelligence Agency, Langley, VA, November 6, 1998.

———. Office of Public Affairs. "Director of Central Intelligence Command Responsibilities." Langley, VA: Central Intelligence Agency, January 1998.

———. Official, DCI Counterterrorist Center. Speech, Naples World Affairs Council on International Terrorism: Challenge and Response, Naples, February 9, 1999.

Central Intelligence Agency. Special assistant to the DCI for Nonproliferation. Statement on the World Wide Biological Warfare Threat, *Hearings*, U.S. House Permanent Select Committee on Intelligence, 106th Cong., 1st sess., March 3, 1999.

Christopher, Warren. "Foreign and Military Intelligence." *Final Report.* U.S. Senate Select Committee on Intelligence Activities, Rept. 94–755, 94th Cong., 2d sess., May 19, 1996.

———. *Hearings*, U.S. Senate Foreign Relations Committee, 103rd Cong., 1st sess., November 4, 1993.

Church, Frank. "Do We Still Plot Murders? Who Will Believe We Don't?" *Los Angeles Times,* June 14, 1983, pt. 2, p. 5.

———. "An Imperative for the CIA: Professionalism Free of Politics and Partisanship." *Congressional Record,* November 11, 1975, 35786–88.

Clarke, Duncan L., and Robert Johnston. "Economic Espionage and Interallied Strategic Cooperation." *Thunderbird International Business Review* 40 (July/August 1998): 413–31.

Clarke, Richard A. "Finding the Right Balance against Bioterrorism." *Emerging Infectious Diseases* 5 (July/August 1999): 497.

Cogan, Charles G. "The New American Intelligence: An Epiphany." *Working Paper no. 3,* Project on the Changing Security Environment and American National Interests, John M. Olin Institute for Strategic Studies. Cambridge, MA: Harvard University, January 1993, 1–46.

———. "Restructuring the CIA." *Foreign Service Journal,* February 1996, 32–38.

Cohen, William S. *Confirmation Hearings*, U.S. Senate Armed Services Committee, 105th Cong., 1st sess., January 22, 1997.

Colby, William E. "Gesprach mit William E. Colby." *Der Spiegel,* January 23, 1978, 114.

———, and Peter Forbath. *Honorable Men: My Life in the CIA.* New York: Simon & Schuster, 1978.

Commission to Assess the Organization of the Federal Government to Combat the Proliferation of Weapons of Mass Destruction (Deutch commission). *Report.* Washington, DC: U.S. Government Printing Office, July 1999.

Connor, William E. *Intelligence Oversight: The Controversy behind the FY 1991 Intelligence Authorization Act.* Intelligence Profession Series no. 11. McLean, VA: Association of Former Intelligence Officers, 1993.

Council on Foreign Relations. *Making Intelligence Smarter.* New York: Council on Foreign Relations, 1996.

Coverdale, Paul. Remarks, "National Security in the 21st Century." Richard B. Russell Symposium, October 26, 1999. University of Georgia, Athens.

Cowan, William. "How to Kill Saddam." *Washington Post,* February 10, 1991, C2.

Cowell, Alan. "Bonn Said to Expel U.S. Envoy Accused of Economic Spying." *New York Times,* March 10, 1997, A6.

Currie, James T. "Iran-Contra and Congressional Oversight of the CIA." *International Journal of Intelligence and Counterintelligence* 11 (Summer 1998): 185–210.

Dabelko, David D., and Geoffrey D. Dabelko. "The International Environment and the U.S. Intelligence Community." *International Journal of Intelligence and Counterintelligence* 6 (Spring 1993): 21–42.

Davis, Jack. "The Challenge of Managing 'Uncertainty': Paul Wolfowitz on Intelligence-Policy Relations." Interview with Paul Wolfowitz, March 1995.

———. "A Policymaker's Perspective on Intelligence Analysis." *Studies in Intelligence* 38 (1995): 7–15.

Deutch, John M. "C.I.A., Bunker Free, Is Declassifying Secrets," Letter to the editor, *New York Times,* May 3, 1996, A10.

———. Memorandum for the president. Washington, DC, April 5, 1996.

———. "Terrorism." *Foreign Policy* 108 (Fall 1997): 10–22.

DeYoung, Karen, and Vernon Loeb. "Documents Show U.S. Knew Pinochet Planned Crackdown in '73." *Washington Post,* July 1, 1999, A23.

Diamond, Jared. *Guns, Germs, and Steel: The Fate of Human Societies.* New York: Norton, 1997.

Doering-Manteuffel, Anselm. "Turning to the Atlantic: The Federal Republic's Ideological Reorientation, 1945–70." *Bulletin of the German Historical Institute* 25 (Fall 1999): 3–21.

Doran, Charles F. "Why Forecasts Fail: The Limits and Potential of Forecasting in International Relations and Economics." *International Studies Review* 1 (Summer 1999): 11–42.

Dorn, A. Walter. "The Cloak and the Blue Beret: Limitations on Intelligence in UN Peacekeeping." *International Journal of Intelligence and Counterintelligence* 12 (Winter 1999): 414–47.

Drozdiak, William. "France Accuses Americans of Spying, Seeks Recall." *Washington Post,* February 23, 1995, A1.

Elliott, Kim Andrew. "Too Many Voices of America." *Foreign Policy* 77 (Winter 1989): 113–31.

Enders, Walter, and Todd Sandler. "Transnational Terrorism in the Post–Cold War Era." *International Studies Quarterly* 43 (March 1999): 145–67.

Erlanger, Steven. "C.I.A.'s Role in Mideast Peace Prompts Outcry and a Call for Senate Hearings." *New York Times,* October 26, 1998, A8.

Ernst, Maurice C. "Economic Intelligence in CIA." *Studies in Intelligence* 28 (Winter 1984): 1–22.

Executive Office of the President. *International Crime Control Strategy.* Washington, DC: Executive Office of the President, May 1998.

———. National Science and Technology Council, Office of Science and Technology Policy. *The National Security Science and Technology Strategy.* Washington, DC: Executive Office of the President, 1996.

Falkenrath, Richard, Robert Newman, and Bradley Thayer. *Biological and Chemical Terrorism and Covert Attack.* Cambridge, MA: MIT Press, 1999.

Fialka, John J. "Stealing the Spark: Why Economic Espionage Works in America." *Washington Quarterly* 19 (1996): 175–89.

Finel, Bernard I., and Kristin M. Lord. "The Surprising Logic of Transparency." *International Studies Quarterly* 43 (June 1999): 315–39.

Fisher, Louis. "How to Avoid Iran-Contras: Review Essay." *California Law Review* 76 (1993): 919–29.

———. *The War Making Powers.* Manhattan: University Press of Kansas, 1996.

Flitner, David Jr. "Presidential Commissions." In Leonard W. Levy and Louis Fisher, eds., *Encyclopedia of the American Presidency,* vol. 1. New York: Simon & Schuster, 1994, 266–69.

Ford, Harold P. *CIA and the Vietnam Policymakers: Three Episodes, 1962–1968.* Washington, DC: National Technical Information Service, 1999.

Fort, Randall M. "Economic Espionage: Problems and Prospects." Washington, DC: Consortium for the Study of Intelligence, 1993.

Fraumann, Edwin. "Economic Espionage: Security Missions Redefined." *Public Administration Review* 57 (July/August 1997): 303–8.

Fredman, Jonathan M. "Covert Action, Loss of Life, and the Prohibition on Assassination." *Studies in Intelligence* 1 (1997): 15–25.

Freeh, Louis. "Economic Espionage." *Hearings,* U.S. Senate Select Committee on Intelligence, 104th Cong., 2d sess., February 28, 1996.

Friedman, Thomas L. "A Manifesto for the Fast World." *New York Times Magazine,* March 28, 1999, 40 ff.

———. "Rattling the Rattler." *New York Times,* January 19, 1999, A23.

Frost, Mike, and Michel Gratton. *Spyworld: Inside the Canadian and American Establishments.* Toronto: Doubleday, 1994.

Gannon, John C. "Intelligence Challenges for the Next Generation." Speech, World Affairs Council meeting, St. Louis, October 8, 1998.

Garrett, Laurie. *The Coming Plague: Newly Emerging Diseases in a World out of Balance.* New York: Farrar, Straus & Giroux, 1994.

Gates, Robert M. *Confirmation Hearings,* U.S. Senate Select Committee on Intelligence, 102d Cong., 1st sess., September 16, 1991.

————. *From the Shadows.* New York: Simon & Schuster, 1996.

————. *Hearings,* U.S. House, Judiciary Committee, Subcommittee on Economic and Commercial Law, 102d Cong., 2d sess., April 29, 1992.

————. "In War, Mistakes Happen." *New York Times,* May 12, 1999, A27.

————. Remarks, Conference on U.S. Intelligence, June 11, 1984, Langley, VA.

————. Speech, Economic Club of Detroit, April 13, 1992, Detroit.

Gatzke, Hans W. *Germany and the United States: A "Special Relationship"?* Cambridge, MA: Harvard University Press, 1980.

Gellert, George A. "International Migration and Control of Communicable Diseases." *Social Science and Medicine,* December 15, 1993, 1489–99.

Gellman, Barton. "U.S. Spied on Iraqi Military via U.N." *Washington Post,* March 2, 1999, A1.

Gerecht, Reuel Marc (aka Edward Shirley). "Alarmism Abets the Terrorists." *New York Times,* December 23, 1999.

Gerth, Jeff. "Nuclear Lapses Known in '96." *New York Times,* March 17, 1999, A12.

————, and David E. Sanger. "Citing Security, U.S. Spurns China on a Satellite Deal." *New York Times,* February 23, 1999, A1.

Gertz, Bill. "Clinton Wants Hill off His Back." *Washington Times,* November 1, 1995, A1.

Goodman, Allan E., Gregory F. Treverton, and Philip Zelikow. *In from the Cold.* New York: Twentieth Century Fund, 1996.

Graham, Bradley. "Military Chiefs Back Anthrax Inoculations." *Washington Post,* October 2, 1996, A1.

Haass, Richard N. "Don't Hobble Intelligence Gathering." *Washington Post,* February 15, 1996, A27.

Halloran, Richard. *To Arm a Nation.* New York: Macmillan, 1986.

Hanrieder, Wolfram F. "The German-American Connection in the 1970s and 1980s: The Maturing of a Relationship." In Carl C. Hodge and Cathal J. Nolan, eds., *Shepherd of Democracy? America and Germany in the 20th Century.* Westport, CT: Greenwood Press, 1992, 105–21.

————. "German-American Relations in the Postwar Decades." In Frank Trommler and Joseph McVeigh, eds., *America and the Germans: An Assessment of a Three-Hundred-Year History.* Philadelphia: University of Pennsylvania Press, 1985.

Hart, C. A., and S. Kariuki. "Antimicrobial Resistance in Developing Countries." *British Medical Journal* 317 (1998): 647–50.

Hastedt, Glenn. "CIA's Organizational Culture and the Problem of Reform." *International Journal of Intelligence and Counterintelligence* 9 (Fall 1996): 249–69.

Hastedt, Glenn. "Controlling Intelligence: The Role of the DCI." *International Journal of Intelligence and Counterintelligence* 1 (1986): 25–40.

———. "Seeking Economic Security through Intelligence." *International Journal of Intelligence and Counterintelligence* 11 (Winter 1998/99): 385–402.

Hedley, John H. "The CIA's New Openness." *International Journal of Intelligence and Counterintelligence* 7 (Summer 1994): 129–42.

———. "The Intelligence Community: Is It Broken? How to Fix It." *Studies in Intelligence* 39 (1996): 11–19.

Henderson, D. A. "Smallpox: Clinical and Epidemiologic Features." *Emerging Infectious Diseases* 5 (July/August 1999): 538–39.

Henig, Robin Marantz. *A Dancing Matrix: Voyages along the Viral Frontier.* New York: Knopf, 1993.

Herman, Michael. *British Intelligence towards the Millennium: Issues and Opportunities.* London Defence Studies no. 38. London: Centre for Defence Studies, 1997.

———. "Diplomacy and Intelligence." *Discussion Paper no. 39*, Diplomatic Studies Programme, Centre for the Study of Diplomacy, Leicester University, March 1998.

———. *Intelligence Power in Peace and War.* Cambridge: Cambridge University Press, 1996.

Hersh, Seymour M. "The Intelligence Gap." *New Yorker*, December 10, 1999, 58–76.

———. "The Missiles of August." *New Yorker*, October 12, 1998, 34–41.

———. "Saddam's Best Friend." *New Yorker*, April 5, 1999, 32–41.

———. "Spy vs. Spy," *New Yorker*, August 8, 1994, 4.

———. "The Traitor." *New Yorker*, January 18, 1999, 26–33.

Hillenbrand, Martin J. *Fragments of Our Time: Memoirs of a Diplomat.* Athens: University of Georgia Press, 1998.

Hirschman, Albert. *National Power and the Structure of Foreign Trade.* Berkeley and Los Angeles: University of California Press, [1945] 1980.

Holt, Robert T. *Radio Free Europe.* Minneapolis: University of Minnesota Press, 1958.

Homer-Dixon, Thomas. "Environmental Scarcities and Conflicts: Evidence from Cases." *International Security* 19 (Summer 1994): 35–62.

———. "Environmental Scarcity, Mass Violence, and the Limits to Ingenuity." *Current History* 95 (November 1996): 359–65.

———. "On the Threshold: Environmental Changes as Acute Causes of Conflict." *International Security* 19 (Fall 1991): 76–116.

———, and Marc Levy. "Correspondence: Environment and Security." *International Security* 20 (Winter 1995/96): 189–198.

———, and Valerie Percival. *Environmental Security and Violent Conflict: Briefing Book.* Toronto: University of Toronto Press, 1996.

Hopgood, Stephen. *American Foreign Environmental Policy and the Power of the State.* New York: Oxford University Press, 1998.

Hughes, Thomas L. "The Power to Speak and the Power to Listen: Reflections in Bureaucratic Politics and a Recommendation on Information Flows." In Thomas M. Franck and Edward Weisband, eds., *Secrecy and Foreign Policy.* New York: Oxford University Press, 1974.

Hulnick, Arthur S. "Openness: Being Public about Secret Intelligence." *International Journal of Intelligence and Counterintelligence* 12 (Winter 1999): 463–83.

———. "The Uneasy Relationship between Intelligence and Private Industry." *International Journal of Intelligence and Counterintelligence* 9 (Spring 1996): 17–32.

Huntington, Samuel P. "The Erosion of American National Interests." *Foreign Affairs* 76 (September/October 1997): 28–49.

Inderfurth, Karl F., and Loch K. Johnson. *Decisions of the Highest Order.* Belmont, CA: Brooks/Cole, 1988.

Inman, Bobby Ray. Interview, *U.S. News & World Report*, December 20, 1982, 32.

Jeffreys-Jones, Rhodri. *The CIA and American Democracy.* New Haven, CT: Yale University Press, 1989.

Johnson, Loch K. *America's Secret Power: The CIA in a Democratic Society.* New York: Oxford University Press, 1989.

———. "Analysis for a New Age." *Intelligence and National Security* 11 (October 1996): 657–71.

———. "Balancing Security and Liberty." *Freedom Review* 28 (Summer 1997): 37–44.

———. "The CIA and the Question of Accountability." In Rhodri Jeffreys-Jones and Christopher Andrew, eds., *Eternal Vigilance? 50 Years of the CIA.* London: Cass, 1997, 132–59; reprinted from *Intelligence and National Security* 12 (January 1997): 178–200.

———. "The CIA: Controlling the Quiet Option." *Foreign Policy* 39 (Summer 1980): 143–52.

———. "Congress and the CIA: Monitoring the Dark Side of Government." *Legislative Studies Quarterly* 5 (1980): 477–99.

———. "The Evolution of CIA Accountability." *American Intelligence Journal* (March 1995): 43–46.

———. "Intelligence and the Challenge of Collaborative Government." *Intelligence and National Security* 13 (Summer 1998): 177–82.

Johnson, Loch K. "Legislative Reform of Intelligence Policy." *Polity* 17 (Spring 1985): 549–73.

———. *The Making of International Agreements: Congress Confronts the Executive.* New York: New York University Press, 1984.

———. "Reinventing the CIA: Strategic Intelligence and the End of the Cold War." In Randall B. Ripley and James M. Lindsay, eds., *U.S. Foreign Policy after the Cold War.* Pittsburgh: University of Pittsburgh Press, 1997, 132–59.

———. *A Season of Inquiry: The Senate Intelligence Investigation.* Lexington: University Press of Kentucky, 1986.

———. *Secret Agencies: U.S. Intelligence in a Hostile World.* New Haven, CT: Yale University Press, 1996.

———. "Smart Intelligence." *Foreign Policy* 89 (Winter 1992/93): 53–70.

———, with Annette Freyberg. "Ambivalent Bedfellows: German-American Intelligence Relations, 1969–1991." *International Journal of Intelligence and Counterintelligence* 10 (Summer 1997): 165–79.

———, with Scott A. Hershovitz. "Strategic Intelligence and Environmental Security." *Research Paper no. 44*, Special Report, Research Institute for European Studies, February 1998, 1–15.

———, with Kevin J. Scheid. "Spending for Spies: Intelligence Budgeting in the Aftermath of the Cold War." *Public Budgeting & Finance* 17 (Winter 1997): 7–27.

———, with Diane C. Snyder. "Beyond the Traditional Intelligence Agenda: Examining the Merits of a World Health Portfolio." *Journal of Conflict Resolution* (Fall 1998): 29–46.

Johnson, Paul. "No Cloak and Dagger Required: Intelligence Support to UN Peacekeeping." *Intelligence and National Security* 12 (October 1997): 102–12.

Johnston, David. "Korean Spy Case Takes More Serious Turn." *New York Times,* October 3, 1996, A5.

Kahn, David. "Big Ear or Big Brother?" *New York Times Magazine,* May 16, 1976, 13 ff.

———. *The Codebreakers.* New York: Macmillan, 1967.

Kaiser, Frederick M. "Congress and the Intelligence Community: Taking the Road Less Traveled." In Roger H. Davidson, ed., *The Post-reform Congress.* New York: St. Martin's Press, 1992.

———. "Impact and Implications of the Iran-Contra Affair on Congressional Oversight of Covert Action." *International Journal of Intelligence and Counterintelligence* 7 (1994): 205–34.

Kaiser, Karl. "Patterns in Partnership." In Steven Muller and Gerhard Schewigler, eds., *From Occupation to Cooperation.* New York: Norton, 1992.

Karacs, Imre. "Germany Expels Three CIA Spies in Secret Deal." *Independent* (London), September 29, 1999, 16.

Kennedy, David M. "Sunshine and Shadow: The CIA and the Soviet Economy." *Case Program* C16–91–1096.0, Kennedy School of Government. Cambridge, MA: Harvard University, 1991.

Kent, Sherman. *Strategic Intelligence for American World Policy*. Princeton, NJ: Princeton University Press, 1949.

Kinkel, Klaus. Speech. Reprinted in *Statements & Speeches* 19, German Information Center, Stuttgart, September 6, 1996.

Kinzer, Stephen. "Where Kurds Seek a Land, Turks Want the Water." *New York Times,* February 28, 1999, E3.

Knott, Stephen F. *Secret and Sanctioned: Covert Operations and the American Presidency*. New York: Oxford University Press, 1996.

Koch, Burkhart. *Germany's New Assertiveness in International Relations: Between Reality and Misperception*. Stanford, CA: Hoover Institution, 1992.

Kohler, Robert. *The Intelligence Industrial Base: Doomed to Extinction?* Working Group on Intelligence Reform. Washington, DC: Consortium for the Study of Intelligence, 1984, 1–22.

Korb, Larry. "Money to Burn at the Pentagon." *New York Times,* September 25, 1998, A27.

Kortepeter, Mark G., and Gerald W. Parker. "Potential Biological Weapons Threats." *Emerging Infectious Diseases* 5 (July/August 1999): 523–27.

Kristof, Nicholas, and Sheryl WuDunn. "Of World Markets, None an Island." *New York Times,* May 2, 1999, sec. 4, p. 1.

Kupperman, Robert H., and David M. Smith. "Coping with Biological Terrorism." In Brad Roberts, ed., *Biological Weapons: Weapons of the Future?* Washington, DC: Center for Strategic and International Studies, 1993.

Lake, Anthony. "Managing Complexity in U.S. Foreign Policy." Washington, DC: U.S. Department of State, Bureau of Public Affairs, March 14, 1978.

Laqueur, Walter. *A World of Secrets: The Uses and Limits of Intelligence*. New York: Basic Books, 1985.

Lasswell, Harold. *What, Where, When, and How*. Chicago: University of Chicago Press, 1936.

Leach, James A. "The New Russian Menace." *New York Times,* September 10, 1999, A27.

Lederberg, Joshua. *Biological Weapons: Limiting the Threat*. Cambridge, MA: MIT Press, 1999.

Levy, Marc. "Is the Environment a National Security Issues?" *International Security* 20 (Fall 1995): 35–63.

Lewis, Anthony. "When We Could Believe." *New York Times,* June 12, 1987, A31.

Lindblom, Charles E. *The Policy-Making Process.* Englewood Cliffs, NJ: Prentice-Hall, 1968.

Lippman, Thomas. "Success Stories, Symbolism Draw Christopher to Africa." *Washington Post,* October 8, 1996, A12.

Livingston, Robert Gerald. "The Quest for Stasi's Old Files." *Los Angeles Times,* December 27, 1998, M2.

Loeb, Vernon. "CIA Still Recuperating from Mole's Aftermath." *Washington Post,* February 22, 1999, A13.

———. "Hobbyists Track down Spies in Sky." *Washington Post,* February 20, 1999, A1.

———. "Spying Intelligence Data Can Be an Open-Book Test." *Washington Post,* March 22, 1999, A17

Lowenthal, Mark M. *Intelligence: From Secrets to Policy.* Washington, DC: CQ Press, 2000.

———. "Keep James Bond out of GM." *International Economy,* July/August 1992, 52–54.

———. *U.S. Intelligence: Evolution and Anatomy.* 2d ed. Westport, CT: Praeger, 1992.

Luard, Evan. *Basic Texts in International Relations.* New York: St. Martin's Press, 1992.

Lundberg, Kirsten, "CIA and the Fall of the Soviet Empire: The Politics of 'Getting It Right,'" *Case Program* C16–94–1251.0. Kennedy School of Government. Cambridge, MA: Harvard University, 1994.

Macartney, John. "NSA, HPSCI Butt Heads over Echelon." *Weekly Intelligence Notes,* Association of Former Intelligence Officers, June 11, 1999, 2.

———. "Reform: Bonanza for Scholars." *Intelligencer,* Academic Exchange Program Newsletter, Association of Former Intelligence Officers 7 (Summer 1996): 3–5.

Maggs, John. "From Swords to Plowshares." *Journal of Commerce,* August 18, 1995, 1.

Mann, Jim. "CIA Papers Detail 1960s Payments to Dalai Lama." *Los Angeles Times,* September 16, 1998, 4.

Marchetti, Victor L., and John D. Marks. *The CIA and the Cult of Intelligence.* New York: Knopf, 1974.

Maslow, Abraham. *Motivation and Personality.* New York: Harper & Row, 1987.

Mastanduno, Michael. "Economics and Security in Statecraft and Scholarship." *International Organization* 4 (Autumn 1998): 825–54.

Matthews, Jessica Tuchman. "Power Shift." *Foreign Affairs* 76 (January/February 1997): 50–66.

———. "Preserving the Global Environment." In Eugene R. Wittkopf, ed., *The Future of American Foreign Policy.* 2d ed. New York: St. Martin's Press, 1994, 108–16.

———. Remarks, "National Security in the 21st Century." Richard B. Russell Symposium, University of Georgia: Athens, October 26, 1999.

May, Ernest R. "Intelligence: Backing into the Future." *Foreign Affairs* 71 (Summer 1992): 63–72.

McClintock, Michael. *Instruments of Statecraft.* New York: Pantheon Books, 1992.

McDonald, Kim A. "NASA Satellites May 'Revolutionize' Earth Sciences." *Chronicle of Higher Education,* July 9, 1999, A20, A22.

McNeil, Donald G. Jr. "AIDS Is the Silent Killer in Africa's Economies." *New York Times,* November 15, 1998, A1.

Melman, Yossi. "Israel's Darkest Secrets." *New York Times,* March 25, 1998, A23.

Menges, Constantine C. *The Future of Germany and the Atlantic Alliance.* Washington, DC: AEI Press, 1991.

Miller, Judith, with William J. Broad. "Clinton Describes Terrorism Threat for 21st Century." *New York Times,* January 22, 1999, A1.

———. "Clinton to Announce That U.S. Will Keep Sample of Lethal Smallpox Virus." *New York Times,* April 22, 1999, A12.

———. "Iranians, Bioweapons in Mind, Lure Needy Ex-Soviet Scientists." *New York Times,* December 8, 1998, A1.

Millis, John. Speech, Central Intelligence Retiree's Association, Langley, VA, October 5, 1998.

Mintz, John. "Lockheed Martin Lawsuit Delayed by Pentagon, CIA." *Washington Post,* February 28, 1996, A13.

Morse, Stephen S. "Controlling Infectious Diseases." *Technology Review* 98 (October 1995): 54–61.

Moynihan, Daniel Patrick. "Do We Still Need the C.I.A.? The State Dept. Can Do the Job," *New York Times,* May 19, 1991, E17.

———. *Secrecy.* New Haven, CT: Yale University Press, 1998.

Muller, Steven, and Gerhard Schewigler, eds. *From Occupation to Cooperation.* New York: Norton, 1992.

National Institute for Public Policy. *Modernizing Intelligence.* Fairfax, VA: National Institute for Public Policy, 1997.

National Intelligence Council. "The Environmental Outlook in Central and

Eastern Europe." *Intelligence Community Assessment*, ICA 96–08D. Washington, DC: National Intelligence Council, December 1997, 1–33.

National Intelligence Council."The Environmental Outlook in Russia." *Intelligence Community Assessment*, ICA 98–08 Washington, DC: National Intelligence Council, January 1999, 1–35.

———. "Global Trends 2010." Langley, VA, November 1997.

National Public Radio. Interview with Apache helicopter pilot in Kosovo, July 7, 1999.

National Research Council. Office of International Affairs. *The Pervasive Role of Science, Technology, and Health in Foreign Policy: Imperatives for the Department of State*. Washington, DC: National Academy Press, 1999.

Neu, C. R. "Comments on Economic Intelligence." Speech, Institute for International Economics, Washington, DC, April 25, 1995.

Neustadt, Richard E. *Presidential Power*. New York: Wiley, 1960.

Newman, David, and Bruce Bueno de Mesquita. "Repeal Order 12333, Legalize 007." *New York Times*, January 26, 1989, A23.

Nivola, Pietro S. "American Trade Policy after the Cold War." In Randall B. Ripley and James M. Lindsay, eds., *U.S. Foreign Policy after the Cold War*. Pittsburgh: University of Pittsburgh Press, 1997, 235–56.

Nye, Joseph S. Jr. *Bound to Lead: The Changing Nature of American Power*. New York: Basic Books, 1990.

———. *Open Hearings*, Aspin-Brown commission. Washington, DC, January 19, 1996.

———."Redefining National Security." *Foreign Affairs* 78 (July/August 1999): 22–35.

Oakley, Phyllis. "Intelligence Support to Diplomacy: Issues and Trends." Speech, Association of Former Intelligence Officers, Langley, VA, November 6, 1998.

O'Connell, Charles T. *The Munich Institute for the Study of the USSR: Origin and Social Composition*. Pittsburgh: University of Pennsylvania Center for Russian and East European Studies, 1990.

Omestad, Tom. "Psychology and the CIA: Leaders on the Couch." *Foreign Policy* 99 (Summer 1994): 105–22.

Omsted, Kathryn. *Challenging the Secret Government: The Post-Watergate Investigations of the CIA and FBI*. Chapel Hill: University of North Carolina, 1996.

Orme, William Jr. "International Study on Water in Mideast Leads to a Warning." *New York Times*, March 3, 1999, A9.

O'Toole, Tara. "Smallpox: An Attack Scenario." *Emerging Infectious Diseases* 5 (July/August 1999): 540–46.

Park, Robert L. "Liars Never Break a Sweat." *New York Times,* July 12, 1999, A19.

Paterson, Matthew, and Michael Grubb. "The International Politics of Climate Change." *International Affairs* 68 (1992): 296.

Perlez, Jane. "Albright Says Hussein's Foes Are Building Unified Front." *New York Times,* May 25, 1999, A4.

———. "Clinton Pushes for Treaty to Ban the Worst Child Labor Practices." *New York Times,* June 17, 1999, A17.

———. "Uncertainty Is Persisting Word on U.S.-Moscow Relationship." *New York Times,* June 20, 1999, A12.

Peters, Ralph. "A Revolution in Military Ethics?" *Parameters* 26 (Summer 1996): 106.

Pincus, Walter. "A Low Profile for CIA Chief." *Washington Post,* January 13, 1998, A13.

———. "Military Espionage Cuts Eyed." *Washington Post,* March 17, 1995, A6.

———. "Rumsfeld Questions Over-Compartmentalization." *Washington Post,* May 5, 1999, A29.

———. "Saddam Hussein's Death Is a Goal." *Washington Post,* February 15, 1998, A36.

———. "Tenet Seeks Coordination of Intelligence Gathering." *Washington Post,* February 12, 1999, A33.

———. "U.S. Preparedness Faulted." *Washington Post,* July 9, 1999, A2.

Pirages, Dennis. "Microsecurity Disease Organisms and Human Well-Being." *Washington Quarterly* 18 (Fall 1995): 5–12.

Porteous, Samuel D. "Looking out for Economic Interests: An Increased Role for Intelligence." *Washington Quarterly* 19 (1996): 191–204.

Powers, Richard Gid. Introduction to *Secrecy,* by Daniel Patrick Moynihan. New Haven, CT: Yale University Press, 1998.

Prados, John. *Presidents' Secret Wars: CIA and Pentagon Covert Operations since World War II.* New York: Morrow, 1986.

Preston, Richard. "The Demon in the Freezer." *New Yorker,* July 13, 1999, 44–61.

———. *Hot Zone.* Random House, 1994.

Pringle, Peter. "Bioterrorism." *Nation,* November 9, 1998, 11–17.

Purver, Ron. "Understanding Past Non-Use of C.B.W. by Terrorists." Presentation, Conference on ChemBio Terrorism: Wave of the Future? Chemical and Biological Arms Control Institute, Washington, DC, April 29, 1996.

Rainey, Hal. *Understanding and Managing Public Organizations.* 2d ed. San Francisco: Jossey-Bass, 1997.

Ranelagh, John. *The Agency: The Rise and Decline of the CIA.* New York: Simon & Schuster, 1986.

Ransom, Harry Howe. *The Intelligence Establishment.* Cambridge, MA: Harvard University Press, 1970.

———. Letter to the editor, *New York Times,* October 30, 1998, A34.

———. "The Politicization of Intelligence." In Stephen J. Cimbala, ed., *Intelligence and Intelligence Policy in a Democratic Society.* Dobbs Ferry, NY: Transnational, 1987, 25–46.

———. "Reflections on Forty Years of Spy-Watching." Unpublished paper, December 7, 1994, 1–14.

Reese, Mary E. *General Reinhard Gehlen: The CIA Connection.* Fairfax, VA: George Mason University Press, 1990.

Richelson, Jeffrey T. *The U.S. Intelligence Community.* 4th ed. Boulder, CO: Westview Press, 1999.

———, and Desmond Ball. *The Ties That Bind: Intelligence Cooperation among the UKUSA Countries.* Boston: Allen & Unwin, 1985.

Rielly, John E. "Americans and the World: A Survey at Century's End." *Foreign Policy* 114 (Spring 1999): 97–114.

———, ed. *American Public Opinion and U.S. Foreign Policy.* Chicago: Chicago Council on Foreign Relations, 1991.

Risen, James. "Bonn Sniffs for Russian Moles, Worrying C.I.A." *New York Times,* June 4, 1998, A1.

———. "C.I.A. Proposal for Iraq Action Reportedly Turned Down." *New York Times,* May 11, 1998, A16.

———. "C.I.A. Sees a North Korean Missile Threat." *New York Times,* February 3, 1999, A6.

———. "Clinton Asks the Views of Top Aides on the Freeing of Pollard." *New York Times,* December 3, 1998, A8.

———. "Clinton Reportedly Orders CIA to Focus on Trade Espionage." *Los Angeles Times,* July 23, 1995, A14.

———. "Energy Secretary Delays Disciplining Staff over Spy Case." *New York Times,* June 10, 1999, A6.

———. "Gore Rejected C.I.A. Evidence of Russian Corruption." *New York Times,* November 23, 1998, A8.

———. "To Bomb Sudan Plant, or Not: A Year Later, Debates Rankle." *New York Times,* October 27, 1999, A1, A12.

———, and Steven Erlanger. "C.I.A. Chief Vowed to Quit If Clinton Freed Israeli Spy." *New York Times,* November 11, 1998, A1.

Ritter, Scott. *Endgame.* New York: Simon & Schuster, 1999.

Robertson, Barbara P. Hull et al. "Yellow Fever: A Decade of Reemergence." *Journal of the American Medical Association*, October 9, 1996, 1157–62.

Robertson, K. G. *Secrecy and Open Government.* New York: Macmillan, 1999.

Rockefeller commission. *Report.* Washington, DC: U.S. Government Printing Office, 1975.

Rockman, Bert A. "America's *Departments* of State." *American Political Science Review*, December 1981, 911–27.

Rohter, Larry. "Haiti Paralysis Brings a Boom in Drug Trade." *New York Times*, October 27, 1998, A1.

Ronnfeldt, C. F. "Three Generations of Environment and Security Research." *Journal of Peace Research* 34 (November 1997): 473–82.

Rosenbaum, David E. "U.S. Official Calls Tallies of Kosovo Slain Too Low." *New York Times*, April 19, 1999, A10.

Ryan, Frank. *Virus X: Tracking the New Killer Plagues.* Boston: Little, Brown, 1997.

Salvetti, Lloyd. Remarks, Joint Intelligence Conference, Defense Intelligence Agency, June 18, 1999.

Sanger, David E., and Tim Weiner. "Emerging Role for the C.I.A.: Economic Spy." *New York Times*, October 15, 1995, A1.

Schelter, Kurt. Speech, Symposium on International Terrorism: Are We Cooperating Enough? New York City, October 23, 1996.

Schick, Allen. *Congress and Money: Budgeting, Spending and Taxing.* Washington, DC: Urban Institute, 1980.

Schmitt, Eric. "In a Fatal Error, C.I.A. Picked a Bombing Target Only Once: The Chinese Embassy." *New York Times*, July 22, 1999, A9.

———. "Leading Senators Demand That U.S. Limit Overtures to China." *New York Times*, March 14, 1999, A6.

———. "Senate Panel and C.I.A. Fight on China Documents." *New York Times*, June 5, 1998, A12.

Schorr, Daniel. "Hypocrisy about Assassination." *Washington Post*, February 3, 1991, C7.

———."Washington Notebook." *New Leader* May 17–31, 1999, 5.

Schumeyer, Colonel Gerard. "Medical Intelligence: Making a Difference." *American Intelligence Journal* 17 (1996): 11–16.

Schweitzer, Glenn E., with Carole C. Dorsch. *Super-Terrorism: Assassins, Mobsters, and Weapons of Mass Destruction.* New York: Plenum Trade, 1998.

Sciolino, Elaine, and Ethan Bronner, "How a President, Distracted by Scandal, Entered Balkan War." *New York Times*, April 18, 1999, A13.

Shenon, Philip. "Suspect North Korean Atom Site Is Empty, U.S. Finds." *New York Times,* May 28, 1999, A3.

Simon, Jeffrey D. *The Terrorist Trap: America's Experience with Terrorism.* Bloomington: Indiana University Press, 1994.

Simpson, Christopher. *Blowback: America's Recruitment of Nazis and Its Effects on the Cold War.* New Haven, CT: Yale University Press, 1990.

———. *National Security Directives of the Reagan and Bush Administrations.* Boulder, CO: Westview Press, 1995.

Smist, Frank J. Jr. *Congress Oversees the United States Intelligence Community, 1947–1989.* Knoxville: University of Tennessee Press, 1990.

Smith, Bradley F. *Sharing Secrets with Stalin: How the Allies Traded Intelligence, 1941–1945.* Lawrence: University Press of Kansas, 1996.

Smith, R. Jeffrey, and Thomas W. Lippmann, "FBI Plans to Expand Overseas." *Washington Post,* August 20, 1996, A1.

Snider, L. Britt. *Sharing Secrets with Lawmakers: Congress as a User of Intelligence.* Intelligence Monograph, Center for the Study of Intelligence, Central Intelligence Agency, Langley, VA, February 1987.

Specter, Michael. "Deep in the Russian Soul, Lethal Darkness." *New York Times,* June 6, 1997, E1.

Steele, Robert D. "Relevant Information and All-Source Analysis: The Emerging Revolution." *American Intelligence Journal* 19 (1999): 23–30.

Steinbruner, John D. "Biological Weapons: A Plague upon All Houses." *Foreign Policy* (Winter 1997/98): 85–96.

———. "Nuclear Decapitation." *Foreign Policy* 40 (Winter 1981/82): 16–28.

Steinhauer, Jennifer, and Judith Miller. "In New York Outbreak, Glimpse of Gaps in Biological Defenses." *New York Times,* October 11, 1999, A1.

Stern, Jessica. "The Prospect of Domestic Bioterrorism." *Emerging Infectious Diseases* 5 (July/August 1999): 517–22.

———. *The Ultimate Terrorists.* Cambridge, MA: Harvard University Press, 1999.

Stolberg, Sheryl Gay. "DDT, Target of Global Ban, Finds Defenders in Experts on Malaria." *New York Times,* August 29, 1999, A1, A6.

Stout, David. "U.S. Photos Show Ground Work at Suspected Site of Mass Grave." *New York Times,* June 10, 1999, A18.

Strong, Maurice. "40 Chernobyls Waiting to Happen." *New York Times,* March 22, 1992, E15.

Talbott, Kirk, and Melissa Brown. "Forest Plunder in Southeast Asia: An Environmental Security Nexus in Burma and Cambodia." In Geoffrey D. Dabelko, ed., *Report: Environmental Change and Security Project,* Woodrow Wilson Center 4 (Spring 1998): 53–60.

Tenet, George J. "Does America Need the CIA?" Speech, Gerald R. Ford Library, Grand Rapids, MI, November 19, 1997.

———. *Hearings*, U.S. Senate Armed Services Committee, 106th Cong., 1st sess., February 2, 1999.

———. Letter to the editor, *New York Times,* July 16, 1998, A18.

———. Remarks, annual dinner, Nashua (NH) Chamber of Commerce, June 28, 1999.

———. "What 'New' Role for the C.I.A.?" *New York Times,* October 27, 1998, A23.

Thomas, Stafford T. "The CIA's Bureaucratic Dimensions." *International Journal of Intelligence and Counterintelligence* 12 (Winter 1999): 399–413.

———. "On the Selection of Directors of Central Intelligence." *Southeastern Political Review* 9 (Spring 1984): 1–59.

———. "Presidential Styles and DCI Selection." *International Journal of Intelligence and Counterintelligence* 7 (Summer 1994): 175–98.

Thompson, Mark. "Why the Pentagon Gets a Free Ride." *Time,* June 5, 1995, 26–27.

Tolba, Mostafa K., with Iwona Fummel-Bulska. *Global Environmental Diplomacy: Negotiating Environmental Agreements for the World, 1973–1992.* Cambridge, MA: MIT Press, 1998.

Traynor, Ian. "Bridge of Spies." *Guardian,* March 26, 1997, 2–3.

Treverton, Gregory F. *Covert Action: The Limits of Intervention in the Postwar World.* New York: Basic Books, 1987.

———. "Intelligence since Cold War's End." In Report of the Twentieth Century Fund Task Force on the Future of U.S. Intelligence, ed., *In from the Cold War.* New York: Twentieth Century Fund Press, 1996, 99–133.

———. "Intelligence: Welcome to the American Government." In Thomas E. Mann, ed., *A Question of Balance: The President, the Congress and Foreign Policy.* Washington, DC: Brookings Institution, 1990, 70–108.

Tucker, Jonathan B. "Chemical/Biological Terrorism" Coping with a New Threat." *Politics and the Life Sciences* 15 (September 1996): 167–85.

Turner, Stansfield. *Democracy and Terrorism.* Boston: Houghton Mifflin, 1991.

———. "Intelligence for a New World Order." *Foreign Affairs* 70 (Fall 1991): 150–66.

———. "Purge the C.I.A. of K.G.B. Types." *New York Times,* October 2, 1991, A19.

———. *Secrecy and Democracy.* Boston: Houghton Mifflin, 1985.

Tyler, Patrick E. "China Concedes That AIDS Virus Infected Common Blood Product." *New York Times,* October 25, 1996, A1.

Tyson, James L. *U.S. International Broadcasting and National Security.* New York: Ramapo Press, 1983.

U.S. Congress. House. *IC21: The Intelligence Community in the 21st Century,* Permanent Select Committee on Intelligence, 104th Cong., 1st sess. Washington, DC: U.S. U.S. Government Printing Office, 1996.

———. House. "Intelligence Authorization Act for Fiscal Year 1997." *H.R. 3259,* 104th Cong., 2d sess. Washington, DC: U.S. Government Printing Office, 1996.

———. House. *Report 102–963,* 102d Cong., 2d sess. Washington, DC: U.S. Government Printing Office, 1992.

———. Office of Technological Assessment. "Proliferation of Weapons of Mass Destruction: Assessing the Risks." Rept. OTA–ISC–559, August 1993.

———. House. Select Committee on U.S. National Security and Military/Commercial Concerns with The People's Republic of China (Cox committee). Report 105–851, 105th Cong., 2d sess. Washington, DC: U.S. Government Printing Office, May 25, 1999.

———. Senate. Select Committee on Intelligence Activities (Church committee). "Alleged Assassination Plots Involving Foreign Leaders." *Interim Report,* 94th Cong., 2d sess., November 1975.

———. Senate. Select Committee on Secret Military Assistance to Iran and the Nicaraguan Opposition and House Select Committee to Investigate Covert Arms Transactions with Iran (Inouye-Hamilton committees). *Report on the Iran-Contra Affair.* S. Rept. 100–216 and H. Rept. 100–433, November 1987.

Walden, Jerrold L. "The CIA: A Study in the Arrogation of Administrative Power." *George Washington Law Review* 39 (October 1970): 66–101.

Walpole, Robert D. "North Korea's Taepo Dong Launch and Some Implications on the Ballistic Missile Threat to the United States." Speech, Center for Strategic and International Affairs, Washington, DC, December 8, 1998.

Warner, Michael, ed. *The CIA under Harry Truman.* Washington, DC: Center for the Study of Intelligence, CIA, 1994.

Weaver, Mary Anne. "The Real bin Laden." *New Yorker,* January 24, 2000, 32–38.

Weber, Ralph E., ed., *Spymasters: Ten CIA Officers in Their Own Words.* Wilmington, DE: SR Books, 1999.

Weiner, Myron, ed., *International Migration and Security.* Boulder, CO: Westview Press, 1993.

Weiner, Tim. "After Errant $2 Billion, Spy Satellite Agency Heads Are Ousted.," *New York Times,* February 27, 1996, A9.

———. "Big Cash Infusion Aims to Rebuild Anemic C.I.A.." *New York Times,* October 22, 1998, A3.

———. "A Blast at Secrecy in Kennedy Killing." *New York Times,* September 29, 1998, A17.

———. "The Case of the Spies without a Country." *New York Times,* January 17, 1999, B6.

———. "C.I.A. Chief Defends Secrecy, in Spending and Spying, to Senate." *New York Times,* February 23, 1996, A5.

———. "C.I.A. Inquiry Asks for an Overhaul." *New York Times,* June 3, 1998, A8.

———. "C.I.A.'s Workaday Cloak." *New York Times,* April 5, 1995, A6.

———. "A Guatemala Officer and the C.I.A.." *New York Times,* March 26, 1995, A6.

———. "House Votes to Bolster a Drug-Trafficking Bill." *New York Times,* November 10, 1999, A8.

———. "Opponents Find That Ousting Hussein Is Easier Said Than Done." *New York Times,* November 16, 1998, A10.

———. "Rethinking the Ban on Political Assassinations." *New York Times,* August 30, 1998, E3.

———. "U.S. Spy Agencies Find Scant Peril on Horizon." *New York Times,* January 29, 1998, A3.

Weiser, Benjamin. "U.S. Officials Say Aid for Terrorists Came through Two Persian Gulf Nations." *New York Times,* July 8, 1999, A8.

Westerfield, Bradford H. "America and the World of Intelligence Liaison." *Intelligence and National Security* 11 (July 1996): 523–60.

———, ed. *Inside CIA's Private World.* New Haven, CT: Yale University Press, 1995.

Whitney, Craig R. "Fewer Bombs Fall on a Cloudy Day in Balkan Battle." *New York Times,* April 12, 1999, A10.

———. "Germany Finds That Spies Are Still Doing Business." *New York Times,* September 9, 1993, A1.

———. "Hunger Strike Continues for Terrorist Called Carlos." *New York Times,* November 15, 1998, A4.

Whitney, Merrill E., and James D. Gaisford. "Economic Espionage as Strategic Trade Policy." *Canadian Journal of Economics* 29 (April 1996): 46–99.

Wildavsky, Aaron. *The Politics of the Budgetary Process.* Boston: Little, Brown, 1964.

———. *Speaking Truth to Power: The Art and Craft of Policy Analysis.* Boston: Little, Brown, 1979.

Williams, Daniel, and John M. Goshko. "Reduced U.S. World Role Outlined but Soon altered.," *Washington Post,* May 26, 1993, A1.

Wilson, Edward O. *The Diversity of Life.* New York: Penguin Books, 1994.

Wilson, James Q. *Bureaucracy.* New York: Basic Books, 1989.

———. *Thinking about Reorganization.* Washington, DC: Consortium for the Study of Intelligence, 1993.

Wilson, Mary E. "Infectious Diseases: An Ecological Perspective." *British Medical Journal,* December 23, 1995, 1681–84.

Wines, Michael. "Straining to See the Real Russia." *New York Times,* May 2, 1999, sec. 4, p. 1.

———."Two Views of Inhumanity Split the World, Even in Victory." *New York Times,* June 13, 1999, sec. 4, p. 1.

Wise, David. *Nightmover.* New York: HarperCollins, 1995.

———."The Spies Who Lost $4 Billion." *George,* October 1998, 82–86.

Woolsey, James R. "The Future Direction of Intelligence." Speech, Center for Strategic and International Studies, Washington, DC, July 18, 1994.

———. *Hearings,* U.S. Senate Select Committee on Intelligence, 103d Cong., 2d sess., March 6, 1993.

———. "World Threat Assessment Brief." Statement for the record, *Hearings,* U.S. Senate Select Committee on Intelligence, 104th Cong., 1st sess., January 10, 1995.

Wren, Christopher S. "A Purer, More Potent Heroin Lures New Users to a Long, Hard Fall, *New York Times,* May 9, 1999, A27.

———. "U.N. to Create Own Satellite Program to Find Illegal Drug Crops." *New York Times,* March 28, 1999, A10.

Wright, Robert. "Private Eyes." *New York Times Magazine,* September 5, 1999, 52, 54.

Zelikow, Philip. "American Economic Intelligence: Past Practice and Future Principles." In Rhodri Jeffreys-Jones and Christopher Andrew, eds., *Eternal Vigilance? 50 Years of the CIA.* London: Case, 1997, 164–77.

———."American Intelligence and the World Economy." In Report of the Twentieth Century Fund Task Force on the Future of U.S. Intelligence, ed., *In from the Cold.* New York: Twentieth Century Fund, 1996, 137–262.

Zumla, Alimuddin, and John Grange. "Tuberculosis." *British Medical Journal* 316 (1998): 1962–65.

# INDEX

# ABOUT THE AUTHOR

Loch K. Johnson is Regents Professor of Political Science at the University of Georgia and author of several books on U.S. national security and politics. He has won the Certificate of Distinction from the National Intelligence Study Center (1986) and the V. O. Key Prize from the Southern Political Science Association. He has served as secretary of the American Political Science Association and president of the International Studies Association, South. Johnson was special assistant to the chair of the Senate Select Committee on Intelligence in 1975–76, staff director of the House Subcommittee on Intelligence Oversight in 1977–79, and special assistant to the chair of the Aspin-Brown Commission on Intelligence in 1995–96.

Born in Auckland, New Zealand, Professor Johnson received his Ph.D. in political science from the University of California at Riverside. At the University of Georgia, he has won the Josiah Meigs Prize, the university's highest teaching honor, as well as the Owens Award, its highest research honor. His extracurricular activities include distance running, alpine skiing, and participation in civic projects.